Perfect Days in ...

PARIS

C000000997

Travel with Insider Tips

www.marco-polo.com

MARCO POLO

Contents

 TOP 10   4

That Paris Feeling   6

For chapters: see inside front cover

Not to be missed!

Our TOP 10 hits – from the absolute No. 1 to No. 10 – help you plan your tour of the most important sights.

1 TOUR EIFFEL ➤ 53

Heavily criticised as an "Iron Monstrosity" at the start of its life, the tower quickly managed to win over the hearts of Parisians. The Eiffel Tower (image left) has become the undisputed emblem of the city – make sure to pay this world famous monument a visit!

2 NOTRE-DAME DE PARIS ➤ 76

The mighty cathedral on the Île de la Cité has shaped the Parisian cityscape for centuries. This breathtaking edifice is seen as a true masterpiece of Gothic architecture.

3 MUSÉE DU LOUVRE ➤ 102

Make a careful plan of attack when tackling the largest and most famous art museum in the world: the motto "less is more" will definitely come in handy.

4 CHAMPS ELYSÉES AND THE ARC DE TRIOMPHE ➤ 108

Oh, Champs-Elysées … you'll get a beautiful view of the oft-serenaded avenue from the Arc de Triomphe. Once built to glorify Napoleon, the arch stands today as a monument to the French nation.

5 SACRÉ-CŒUR ➤ 154

The basilica's white, almost oriental-looking domes attract huge flocks of tourists up to visit the hill of Montmartre.

6 LE MARAIS AND THE PLACE DES VOSGES ➤ 130

Elegant mansions surround what is probably the most beautiful square in the city. The quarter has now become "chic" once again.

7 MONTMARTRE ➤ 156

This quarter is full of picturesque spots bearing traces left behind by the bohemians of the Belle Époque. Pleasure is still king here today, just as it was back then.

8 ÎLE DE LA CITÉ AND THE CONCIERGERIE ➤ 82

This island, lapped by the Seine, is regarded as the birthplace of the city. If you walk across the Île, stroll past the Conciergerie – once the "Antechamber to the Guillotine".

9 MUSÉE D'ORSAY ➤ 56

French painting at its finest is housed under the elegant glass roof of this imposing former Belle Époque railway station.

10 CENTRE GEORGES-POMPIDOU ➤ 133

This futuristic web of pipes is home to one of the largest collections of modern Art in the world.

THAT
PARIS

Find out what makes the city tick and experience its unique flair – just like the Parisians themselves.

SOUS LES PONTS DE PARIS

"Under the Bridges of Paris…" so goes the old hit tune that can be heard sung with accordion accompaniment all over the city.

You'll know you've really arrived in Paris when you're standing on the banks of the Seine. It's particularly impressive when the evening light places a silken, impressionistic sheen on the surface of the water, setting the golden splendour of the bridges off to their full advantage. Paris's many bridges are just waiting to be discovered by bike. For info about bike rentals, visit www.velib.paris.fr.

A CITY WITH HISTORY

Each cobblestone bears witness to the city's long history. In contrast to other European cities, Paris was not destroyed during the war. Careful restoration and the patina of old age make Paris look like the backdrop of a period film. The 18th-century shopping arcades (►113) and Montmartre's almost village-like feel are particularly nostalgia-inducing (►156).

PERFECTLY ILLUMINATED MONUMENTS

Paris – City of Light: it wasn't just the Sun King who knew how to put himself in a good light. Visitors are amazed by the illuminations at such sites as the Place de la Concorde (►114), Les Invalides (►63), the Arc de Triomphe (►108) and other magnificent monuments. You can catch a first glimpse of their radiance on a round-trip of the city in an open-top double decker bus (www.parislopentour.com).

PARIS, MON AMOUR

Doisneau's photo of a kiss at the Hôtel de Ville helped cement Paris's long-held reputation as the City of Love. The city radiates pure romance at every corner – perhaps that's why more marriage proposals are made here than anywhere else in the world. Get a taste of the romance by going tango dancing on a balmy summer's evening at the Trocadéro or at the Quai Saint Bernard on the banks of the Seine (►16).

FEELING

Evening atmosphere on the banks of the Seine

That Paris Feeling

BASTION OF FASHION

With such labels as Dior, Chanel, Lacroix, Givenchy and Yves Saint-Laurent embodying elegance, style and luxury, it should come as no surprise to discover that the word "chic" is French. Even if you don't want to take an expensive scarf, fine jewellery, or a bewitching perfume home with you as a souvenir, it's still an intoxicating feeling to saunter along the Avenue Montaigne (➤ 122) and totally immerse yourself in opulence.

DIVE INTO ART

The gigantic Musée du Louvre isn't the only treat awaiting the art lovers among you. Many parts of the city also play host to a variety of completely different small museums that are just waiting to be discovered. Even locals will queue patiently to get into a particularly exciting special exhibition. You'll find helpful information about current exhibitions, the gigantic schedule of films and the excellent selection of operas and concerts in *Pariscope,* the weekly events magazine (www.spectacles. premiere.fr).

EAT LIKE A FRENCH KING

Nowhere in the world can boast more top-class food hotspots than Paris. The best cuisine from all over France has been collected and refined in this gourmet capital for centuries. And because your eyes deserve a feast as well, the window displays of some patisseries look like they come from jewellers' shops. Desserts decorated with real gold leaf are just one of the exquisite temptations available to foodies. Bon appétit!

You'll also see Paris's multicultural flair in many shops

MULTICULTURAL WORLD CITY

When you hear the beat of African drums in Barbès at the foot of Montmartre, catch the scent of Indian spices in the Passage Brady, enjoy Jewish delicacies in the Rue des Rosiers in le Marais and browse through Chinese trinkets around the Place d'Italie, you'll get the feeling that Paris can magically attract people from all over the world. Multiculturalism shapes Paris and contributes to its particular flair. A visit to a single city can make you feel like you've travelled the globe...

The Magazine

Liberté and all that

"Is it a revolt?" the incompetent, indecisive King Louis XVI is said to have enquired on hearing of the fall of the Bastille in 1789. "No, sire," replied a duke, "it's a revolution!" The following decade brought both the guillotine and the Reign of Terror, but times were tough even before Louis lost his head.

Since the reign of Louis XIV a century earlier, the expensive cult of absolute monarchy had glorified France abroad and enriched its aristocrats and courtiers at home. But for the poor and the middle classes – heavily over-taxed and under-represented – the story was dramatically different. Things came to a head when a bad harvest in 1788 sent bread prices soaring while wages sagged to a new low. As an out-of-touch king dithered about how to regain control of a disaffected populace, and his unpopular queen, Marie-Antoinette, depleted the coffers, the masses took to the streets. On 14 July 1789 they raided Les Invalides (►63) for weapons and stormed the fortress-prison of the Bastille, the ultimate symbol of royal

> "By mid-1794, some 17,000 people had been beheaded"

repression, massacring its defenders and releasing its prisoners – all seven of them! Later that year, a mob removed the despised king and queen from Versailles (►171), to keep them as virtual prisoners in the Palais des Tuileries (►110). Little did they both realize that the building of the palace at Versailles was to be one of the last grand gestures of the French monarchy as, following the events of the 1780s – apart from the brief reigns of Louis XVIII and Charles X – France has remained a republic.

View of the Tuileries from Place de la Révolution, painted by Thomas Naudet in 1799

Revolution!

At first the Revolution was led by relative moderates called Girondins, and France was declared a constitutional monarchy. Following external threats to their new government by Austria, Prussia and exiled French nobles, the masses rallied patriotically together, and soon the conservative Girondins had lost power to the extremist Jacobins, the most famous anti-royalist political group of the Revolution. They abolished the monarchy, revoked religious freedom and deconsecrated churches, established a "Revolutionary Convention" and, in September 1792, declared the First People's Republic of France.

Terror and the Guillotine

This marked the start of the dreaded two-year "Reign of Terror", a period governed by the ruthless, power-crazed Jacobin leaders Maximilien Robespierre and Georges Danton, during which revolutionary ideals waned as more and more heroes were tried on unlikely charges of treason, and beheaded. The king was convicted of "conspiring against the liberty of the nation" and in January 1793 was guillotined on the newly named Place de la Révolution (formerly Place Louis XV, now Place de la Concorde, ►114), followed by Marie-Antoinette in October, and a further 1,343 "enemies of the Revolution". By mid-1794 some 17,000 people had been beheaded and the Revolution had reached such a frenzy of bloodlust that it turned on itself, even executing Danton and Robespierre.

A leading protagonist in this last stage of the Revolution was Paul Barras, a moderate Republican who, with four others, established the "Directoire" as the Republic's ruling body. And waiting in the wings was a young Napoleon Bonaparte, who, within a decade, was to work his way up to eventually become "Emperor of the French".

A Hungry King

Even in the face of death, poor King Louis XVI didn't lose his appetite. During his trial, he became hopelessly distracted by a plate of filled rolls. In tears, and unable to concentrate on the questions put to him, he eventually blurted out, "Please might I have one of those?" Just before having his head removed, he ate 16 pork chops!

PARIS
FASHION CHIC

No matter what this year's fashion fad is, it always contains one vital ingredient – the distinctive *"je ne sais quoi"* of French chic. In the inimitable words of Coco Chanel, "fashions pass away; style lives on".

Above: Christian Dior show; middle: St-Ouen flea market; right: Coco Chanel and models

It may be the household names of the fashion world – the Diors and the Gaultiers – with their lavish *haute-couture* creations, who receive the praise, but their success has spawned an entire industry. The annual Fashion Weeks flood Paris with journalists, buyers and hangers-on, while a hip cauldron of vintage and one-off designer stores bubbles beneath the surface. The success of Paris's fashion industry, especially its *haute couture* sector, depends on *les petites mains*, literally "the little hands" – the team of seamstresses, button- and bead-makers, embroiderers and other rarely acknowledged artisans who create the vital accessories.

English Influence
Ironically it was an Englishman, Charles Frederick Worth, who founded French *haute couture*. After moving to Paris from London in 1845, aged 20, he worked in a draper's shop until he could afford a shop of his own, 13 years later, at 7 Rue de la Paix. Specializing in well-cut clothes, he radically changed the female silhouette and introduced the rhythm of the seasons to fashion by preparing his collections in advance. Another of his innovations was the use of live models for fashion shows.

The most extravagant and prestigious shows are staged at the Carrousel du Louvre every January and July, in front of 2,000 journalists and celebrities and 800 buyers. The atmosphere is electric, and tickets are virtually impossible to obtain. Some of the seats are reserved for *les petites mains*, who can watch their handiwork come alive in movement as the world's top models step out on to the catwalk, in a pivoting swirl of silk, chiffon, brocade, organza and moiré. Many designers parade their work in increasingly innovative locations: in 2011 Christian Dior held their show in the rose-lined gardens of the Rodin Museum; Georges Chakra conducted his at the Palais de Tokyo art museum. The *prêt-à-porter*, or "off-the-peg", collections have their own fashion weeks in October and March. They are no less extravagant but are a little more visible, with a greater number of models and designers frequenting Paris's hottest post-show spots.

Vintage Paris

Want to give a classic item of Chanel a brand new home? Ever wondered where unloved pieces of Dior are put out to pasture? Even top celebrities have been spotted snooping through the vintage stores that stud the streets of the Marais and Oberkampf, and especially around the 6th *arrondissement*.

A cut above the crowd is tiny Les Trois Marches de Catherine B in St-Germain-des-Prés (1 Rue Guisarde, 75006; tel: 01 43 54 74 18; www.catherine-b.com), an upmarket *haute-couture* flea-market store. Pricey, but oh-so-elegant, is Didier Ludot (20–24 Galerie de Montpensier) by the Palais Royal. Fashionistas hunting down 1970s knit dresses rather than vintage Hermès bags should try Free P Star (▶ 147). Those who like to rummage should hit Marché aux Puces de Saint-Ouen (▶ 163).

PICNIC
PARIS

You'll be hard-pressed to find any restaurant's décor that can compete with Paris's architectural beauty. From verdant parks to the Seine at sunset, here's where to find the tastiest Parisian fare and the perfect spots to eat it.

SOURCE IT
Food Halls, Shops and *Épiceries*

Locals shop in the Rue St-Louis-en-l'Île (► 89) on the Île Saint-Louis, Rue des Abbesses (► 166) in Montmartre and Rue Montorgueil (► 147) off Jardin des Halles. All three are lined with *charcuteries* (selling cured meats), cheese stores and *pâtisseries*. Le Bon Marché's (► 69) ground-floor food hall stocks everything from miniature *crudités* to mint-laced tabbouleh. As it caters to the *crème* of Parisian society, prices can be expensive. It may be a bit of a hike to Montmartre, but who can resist the best baguette in Paris? Winner of the 2011 annual competition, Pascal Barillon of Au Levain d'Antan (6 Rue des Abbesses, 75018; tel: 01 42 64 97 83; Metro: Abbesses) gets a contract to supply President Sarkozy with their daily bread.

Farmers' Markets

Le Marché Couvert St-Germain (open Tue–Sun, ► 69) has its own *cave*, or wine cellar, as well as stalls selling Greek, Italian and East Asian dishes to take away. The sprawling Marché Bastille (Boulevard Richard Lenoir, 75011;

Thu and Sun; Metro: Bastille) offers some of the city's best prices on local produce.

Organic

On a Sunday, drop by Paris's largest organic market, Marché Biologique Raspail (Boulevard Raspail, 75006; Sun 9–1:30; Metro: Sèvres-Babylone). Alternatively, Le Marché des Enfants-Rouges (39 Rue de Bretagne, 75003; Tue–Sun; Metro: Filles du Calvaire) is home to an organic stall with a large selection of fruit and vegetables. For a list of all of the city's organic outlets, pick up a copy of *Paris Nature et Bio* (in English and French), published by *L'Indispensable* in 2009 and available from most newsagent kiosks.

EAT IT
Jardins du Trocadéro

Offering breathtaking views over the Seine to the Eiffel Tower, the Trocadéro gardens tumble down from the Palais de Chaillot to the Pont d'Iéna below. Be sure to access the gardens from Place du Trocadéro, as the hike up from the river is long and relatively steep.

Place des Vosges

Located within the elegant and picturesque Place des Vosges in the Marais, this park is neatly fenced in, making it a great place to picnic with little ones. On weekends, make sure to stake out a spot early, as the park tends to fill up quickly.

Île de la Cité

Halfway across Pont Neuf, two sets of steps lead down to pretty Place du Pont Neuf. Bypass the few visitors waiting to board Les Vedettes (▶ 182), and wander to the western tip of the island. **Insider Tip** Expect envious stares from both sides of the Seine, as observers wonder how you found such a perfect picnic spot in the dead centre of Paris.

Markets in Paris sell all manner of fresh produce including bread, cheeses, olives and salamis – perfect for a picnic

The **SEINE**

It is no coincidence that the inscription on Paris's coat-of-arms reads: "She is buffeted by the waves but does not sink".
The city's history has been inextricably linked with the Seine since its earliest origins as a Gaulish village on the Île de la Cité, an islet in the river. The river represents the very lifeblood of Paris, flowing through its heart, animating the city, defining the capital geographically and reflecting its history in its many fine buildings.

View along the *quais* on the River Seine at Île St-Louis

Yet, as tourist boats peacefully ply the river today, it is easy to forget that, in the ninth century, the Seine was used by 700 Viking warships to invade Paris, or that thousands of bodies floated through the city in 1572, victims of the Saint Bartholomew's Day Massacre of Protestants.

"Sand and sun-loungers spread out along the city's Right Bank each summer"

Just three centuries ago, the Seine served a multitude of purposes: it was both the city's sewer and the main source of drinking water; washerwomen did their washing in it, laying the clothing out to dry on the watersides; workshops churned their waste into it; horses drank from it; workers at the floating fish market near the Île de la Cité threw fish heads into it; and Parisians bathed in it – a fashion introduced by the flamboyant Henri IV

Picnics and sunbathing on Quai de Bourbon, Île Saint-Louis

in the swelteringly hot summer of 1609, when he took to nude bathing. By mid-August that year, as many as 4,000 of his male subjects could be seen frolicking naked in the river – much to the delight of onlooking ladies!

The Seine was also a major trading route. During the 17th and 18th centuries a large port grew up near the Louvre to supply the court with coal, wood, hay and food. Before the invention of engines powered by steam and gas, barges travelling upstream had to be towed by men or horses. To navigate the narrow arches of the bridges, expert boat-handlers known as "bridge-swallowers" were employed to haul the barges through with the help of poles, ropes and rings.

During the 18th century, as the port went from strength to strength, the construction of waterfronts (built to ward off the then-frequent danger of flooding), corbelled houses and mills started to encroach on the river. Near Châtelet, the river is 43m (47 yards) narrower than it was during the Middle Ages. Nowadays, it is cleverly regulated by locks upstream and the Suresnes dam downstream. Paris remains the country's leading river port and its water is less polluted than it has been for years. But the "cross-Seine swim" is a thing of the past – you could well be decapitated by one of the many *bateaux-mouches* that ply the city-centre stretch of the river.

Paris-on-Sea

Sand and sunloungers spread out along the Right Bank each summer in an exercise known as Paris-Plage. The "beach" features volleyball nets, a toddlers' area, mist fountains, palm trees, bars and places to relax. Floating swimming pools were popular along the river from the 18th century onwards. Although the last one sank in 1993, a fresh breed of *piscine flottante* was inaugurated in 2006. The new Josephine Baker swimming pool by the Bibliothèque François-Mitterrand has a removable roof and paddling pool, and is another excuse to pack your swimwear.

Bridges Ancient and Modern

The city's 37 bridges reflect the architectural history of Paris, representing every period and built in every style. The oldest and most famous, ironically called Pont Neuf (New Bridge), dates back to 1604, and was erected to ease Henri IV's journey between the Louvre Palace and the abbey of St-Germain-des-Prés. The newest, inaugurated in 2006, is the Passerelle Simone-de-Beauvoir, a steel pedestrian and cycle bridge by Quai de la Gare Metro station, a few kilometres east of the centre. But the most photogenic is Pont Alexandre III, with its ornate candelabra-style lamps, its winged horses, lions, gilded nymphs and garlands.

DID YOU KNOW?

■ The Seine runs 776km (482mi) from Burgundy to the English Channel. It was named by Gaius Julius Caesar.

■ In his will, Napoleon asked for his ashes to be sprinkled on the Seine after his death in forced exile on the island of Saint Helena. They were eventually interred in Les Invalides, where his mausoleum can be visited today (▶63).

■ In 1985 the artist Christo wrapped the Pont Neuf in reams of cloth to celebrate the Fête de la Musique (Festival of Music).

■ From the 17th century onwards, canaries, blackbirds, warblers and other birds were sold between the Pont au Change and Pont Neuf, and there's still a bird market today on the Île de la Cité (▶82).

■ In 1765, William Cole, a visitor to Paris, described the Seine as "a dirty, nasty ditch of a river", and in 1862, celebrated French poet Paul Verlaine referred to it as "a muddy old snake".

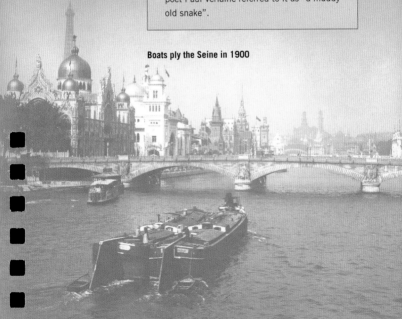

Boats ply the Seine in 1900

The Magazine

ROMANCING IN PARIS

Paris revels in its reputation as the world's most romantic city. Cross any boulevard or stroll along the Seine at sunset and you'll find lovestruck locals and canoodling couples at every turn. Prince or pauper, there's always a way to impress a date in the City of Love.

LOVE IN THE LAP OF LUXURY

Breakfast: The morning menu at the Ritz's L'Espadon restaurant (15 Place Vendôme, 75001; tel: 01 43 16 30 80) includes both Japanese and Parisian set breakfasts, the former with grilled salmon, the latter with a glass of champagne.

Private cruise: Whizz past the group cruises on your own bespoke speedboat tour of the capital, courtesy of River Limousine (www.river-limousine.com). Like Venice, but much faster and way cooler.

Lunch: Get dropped off at Pont de la Concorde from where it's a two-minute stroll to the glamorous Hôtel de Crillon (▶ 40). Keep lunch light with their "My Paris Bento" lunchbox of smoked salmon, crab and avocado salad served each weekday.

Love in the Louvre: It's a 10-minute walk through the Jardin des Tuileries (▶ 110) to Paris's finest museum (▶ 102) for a private tour from Paris Muse (www.parismuse.com). Take a peek at Rubens's magically romantic Marie de Médicis cycle.

Shopping: It's straight over the Pont Neuf to the boutiques of St-Germain (▶ 69).

Dinner: Take a leisurely stroll along the Seine to the Eiffel Tower (▶ 53), as it's totally romantic to say "I love you" on the top floor. Nip down one level to Alain Ducasse's Le Jules Verne (▶ 67), for there's nothing tastier than savouring poached lobster while overlooking Paris.

STARRY-EYED ON A SHOESTRING

Breakfast: The pedestrianized Pont des Arts is the city's most romantic bridge and couples have been known to set up tables for a candlelit dinner here. Make do with fresh morning croissants and coffee from nearby Les Délices de Manon (400 Rue St Honoré, 75001).

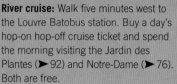

River cruise: Walk five minutes west to the Louvre Batobus station. Buy a day's hop-on hop-off cruise ticket and spend the morning visiting the Jardin des Plantes (➤ 92) and Notre-Dame (➤ 76). Both are free.

Lunch: Alight for the last time at St-Germain and window-shop through the boutiques to Le Pré Verre (➤ 94) for Asian-inspired gourmet cuisine without the hefty price tag.

Reader's digest: Stumble around the corner to the city's finest park, the Jardin du Luxembourg (➤ 65), where Parisians come to lounge with a novel or doze by the grand fountain.

Two wheels: Pick up a Vélib' bike (➤ 38) from outside the park and pack a bag full of treats from Le Bon Marché (➤ 69) five minutes away. It's the finest food hall in Paris.

Dinner: Park your bike on tranquil Île St-Louis (➤ 88). The small number of visitors all leave in the evening, so it's easy to find a peaceful picnic spot all to yourself. And there are *charcuteries* and bakers on the narrow Rue St-Louis (➤ 95) in case you run out of food.

TOP left: On the Pont des Arts at dusk
TOP right: A couple seated near the Seine

STAY OVERNIGHT IN ...
... the Blowout Hotel:
For discreet calm and crisp linen sheets, check into the Villa Madame (above; ➤ 42), a stone's throw from the Jardin du Luxembourg.

... the Budget Hotel:
Friendly, freshly painted and an absolute bargain, rest your head at the Hotel du Séjour (➤ 41), around the corner from the Pompidou Centre.

ART & ARTISANS
The Second Revolution

Paris first attracted artists on a major scale during the reign of Louis XIV, and the city's position as the artistic cradle of Europe only continued to grow: it was here that some of art history's most important movements developed.

It was Claude Monet's 1873 painting *Impression, soleil levant (Impression, sunrise)* that coined the term "Impressionism". Frequently attributed to Monet's failing eyesight, this style of painting placed prominence on light and movement, rather than distinct lines or realistic portrayal. The movement took the Parisian art world by storm. Often joined by friends and fellow former students Pierre-Auguste Renoir, Frédéric Bazille and Alfred Sisley, Monet painted outdoors, eventually moving his base to a picturesque cottage in Giverny (► 169). The artist's world-renowned water lily paintings were completed here.

21ST-CENTURY ART
Paris continues to cultivate creativity. In late 2008, a 19th-century funeral parlour in one of the city's northeastern neighbourhoods was transformed into Centquatre (▶ 141): contemporary artisans work in small ateliers, often open to the public, which ring the vast exhibition spaces.

Around the same period, Auguste Rodin stunned the world with his contemporary approach to sculpture. Rather than depicting a physical or mythical ideal, his marble and bronze sculptures portrayed realistic human forms. Early works, including *The Age of Bronze* and *St John the Baptist Preaching*, slowly helped the artist to establish a name for himself, while sculptures *The Kiss* and *The Thinker* are Rodin's most famous.

Beyond Impressionism
Paul Gauguin took the Impressionist movement a few steps further, as did his friends Henri de Toulouse-Lautrec and Vincent van Gogh. Loosely grouped under the unimaginative post-Impressionism label, all three artists favoured boldly coloured, exotic images, and often strikingly unrealistic proportions. Toulouse-Lautrec, in particular, is synonymous with Montmartre and the Moulin Rouge dancers of the late 19th century.

Short but explosive, the fauvist movement followed, led by Henri Matisse and André Derain in the early 20th century. Traditional, flattering colours were eschewed in favour of olive green highlights, or bursts of crimson and tangerine. Critics and the public considered the Fauves to be on the brink of insanity, but when collectors began to purchase their work the movement acquired a more positive reputation.

TOP left to right: A Toulouse-Lautrec-designed poster; *Le déjeuner des canotiers* **(1881) by Pierre-Auguste Renoir; Claude Monet's** *Impression, soleil levant* **(1873)**

The Magazine

Cubism and Surrealism

It was in 1907 that Spanish artist Pablo Picasso, who had been resident in the French capital since 1900, broke through the boundaries of art once more by painting his first cubist work, *Les Demoiselles d'Avignon* ('The Young Ladies of Avignon'), at the Bateau-Lavoir (▶ 159) in Montmartre. It was here, in a warren of tiny ateliers shared with other artists, including the Italian painter and sculptor Amedeo Modigliani, that Picasso, Georges Braque and Juan Gris developed cubism, a painting technique that depicted images transformed into a semi-abstract range of piecemeal shapes, such as basic spheres, cubes and cylinders. As with other movements during this period, cubist theory soon spread, and it was taken up in various forms within the disciplines of architecture, poetry and ballet.

The Zurich-based Dadaist movement, defined by proponents like Man Ray and Max Ernst as "anti-art", laid the groundwork for the city's next artistic craze: surrealism. Burgeoning to life with André Breton's "automatic writings" at the beginning of the 1920s, surrealist art sought to transcribe the subconscious unaltered, often in the form of un-censored dreams, through painting, film and three-dimensional objects. The most famous surrealist artist was Salvador Dalí, although Yves Tanguy, Joan Miró, Marcel Duchamp and Paul Éluard were also major players in the movement.

MAP THE MOVEMENTS

Each artistic movement may have left the city reeling, but between the late 19th and early 20th centuries virtually all of the world's most enduring international artists lived and worked in Paris. Trace their creative waves at the following spots:

- **Impressionism:** Monet's ethereal water lilies, along with his *Coquelicots (Poppies)*, plus works by Degas, Manet, Renoir and (early) Cézanne can be seen at the Musée d'Orsay (▶ 56).
- **Stunning sculpture:** Visit Rodin's former home and sculpture garden, now the Musée Rodin (▶ 63).
- **Post-Impressionism:** Pop into the Musée de Montmartre (▶ 161) for a peek at Toulouse-Lautrec's take on the Moulin Rouge.
- **Fauvism:** The Salle Matisse, located in the Musée d'Art Moderne, holds the Fauvist master's famous triptych, *La Danse* (11 Avenue du Président Wilson, 75116; tel: 01 53 67 40 00; www.mam.paris.fr; Tue–Sun 10–6, Thu 10–10 for exhibitions only; Metro: Alma-Marceau).
- **Cubism:** Compare and contrast Picasso's *Le Violon, 1914* and Braque's *L'Homme à la guitare, printemps 1914*, both on the fifth floor of the Centre Georges Pompidou (▶ 133).
- **Surrealism:** See Salvador Dalí's sculptures, graphics and many other works of art at the fantastical Espace Montmartre Salvador Dalí (▶ 160).

A WALK
in the Park

Never before has Paris been greener. More than 400 parks and gardens enliven the city, each with its own character. Some are *à la française* (symmetrical rows of lawns, trees and pathways), some *à l'anglaise* (freely landscaped), others are totally modern; some are ideal for kids, others for a riverside stroll, for romance or a game of tennis or *boules*.

What's more, the green space on offer in Paris is almost entirely public, so visitors can flop down on a park bench almost anywhere in the city. In the last few years bike tracks have been routed around the larger parks, while the smaller ones in the centre often offer WiFi.

Jardin des Tuileries and Jardin du Luxembourg
Many of the mature parks serve as reminders of the capital's illustrious past. The oldest – the Jardin des Tuileries (► 110) – was created for Catherine de Médicis in the 16th century, with later modifications by the great master of the French-style garden, André Le Nôtre, designer of

Relaxing in the Jardin des Tuileries

The Magazine

the gardens of Versailles (▶171). Marie de Médicis' Jardin du Luxembourg (▶65), originally a private garden like the Tuileries, has hardly changed in character since the early 1800s although, in recent years, several hundred comfy garden chairs have been liberally scattered around the fountains, tennis courts and shady copses.

Bois de Vincennes and Bois de Boulogne

Gardens featured high on Napoleon III's priorities during his transformation of Paris into a more resident-friendly city, including the development of the Bois de Boulogne and the Bois de Vincennes, both ancient royal hunting forests that encircled Paris in the Middle Ages. These wild, unkempt parks make you feel you've escaped Paris altogether. The Bois de Vincennes to the east also contains a magnificent château and a zoo, while the Bois de Boulogne to the west, inspired by London's Hyde Park, is better known for its beautiful Parc de Bagatelle with strutting peacocks, its Jardin d'Acclimatation (a children's amusement park) and, by night, when it can be dangerous, for its prostitutes. Both parks have Vélib' cycle points stationed in them.

> "The green space on offer in Paris is almost entirely public"

Les Halles, La Villette, Parc André-Citroën, Parc de Bercy and Jardins d'Éole

The late President Mitterrand's architectural renaissance of the 1980s and 1990s (▶30) revived interest in gardens, with several new parks. These include Les Halles, La Villette (▶162), the Parc André-Citroën and Parc de Bercy. The futuristic Parc André-Citroën was the most ambitious: built in 1992 on the site of the old Citroën car factories in southwestern Paris, it has two juxtaposed gardens (Jardin Blanc and Jardin Noir)

A couple play chess in the Jardin du Luxembourg (left); Les Halles (right)

dominated by gigantic high-tech greenhouses, six sophisticated areas – les Jardins Sériels – each associated with the colour of a metal, computer-ized water features for children and a striking river perspective. By contrast, the more classical Parc de Bercy, also on the Seine, was created in 1997 as part of a vast programme of urban renewal for eastern Paris, and comprises several themed gardens, including the Jardin des Plantes Aromatiques for the visually impaired. The city's newest park, the Jardins d'Éole, sprang to life in 2007. It focuses on sustainable outdoor develop-ment and boasts a wild prairie zone filled with wildflowers.

Musée de la Sculpture en Plein Air and the Promenade Plantée

Finally, for a pleasant stroll, try either of the city's two most innovative parks: the Musée de la Sculpture en Plein Air (Open Air Sculpture Museum, ►92), squeezed between the Seine and the Jardin des Plantes (►92), and the Promenade Plantée, on an abandoned rail viaduct stretching from Bastille to the Bois de Vincennes, which is now a 4.5km (3-mile) long elevated walkway lined with vines, trees and flowers that passes over shopping arcades en route to the Gare de Lyon.

Secret Gardens

For a quick dose of greenery in the city centre, make for the square de la Tour St-Jacques near the Louvre, a small, grassy retreat surrounding an ornate Gothic tower, all that remains of an ancient church, or the river-lapped square du Vert-Galant at the western point of the Île de la Cité. This magical park bears the nickname of amorous King Henri IV and is one of the most romantic corners of Paris.

The Jardin Sauvage de St-Vincent comes as a surprise in the heart of Montmartre – a totally wild patch of land, established to encourage natural flora and fauna – and don't overlook the gardens attached to many museums, most notably the extensive statue-studded grounds of the Musée Rodin (►63).

The Promenade Plantée stretches from Bastille (left); Buttes Chaumont (right)

CAFÉ CULTURE

Nothing is more Parisian than the café. From the famous, fashionable and exotic to the local neighbourhood haunt, Paris would not be Paris without its 10,000 or so cafés.

There is one at virtually every crossroads, a place to meet friends and to people-watch. Café life is an essential part of everyday Paris, from the traditional zinc café (named after its zinc-lined counter top) and Left Bank philo-café (made famous by its "arty" patrons), to Eastern tea gardens and 21st-century designer cafés.

Café Beaubourg
This sleek, postmodern café, overlooking the Centre Pompidou, is the ultimate 1980s designer café. Its interior, by Christian de Portzamparc, is spacious, comfortable and unabashedly sophisticated (► 145).

Café Marly
Some famous architects have designed cafés throughout Paris, giving them immediate cachet. This one in the Louvre (► 102), by Olivier Gagnère, boasts a glamorous setting, IM Pei's glass pyramid.

La Closerie des Lilas
The brass plaques on the tables of this pleasant, historic café (171 Boulevard du Montparnasse, 76006; tel: 01 40 51 34 50; Metro: Vavin) help you enjoy your drink where poets Baudelaire and Apollinaire and author Hemingway once sat. Picasso dropped by every week for the poetry readings; Lenin and Trotsky were also fans in their time.

Above left to right: Outdoor café in 1938; Café de la Paix; Café Marly

Les Deux Magots and Café de Flore

Parisian cafés are best known as popular rendezvous for the literary élite, and none more so than these two neighbours. Les Deux Magots (►64), made famous in the early 20th century by Picasso and poets Verlaine and Breton, has been the watering hole of choice of almost every Paris intellectual. The more cosmopolitan Café de Flore (172 Boulevard St-Germain, 75006; tel: 01 45 48 55 26; Metro: St-Germain-des-Prés) is famous for its existentialist clientele – notably author-philosophers Albert Camus, Simone de Beauvoir and Jean-Paul Sartre.

Le Zinc

For the traditional Parisian zinc café experience, head to the stylish Café de l'Industrie on Rue St-Sabin near the Bastille (Metro: Bréguet-Sabin), La Palette on Rue de Seine (Metro: St-Germain-des-Prés), frequented by art dealers and students of the Académie des Beaux-Arts, or Le Cochon à l'Oreille at 15 Rue Montmartre (Metro: Les Halles). In its heyday, this tiny workers' café was famous for its onion soup served at dawn.

Insider Tip

Full of Eastern Promise

For a change of scene, visit the exotic Café Maure de la Mosquée (39 Rue Geoffroy-St-Hilaire, 75005; Metro: Place Monge) for a refreshing glass of mint tea in beautiful Moorish surroundings.

Oberkampf

The current fashionable café district is the Ménilmontant end of Rue Oberkampf, 75011; Metro: Parmentier. Café Charbon at No 109 is a former dance hall; old dance hall murals evoke a 1920s neighbourhood café. Cithéa Nova at No 112 is popular for its electro evenings, while tiny Kitsch, down the road at No 10, is a visual fiesta of Formica tabletops and 1940s magazine cut-outs.

GRANDS
Travaux

Over the centuries, French leaders have sought to glorify themselves by carrying out ambitious and monumental public building schemes in Paris, which have come to be known as *les grands travaux*. But are they self-promoting ego trips or inspired designs for the future?

Louis XIV, the Sun King, was the first to use architecture to aggrandize the institution of absolute monarchy, with the construction of imposing squares, theatres, aristocratic *hôtels particuliers* (mansions), Les Invalides (►63) and the château of Versailles (►171). His breathtaking extravagance, combined with the wars he waged against neighbouring countries, led to a crippling decline of the monarchy's coffers.

The second major, perhaps most radical, transformation of Paris took place in the mid-19th century under Napoleon III, when Baron Haussmann transformed it into the most magnificent city in Europe. He demolished the crowded, insanitary streets of the medieval city and replaced them with a much more clearly ordered, sometimes chess-board-like system of broad boulevards that linked such focal points as the new Opéra Garnier (►113), the Gare de l'Est and the Arc de Triomphe (►108). His vision can best be appreciated from the top of the Arc de Triomphe, which looks out over 12 grand avenues – including the Champs-Élysées itself – that radiate like the points of a star from la Place Charles-de-Gaulle.

Presidential Vision
In the latter half of the 20th century it was the turn of politicians to leave their stamp on the city. To the initial dismay of Parisians, President Georges Pompidou constructed the now much-loved Centre Georges Pompidou (►133). His successor Giscard d'Estaing played a key part in transforming a derelict railway station into the glorious Musée d'Orsay (►56).

But the late President François Mitterrand surpassed them both in his achievements of the 1980s and 1990s. His programme of *grands travaux* excited mounting controversy as to whether the city was changing too drastically. One of the greatest advocates of urban renewal, Mitterrand feared that Paris was becoming a museum.

Mitterrand's *Grands Travaux*

Many of Mitterrand's projects were greeted with initial horror, in particular his first and most daring construction – the Louvre pyramid (►104). His buzzword for transforming the city was "transparency": take a look at the Fondation Cartier (261 Boulevard Raspail, 75014; Metro: Raspail), with its clever glass slices, and the Institut du Monde Arabe (►89), with its extraordinary aperture-effect glass panels. Other dramatic constructions included the glass-fronted Opéra Bastille (►140) and La Grande Arche (►118), which gave the district of La Défense a badly needed monument and focal point. It also completed his Grand Axis, a line linking the Arc de Triomphe, the Champs-Élysées, his Pyramide and the Louvre. The new national library was completed following Mitterrand's death in January 1996, and renamed the Bibliothèque Nationale de France François-Mitterrand (11 Quai François-Mauriac, 75013) in his honour.

One of Paris's lower-profile "Mitterrand buildings" is the dazzling white Cité de la Musique, designed by Christian de Portzamparc. Part of the La Villette complex (►162), it is home to the National Conservatory of Music and Dance. De Portzamparc chose undulating and conic forms to translate the sensations of music into architecture.

21st-Century Innovation

The most famous mark of ex-President – and former mayor of Paris – Jacques Chirac on the city's skyline is the 2006 Musée du Quai Branly (►62). His fast-talking successor, Nicolas Sarkozy, is planning a somewhat grander architectural legacy. Announced in 2009 was a reinvigoration plan for the business district of La Défense, which includes Norman Foster-designed twin towers, tapering upwards to the heavens, set for completion in 2019. Also on the agenda is a plan to extend Paris to the English Channel along the Seine, a project envisaged by Napoleon, to whom Sarkozy is regularly likened. Critics will have to wait and see if this swathe of urbanization is a new chapter in Paris's architectural story.

The Grande Arche de La Défense, completed in 1989, faces the Arc de Triomphe

A Star-Studded
HISTORY

Great cities are moulded as much by their citizens as by the skills of their architects and masons, and Paris has had more than its fair share of celebrated residents. Thomas Jefferson, who lived here for a while before becoming US President in 1801, declared the city "everyone's second home".

Above: Author Marcel Proust; above right: Singer Edith Piaf

The incredible appeal of the beautiful city on the river Seine can be traced back to the 13th century, when the Sorbonne University was founded. The French capital became one of the leading creative and academic centres of the Western world, attracting many scholars and intellectuals, all under the spell of the city's style and distinctive charm. As Cardinal Eudes de Châteauroux remarked at that time: "France is the oven in which humanity's intellectual bread is baked."

In the 18th century, Paris charmed its international visitors, achieving notoriety as "the most romantic city in Europe"; it thereby became a popular place for people from all over the world to visit or to live in.

Paris in Words

Paris has been the focus of countless literary masterpieces. "In Paris one can lose one's mind, but one can never lose one's way," claimed Oscar Wilde. He lost both, however, dying in a run-down hostel simply called L'Hôtel, now one of the few luxury hotels of the Left Bank (▶ 48).

Other writers include 17th-century playwright Molière, who helped create the Comédie-Française (➤ 124), France's national theatre, while Jean Racine (1639–99) premiered some of his plays at the Théâtre de l'Odéon. The 19th century saw the genius of novelists Balzac, Zola, Flaubert and Hugo. Among the countless 20th-century writers, Marcel Proust, F Scott Fitzgerald, Samuel Beckett, Henry Miller and Anaïs Nin, Jean-Paul Sartre and Simone de Beauvoir all resided in Paris; the city, society and urban culture of the era influenced their writings extensively.

Paris in Music

Musicians, too, have been attracted to the city: Rameau (1683–1764), pioneer of harmony, Berlioz (1803–69) and Liszt (1811–86) are all associated with Église St-Eustache (➤ 137), while the great organist family, the Couperins, gave frequent recitals in various churches, and Offenbach (1819–80) composed his famous cancan here. Mozart (1756–91) visited Paris often as a child. His final trip, however, was a disaster. He was no

Above left to right: American lyricist Cole Porter; French singer Vanessa Paradis

longer acknowledged as a prodigy, and his mother died during their stay. Mozart left in 1788, utterly contemptuous of Parisian society.

The Opéra Garnier (➤ 113), one of the most prestigious opera houses in the world, has staged such premieres as Wagner's *Tannhäuser*, Bizet's *Carmen* and Debussy's *Pelléas et Mélisande*; and soprano Maria Callas gave numerous acclaimed performances here.

Jazz has thrived in Paris since its heyday in the 1920s, when Cole Porter lived here and Gershwin composed his *American in Paris*. Today a host of clubs, including Le Duc des Lombards (21 Boulevard de Sébastopol, 75001; tel: 01 42 33 22 88) and the Lionel Hampton Jazz Club (Hôtel Le Méridien-Étoile, 81 Boulevard Gouvion-St-Cyr, 75017; tel: 01 40 68 30 42), continue to attract top international performers. The city's most celebrated *chanteuse*, however, is Edith Piaf (➤ 142), famous for her powerful, emotional voice and her nostalgic songs of street life, lost loves, drugs, death and prostitutes, which are still performed in the bars and cafés of Montmartre.

The Magazine

Paris in Film

The city's spacious promenades and Seine-side riverbanks have played a starring role in hundreds of films. First-time visitors to the city will find the winding alleys and well-documented landmarks eerily familiar.

Paris has been a choice stage since the 1950s. From French new wave *(nouvelle vague)* directors Jean-Luc Godard and Claude Chabrol to surrealist Luis Buñuel (*Belle de Jour*, with Catherine Deneuve), they have all opted to set their groundbreaking films in *la Ville-Lumière (the City of Light)*. Audrey Hepburn visited in the 1960s, for *Charade* and *How to Steal a Million*, and Paris was the 1972 backdrop for Bernardo Bertolucci's *Last Tango in Paris*, starring Marlon Brando. *Amélie* (2001), Jean-Pierre Jeunet's romantic comedy starring Audrey Tautou, was set in Montmartre; Nicole Kidman and Ewan McGregor danced in the eponymous *Moulin Rouge;* and the film adaptation of *The Da Vinci Code* (2006), starring Tom Hanks and Audrey Tautou, was set largely in Paris. Most recently, the city was the star of Woody Allen's comedy *Midnight in Paris* (2011).

Above left to right: Actress Sophie Marceau; American author Henry Miller

Star-Gazing

Today's city celebrities include film stars Sophie Marceau, Audrey Tautou, Julie Delpy, Juliette Binoche and Catherine Deneuve; among Paris's fashion gurus are Christian Lacroix and wacky Jean-Paul Gaultier, who brings life and colour to the Parisian fashion scene with his quirky clothing, perfume and accessories.

The Grave Side of Stardom

Since 1804, Père-Lachaise (► 141), the city's largest cemetery, has been the place to be interred – the ultimate status symbol for the rich and famous, from playwright Molière to lovers Abélard and Héloïse, from opera singer Maria Callas, authors Gertrude Stein and Alice B Toklas to writer and wit Oscar Wilde and dancer Isadora Duncan.

The most visited grave is that of Jim Morrison, lead singer of The Doors, who died in 1971 from a drug overdose while living in Paris.

Finding your Feet

First Two Hours

Don't be daunted by the size of Paris. It's actually quite a small city and finding your way to the centre on arrival is surprisingly straightforward, thanks to the efficient and easy-to-use public transport systems.

Roissy Charles de Gaulle Airport

Roissy Charles de Gaulle (www.adp.fr) is Paris's main airport, 25km (16mi) northeast of the city centre. There are three terminals. Air France uses Terminal 2. You can get to the city in three ways:

- **By bus:** Air France operates a bus service to Montparnasse every 30 minutes 7am–9pm, and to the Arc de Triomphe every 15 minutes 5:45am–11pm. (You needn't have flown on Air France to use this service.) Alternatively, the Roissybus (www.ratp.fr) runs every 15 minutes to Opéra 6am–11pm (every 20 minutes after 7pm), taking 45 minutes to 1 hour.
- **By taxi:** A taxi to the centre costs around €50 and takes 30 minutes to 1 hour, depending on the traffic. Note that fares can increase by up to 15 per cent between 5pm and 10am, and on Sundays and public holidays. For heavy luggage, an additional charge of €1 per item is payable.
- **By train:** The RER (Réseau Express Régional – a suburban express train network) line B takes around 35 minutes into central Paris. Trains leave every 4 to 15 minutes (4:55am–11:55pm).

Orly Airport

Orly Airport (www.adp.fr) lies 15km (9mi) south of Paris, and is therefore much closer to the city centre than Roissy. There are two terminals: Orly-Sud for most international flights; and Orly-Ouest for domestic flights, Air France and some international carriers. Although there are no direct public transport links, access to the city centre is swift and easy.

- **By bus:** Unless you're staying on the south side of the city, it's unlikely that the Orlybus (6am–11:30pm) to Denfert-Rochereau Metro will be convenient. Instead, opt for the Air France shuttle buses to Les Invalides and Gare Montparnasse, which depart daily every 15 minutes 6am–11:30pm. The trip takes about 30 minutes.
- **By taxi:** A taxi will cost around €35 to the city centre, and takes around 15 to 30 minutes. Fares increase at night, on Sundays and public holidays.
- **By train:** The Orlyval train, which operates every 4 to 8 minutes daily 6am–11pm, will take you two stops to Antony, where you can change on to the main Paris RER rail system (line B). From here it takes around 30 minutes to reach the city centre.

Gare du Nord – Arrival Point for Eurostar

This is probably the easiest way to arrive in Paris. The train (www.eurostar.com) takes you right into the heart of Paris, just 3km (2mi) from the official centre, and, as all the customs and immigration formalities are completed before arrival, you can head straight into the city from the station.

- The **Eurostar terminal** is on the upper level of the Gare du Nord, and includes a currency exchange bureau, a newsagent, cafés and bars.
- The **Gare du Nord** station is on two Metro (underground) lines and three RER (overland) lines (▶ right).
- **Taxi** queues are depressingly long when a Eurostar train arrives but they move fairly quickly. Be aware of extra charges for baggage.

Getting Around

The city can be divided into two halves; the Right Bank or la Rive Droite and the Left Bank or la Rive Gauche. Its official centre is Notre-Dame cathedral (► 76). Most of the top sights are within an 8km (5-mile) radius.

Arrondissements

For more than a century, Paris has been divided into 20 *arrondissements* (districts), which spiral out clockwise from the city centre like a snail's shell. The central *arrondissements* are logically numbered from 1 to 8:

- **1er** (75001) heart of the Right Bank, centred on the Louvre and part of the Île de la Cité.
- **2e** (75002) the commercial district to the east of the Opéra.
- **3e/4e** (75003/4) the Marais, part of Île de la Cité, and Île St-Louis.
- **5e** (75005) Latin Quarter on the Left Bank.
- **6e** (75006) St-Germain district.
- **7e** (75007) residential Faubourg St-Germain and the Eiffel Tower.
- **8e** (75008) chic district of avenues radiating from the Arc de Triomphe.

City Centre Tourist Offices

Paris's tourist offices are good for maps and information about what's on. They will also help you to sort out accommodation. Department stores Au Printemps and Galeries Lafayette offer free tourist maps.

Office du Tourisme (main office) ✉ 25 Rue des Pyramides, 75001 ☎ 08 92 68 30 00 🕐 Jun–Oct daily 9–7; Nov–May Mon–Sat 10–7, Sun and public hols 11–7 🚇 Pyramides

Île de France ✉ Carrousel du Louvre, 99 Rue de Rivoli, 75001 ☎ 08 92 68 30 00 🕐 Daily 10–6. Closed public hols 🚇 Palais Royal-Musée du Louvre

Anvers Office ✉ boulevard de Rochechouart (opposite No 72), 75018 🕐 Daily 10–6. Closed public hols 🚇 Anvers

Montmartre ✉ 21 Place du Tertre, 75018 ☎ 01 42 62 21 21 🕐 Daily 10–7. Closed 1 May 🚇 Abbesses

Gare de Lyon ✉ 20 Boulevard Diderot, 75012 ☎ 08 92 68 30 00 🕐 Mon–Sat 8–6. Closed public hols 🚇 Gare de Lyon

Gare du Nord ✉ 18 Rue de Dunkerque, 75010 ☎ 08 92 68 30 00 🕐 Daily 8–6. Closed public hols 🚇 Gare du Nord

Paris Expo Office ✉ 1 Place de la Porte de Versailles, 75015 ☎ 08 92 68 30 00 🕐 Daily 11–7 during fairs and exhibitions 🚇 Porte de Versailles

Public Transport

Buses are good for sightseeing; routes are clearly marked on bus stops and in the buses. The transport of choice is the Métropolitain or RER, two separate but linked systems. The RER is a suburban rail network that passes through the city centre, while the Metro (underground) has 16 lines and more than 300 stations. Both are cheap and efficient and function in the same way; tickets are interchangeable. For transport information in English,

Finding your Feet

call 08 92 69 32 46 or visit the website: www.ratp.fr. People with limited mobility as well as those with partial sight can contact Infomobi (➤ 196).

How to Use the Metro
- **There is a Metro map inside the back cover of this book.**
- **Metro lines** are identified by their end-station, a colour and a number.
- The Metro operates from 5:30am to around 1:15am (2:15am Fri–Sat).
- The city is divided into **five fare zones**, but for everything covered in this book you will just need zone 1, apart from La Défense (zone 3), the excursions and the airports (zone 4: Orly, zone 5: Roissy).
- Buy a **Carnet Ticket-t** of 10 tickets for zone 1 – it costs about the same as seven single tickets.
- You can get an unlimited *Paris Visite* travel pass for one, two, three or five days for zones 1–3 or 1–6. Tickets are available from all main stations.
- **Validate your ticket** on entering the station by placing it in the slot on the side of the barrier; remove it from the second slot on top before passing through the turnstile. Keep it as inspectors fine ticketless travellers.

Batobus
The Batobus shuttle boat (tel: 08 25 05 01 01; www.batobus.com) operates all year (except early Jan to early Feb) every 17 to 35 minutes: 10–9:30 in summer; 10–7 in spring and autumn; 10:30–4:30 in winter. It stops at the Eiffel Tower, Musée d'Orsay, St-Germain-des-Prés, Notre-Dame, Hôtel de Ville, Louvre, Jardin des Plantes and the Champs-Élysées. Tickets can be purchased for single trips, one, two or five days, or a full month.

Taxis
Taxis can be hailed in the street if the white roof sign is illuminated, or there are taxi ranks at most main sights. Calling the City of Paris taxi service (tel: 01 45 30 30 30) will put you in touch with a taxi at the rank nearest you.

Car
Parking is difficult and expensive (although www.parkingdeparis.com can offer reduced fees if booked in advance), filling stations are hard to find, and the one-way systems can make driving a nightmare. The city speed limit is 50kph (31mph) and safety belts must be worn. For advice, visit www.theaa.com/motoring_advice/overseas.

Car Rental
All the main car-rental companies have desks at Roissy CDG airport, and in the city centre. Contact Avis (tel: 08 20 05 05 05), Hertz (tel: 08 25 86 18 61) or Europcar (tel: 08 25 01 13 31) for details.

Bicycles
Paris's Vélib' bike-hire scheme was launched in 2007 (tel: 01 30 79 79 30; www.velib.paris.fr). Journeys under 30 minutes are free; a day's ticket costs €1.70; a weekly one €8. A credit card deposit is required. Tickets are available at the many docking stations or online (no need to pre-register).

Discount Passes
A **Paris Museum Pass** (www.parismuseumpass.com) offers unlimited access to more than 60 sights and museums (not temporary exhibitions) over a two-, four- or six-consecutive day period. It is available at tourist offices, railway stations and museums, and online through FNAC.

Accommodation

From luxurious palaces to guest houses for every budget, Paris offers visitors a range of accommodation possibilities – only be sure to reserve well in advance, particularly in the spring and autumn.

Reservations

An excellent reservation service for both hotels and restaurants is provided by the website of the Paris Tourist Office (www.parisinfo.com), which offers discounts, as well as suggestions for special occasions. Many hotels will offer deals either through their own websites or on hotel booking websites, so shop around if you have time. Remember it's also useful to check out online reviews; Expedia has customer ratings and reviews as does Tripadvisor.

Multinational Chains

Multinational chains are encroaching here as elsewhere, and though their hotels offer relatively good accommodation, they are rather soulless, without real national identity. Often, because of their size, service is more automated than personal. However, they are a useful standby when the city gets booked up during trade fairs in spring and autumn. **Holiday Inn** (tel: UK: 0800 40 50 60, France: 08 00 91 16 17; www.holidayinn.com) has 26 hotels in and around the city. Accor Hotels (tel: 08 92 23 02 00; www.accorhotels.com) own 165 hotels in Paris, shared between the discount **Ibis**, **Étap** and **Formule 1** chains and the more upscale **Mercure** and **Sofitel.**

Apartments

Renting an apartment makes practical and financial sense: it is like having your own private address, and the facilities are excellent. All are serviced on a daily basis. Rooms are comfortable and spacious, with lots of storage space. Bathrooms are up to date and well maintained. Galley kitchens provide the necessary items for self-catering. **Paris Appartements Services** (20 Rue Bachaumont, 75002; tel: 01 40 28 01 28; www.paris-apts.com) offers a good selection. There are plenty to choose from at www.feelparis. com, www.specialapartments.com or, at the high-end, www.rentapart.com.

Hostels

Hostels provide budget rooms that are generally shared with others and may not have their own bathrooms. Most are geared towards the under-35s. The best contact point is the main tourist office: **Office de Tourisme de Paris**, 25 Rue des Pyramides, 75001; tel: 08 92 68 30 00; June–Oct daily 9–7, Nov–May Mon–Sat 10–7, Sun and public hols 11–7; Metro: Pyramides/ Tuileries. Arrive as early as possible because queues soon build up. The city's youth hostels include **Auberge Internationale des Jeunes** in Bastille (10 Rue Trousseau, 75011; tel: 01 47 00 62 00; www.aijparis.com; Metro: Bastille/ Ledru Rollin), with rooms for up to four people, and **Auberge de Jeunesse de Paris Jules Ferry** (8 Boulevard Jules Ferry, 75011; tel: 01 43 57 55 60; www.fuaj.org/Paris-Jules-Ferry; Metro: Goncourt), with rooms for up to six.

Bed-and-Breakfasts

For B&B, and sometimes dinner, in private homes contact **France Lodge**, 2 Rue Meissonier, 75017; tel: 01 56 33 85 85; www.francelodge.fr; Metro: Wagram. The selection on pages ➤ 40–42 represents a small cross-section of some of Paris's best, most characterful hotels.

Finding your Feet

Four Seasons George V €€€€

Expertly managed, this *grande dame* hotel is stylish, not stuffy. The public areas, built around the scented courtyard garden, are filled with natural light and laden with exotic plants. Downstairs, the highly acclaimed spa, which is open to non-guests, uses Carita and Sodashi products to relieve jetlag and stress, or simply to pamper. Rooms are sumptuous and elegant.

✚ 202 C4 ✉ 31 Avenue George V, 75008
☎ 01 49 52 70 00; www.fourseasons.com/paris
Ⓜ George V

L'Hôtel €€€€

Formerly the Hôtel d'Alsace, and now an award-winning classy hotel, this is where Oscar Wilde died in 1900. Restored and re-opened in 1968 by the present owners, it retains many original features, including a reconstruction of Wilde's modest room. By contrast, bedrooms are now tastefully styled throughout. There's room service until 2am, a *hammam* and an indoor pool.

✚ 204 C1 ✉ 13 Rue des Beaux-Arts, 75006
☎ 01 44 41 99 00; www.l-hotel.com
Ⓜ St-Germain-des-Prés

Hôtel Agora €/€€

In a central location near Les Halles and the Centre Pompidou, this is an attractively decorated hotel with small rooms and good-value prices. There are five floors, with a lift; the bedrooms on the top floor are the most characterful, with sloping ceilings. All have a shower and toilet; larger rooms have bathtubs too.

Insider Tip

✚ 205 E3 ✉ 7 Rue de la Cossonnerie, 75001
☎ 01 42 33 46 02; www.hotel-paris-agora.com
Ⓜ Les Halles

Hôtel Caron de Beaumarchais €€

This historic hotel is named after the author of *Le Mariage de Figaro*, which inspired Mozart to write his famous opera. Take a romantic journey back to the 18th century here; the hotel's 19 rooms are soundproofed and equipped with all modern conveniences: en suites, air conditioning, satellite TV, high-speed WiFi internet connection. Breakfast is served until noon.

✚ 206 A2 ✉ 12 Rue Vieille-du-Temple, 75004
☎ 01 42 72 34 12; www.carondebeaumarchais.com Ⓜ Hôtel de Ville

Hôtel de Crillon €€€€

The Crillon vies for the accolade of finest hotel in Paris, and is the preferred place to bed down of both presidents and royalty, from Theodore Roosevelt to the Dalai Lama. The 94 guest rooms and 43 suites are exquisite. Annick Goutal products are available in the marble-clad bathrooms. Many overlook Place de la Concorde, or the American Embassy. Ask about early arrival and late weekend check-out options.

✚ 204 A3 ✉ 10 Place de la Concorde, 75008
☎ 01 44 71 15 00; www.crillon.com Ⓜ Concorde

Hôtel Design de La Sorbonne €€/€€€

A very chic hotel on the doorstep of the Sorbonne University, although one designed with the guest, not a style guru, in mind. The Mac computers in each room, framed by fine linen and a bold colour scheme, are for watching DVDs and web surfing. Book in advance for a discount.

✚ 209 E4 ✉ 6 Rue Victor Cousin, 75005
☎ 01 43 54 58 08; www.hotelsorbonne.com
Ⓜ Cluny-La Sorbonne

Hôtel Gabriel €€/€€€€

This detox design hotel equates comfort with style, and has been wildly popular since its inception in early 2009. The calm white rooms feature hardwood floors and freestanding bathtubs. Hi-tech innovations include LED patterns that stud the walls and a NightCove machine, which emits soft sounds and coloured lights to aid restful sleep. Paris's finest tea, Kusmi, is served with the buffet breakfast.

🏨 206 C4 ✉ 25 Rue du Grand-Prieuré, 75011 ☎ 01 47 00 13 38; www.hotel-gabriel-paris.com Ⓜ Oberkampf

Hôtel du Levant €/€€

This family-run hotel in the heart of the Latin Quarter, a five-minute walk from Notre-Dame, is full of Parisian charm. The 47 rooms have air conditioning and internet access. The buffet breakfast is included in the bargain room rate. Direct RER trains go to the airports and Gare du Nord.

🏨 209 F5 ✉ 18 Rue de la Harpe, 75005 ☎ 01 46 34 11 00; www.hoteldulevant.com Ⓜ St-Michel

Hôtel du Louvre €€€€

This historic hotel, facing the Opéra Garnier and the Louvre Museum, was built in 1855 at the behest of Napoleon III and, at the time, was considered France's foremost luxury hotel. At the heart of the hotel are the dark wood and club chairs of the exclusive Defender Bar. The 177 rooms all have WiFi and are stocked with Annick Goutal beauty products. As well as offering cooking courses and late checkout times, the hotel also organises romantic breaks and shopping trips.

🏨 204 C3 ✉ place André Malraux, 75001 ☎ 01 44 58 38 38; www.hoteldulouvre.com Ⓜ Palais Royal-Musée du Louvre

Hôtel Madison €€/€€€

Albert Camus was a regular and finished his famous novel L'Étranger here. Rooms are elegantly and classically furnished on the lower floors, while those on higher floors are more cool and contemporary. The celebrated café Les Deux Magots is opposite.

🏨 204 C1 ✉ 143 Boulevard St-Germain, 75006 ☎ 01 40 51 60 00; www.hotel-madison. com Ⓜ St-Germain-des-Prés

Hôtel de la Place du Louvre €€

From rooms with a view at this laid-back, welcoming hotel, you can admire the gargoyles of St-Germain l'Auxerrois and the Louvre. Each of the 20 spacious bedrooms comes complete with a sparkling bathroom and free WiFi. Although simple French breakfasts are served in the atmospheric Musketeers' Cellar, sample the city's best croissants at Cador, a venerable salon de thé at the end of the street.

🏨 205 DF2 ✉ 21 Rue des Prêtres St-Germain-l'Auxerrois, 75001 ☎ 01 42 33 78 68; www.paris-hotel-place-du-louvre.com Ⓜ Louvre-Rivoli/Pont Neuf

Hôtel Relais St-Germain €€€

Set in a charming 17th-century town house, this idyllic hotel almost feels as though it is in the countryside. This is due not only to sound-proof double-glazing and an abundance of flowers, but also to carved stonework, parquet flooring and wooden beams in most rooms. Ranging from intimate standards to large suites, most of the 22 rooms have a separate bathroom, and are named after French writers. The hotel's literary theme is reinforced by an enticing reading room off the lobby, where you can pick French classics off the shelves.

🏨 209 E4 ✉ 9 carrefour de l'Odéon, 75006 ☎ 01 44 27 07 97; www.hotelrsg.com Ⓜ Odéon

Hôtel du Séjour €

Insider Tip

Friendly and freshly painted, the hotel is perfectly located five minutes from the Centre Georges Pompidou. The rooms in this family-run hotel – and don't be surprised to see the said family sharing dinner in the first floor reception room – are a little like Granny's spare room: dated, but not too poky. Some share a bathroom and toilet, and all are reached by the same narrow staircase.

Finding your Feet

⊞ 205 F3 ✉ 36, Rue Grenier Saint Lazare, 75003 ☎ 01 48 87 40 36; www.hoteldusejour.com 🚇 Rambuteau

Terrass Hôtel €€€
At the foot of the Butte Montmartre and close to Sacré-Cœur, the Terrass has been run by the same family for four generations. The 98 comfortable rooms include 13 suites, and the seventh-floor restaurant (May–Sep only) and bar lounge have superb views, shared by front-facing rooms on the fourth to sixth floors. The ground-floor restaurant is open year-round (but closed Sun eve and Mon).
⊞ 200 B3 ✉ 12 Rue Joseph-de-Maistre, 75018 ☎ 01 46 06 72 85; www.terrass-hotel.com 🚇 Blanche/Place de Clichy

Villa Madame €€/€€€
A discreet oasis a stone's throw from the Jardin du Luxembourg. Following a renovation, cooling grey colours are used throughout the hotel, with orchids outside every soundproofed room and Hermès products inside the marble bathrooms. Breakfast is a selection of fresh fruit, organic yoghurt and pastries, and can be taken in the petite garden in summer. As you'd expect from a hotel of this calibre, there's free WiFi and an art-filled lobby in which to relax.
⊞ 209 D4 ✉ 44 Rue Madame, 75006 ☎ 01 45 48 02 81; www.hotelvillamadameparis.com 🚇 St-Sulpice

La Villa Saint-Germain €€€
For designer chic and cutting-edge décor, you can't go wrong with this gem, popular with celebrities. No period furnishings here but comfort is not sacrificed. Bedrooms and bathrooms are stylish and modern. A smart place-to-be-seen bar is on the ground floor. Check out their reduced-rate internet prices.
⊞ 204 C1 ✉ 29 Rue Jacob, 75006 ☎ 01 43 26 60 00; www.villa-saintgermain.com 🚇 St-Germain-des-Prés

Food and Drink

Paris enjoys an international reputation as the world capital of gastronomy. No trip to Paris would be complete without visiting some of its countless restaurants, brasseries, bistros and cafés. For Parisians, gastronomy, or the art and science of good eating and drinking, is more than a pastime – it is a way of life in a city where the inhabitants spend a greater proportion of their income on food than they do on almost anything else. A selection of restaurants is included at the end of each chapter in this guide.

More than One Type of Cuisine
In his 32-volume *La France Gastronomique*, Curnonsky, the famous French gastronome and author who died in 1956, identified four distinct types of French cookery: *"La Haute cuisine, la cuisine Bourgeoise, la cuisine Régionale* and *la cuisine Improvisée"*. His categories still stand today.
- **Haute cuisine**, based on a solid classical foundation and built on long, hardworking and rigorous apprenticeships and great techniques, is professional cooking by chefs of the highest achievement. In current terms it describes accurately the cooking of multi-starred Michelin chefs such as Alain Ducasse (►119) and Guy Savoy (►66).
- **Nouvelle cuisine** is (or was) a modern interpretation of *haute cuisine*, in which top chefs reconstructed classic French dishes in response to demand in the 1980s for lighter, more decorative and fanciful food that relied heavily on much-reduced sauces to carry the flavours. In its original form, the style was short-lived. However, *nouvelle cuisine* has left a

distinctive mark on French *haute cuisine*, where classic dishes are now prepared in a much lighter vein than 25 years ago.

■ By contrast, **cuisine improvisée** is peasant or rustic in origin and execution: in other words, old-fashioned farmhouse dishes using simple ingredients.

■ It is the two remaining categories that have most shaped the culinary map of Paris. **Cuisine bourgeoise**, French provincial cooking, is based on the simple day-to-day dishes of ordinary middle-class French cookery. **Cuisine régionale**, meanwhile, features the great regional specialities reflecting the produce of the regions, with classic dishes such as *bouillabaisse* (fish stew) and *estouffade de bœuf* (beef stew) from Provence, pike with *beurre blanc* (creamy sauce) from the Loire, *coq au vin* (chicken in red wine) from Burgundy and *cassoulet* (meat and bean stew) from Toulouse.

Opening Times

Most restaurants open for lunch at 12 and close at 2:30 or 3, then open again at around 7 for dinner until 10 or 10:30. Note that many of the better restaurants close at the weekends, too, and nearly all for the whole of July or August.

Bistros, Brasseries and Restaurants

Visitors to Paris are often confused by the distinctions between bistros, brasseries and restaurants.

Bistro

■ A bistro is basically a small, modest establishment with a short menu of **traditional, home-style cooking,** together with a good selection of local cheeses.

■ **Wine** is offered by the carafe or *pichet* (jug), with only a small selection available by the bottle.

Brasserie

■ *Brasserie* is the French word for brewery, but the word nowadays describes a lively, smart, yet **informal** restaurant that serves food at any time of the day and often late into the night.

■ **Beer** remains a feature; some brasseries offer an extensive selection.

■ **Typical dishes** are *choucroute*, a hearty blend of sauerkraut and assorted sausages, *blanquette de veau* (veal in a cream sauce) and **steak frites** (steak with chips or fries). Shellfish plays a major part, as witnessed by the mountainous displays outside many brasseries on Paris's boulevards.

Restaurant

■ Fully fledged restaurants offer elegant, classic **haute cuisine** in a more refined setting. Prices are higher, but frequently these restaurants offer **fixed-price menus** of surprisingly good value, especially at lunch time.

■ Some **specialize** in creative modern cooking, others in seafood or classic regional dishes.

■ Whereas in a bistro or brasserie it is usual to order the house wine, restaurants often have long-standing **wine cellars** and *sommeliers* (wine waiters) who will happily give advice on what to order with the food.

■ At top restaurants it is absolutely essential to **reserve your table** well in advance, often weeks or months.

■ For dinner especially, both sexes should **dress smartly**, men with jacket and tie, though in trendier establishments ties are not *de rigueur*.

Finding your Feet

Recommended Restaurants

Le Chamarré (➤ 164, www.chamarre-montmartre.com) – romantic setting, with a terrace, and serving exotic, contemporary food.

L'Ambroisie (➤ 144; www.ambroisie-paris.com) – elegant surroundings in a town house on the Place des Vosges.

Pierre Gagnaire (➤ 121; www.pierre-gagnaire.com) – inventive, imaginative cuisine from one of France's most creative chefs.

Le Gaigne (➤ 146; www.restaurantlegaigne.fr) – fine organic cuisine; the lunchtime menu is good value for money.

Alain Ducasse (➤ 119; www.alain-ducasse.com) – one of France's top chefs reinterprets classic *haute cuisine*.

Cafés and Bars

- There are around **10,000 cafés and bars** in Paris. Cafés with rows of seats facing out into the street are as typically French as the baguette.

- **Coffee and beer** (*café* and *bière)* are the main drinks; tea is usually mediocre (except in *salons de thé*). Drink coffee black and order draught beer (*une pression*) – it's cheaper. **Hot chocolate** (*chocolat chaud*; often made with real chocolate) is superb.

- A **service charge** is automatically applied to all café bills, which you settle when you're ready to leave; *service compris* means service is included.

- Staff should be addressed politely as "*monsieur*" or "*mademoiselle*": never call "*garçon!*" or snap your fingers.

- The hub of Paris café society is **St-Germain-des-Prés**: here you will find **Café de Flore** (➤ 29) and **Les Deux Magots** (➤ 64), once the haunts of bohemian existentialists, now pricey, sought-after tourist attractions.

Recommended Breakfast Venues

Café Beaubourg (➤ 145) – stylish café overlooking the Pompidou Centre.

Le Cochon à l'Oreille (➤ 29) – legendary workers' café near Les Halles, famous for its early snacks.

Recommended Tea Salons

Angélina ✚ 204 B3 ✉ 226 Rue de Rivoli, 75001 – great hot chocolate.

L'Ébouillanté ✚ 206 A2 ✉ 6 Rue des Barres, 75004 (www.restaurant-ebouillante.com) – tiny tea shop with delicious pastries.

Ladurée ✚ 204 A4 ✉ 16 Rue Royale, 75008 (www.laduree.fr) – old-fashioned tea room known for its macaroons.

Mariage Frères (➤ 65) – chic and expensive tea shop.

Recommended Aperitif Venues

Café de la Musique ✚ 206 off C5 ✉ 213 Avenue Jean-Jaurès, 75019 (www.cite-musique.fr) – modern cocktail bar in Cité de la Musique complex.

La Gueuze (➤ 94) – a temple to beer, 130 brands from around the world.

Le Baron Rouge ✚ 206 off C1 ✉ 1 Rue Théophile Roussel, 75012 – part bar, part wine shop.

Le Fumoir ✚ 205 D2 ✉ 6 Rue de l'amiral de Coligny, 75001 – vintage, stylish bar close to the Louvre with happy hour (6–8pm).

Restaurant Prices

The prices refer to a set menu, excluding drinks:

€ under €25   €€ €25–€50   €€€ €51–€100   €€€€ over €100

Shopping

Paris excels in two notable areas: *haute couture* and *haute cuisine*. This is one of the style capitals of the world. One of the many pleasures of visiting this vibrant but often expensive capital, and one that will not affect your pocket, is window-shopping, admiring the exhilarating displays on offer.

■ Best for **exclusive shopping** is the Right Bank, in an area contained within Boulevard de Sébastopol to the east, Boulevard Haussmann to the north, and Rue Washington and Avenue George V to the west.

■ The major **department stores** are also here (with the exception of Bon Marché in the **7th *arrondissement***, ➤ 69). These were the first in the world, designed as showplaces for affordable fashion and jewellery.

■ Some of the more exclusive shops require you to be **dressed in a suitable manner**: scruffy attire is frowned upon.

■ Shopping on the **Left Bank** is a more hit-and-miss affair, but the numerous narrow, crowded streets off Boulevard St-Germain are worth exploring.

■ To the east is the **5th *arrondissement***, the student quarter, with its numerous bookshops.

■ The **6th and 7th *arrondissements*** are home to a sumptuous array of antiques shops and individual boutiques, though the 7th, consisting largely of wealthy residential areas and government properties, lacks a good network of Metro connections: if you're prepared to do the legwork, however, there are some superb shops to be discovered.

Cosmetics and Fragrances
■ Cosmetics and perfumes aren't much cheaper than at home, so have your home stores' prices to hand to enable you to **make comparisons**.

■ The major perfume houses often launch their new fragrances in the large department stores such as Galeries Lafayette: it's well worth paying them a visit to check out the **introductory offers**.

Gourmet Foods
■ Paris is a Mecca for foodies. It is a city of wonderful **pastry and chocolate shops**. Hévin (➤ 123) is a must for chocolate fans.

■ For **cheeses** try Alléosse (➤ 123) in the 17th *arrondissement*, Barthélémy and Marie-Anne Cantin in the 7th (➤ 69) and La Ferme St-Aubin (➤ 95) in the 4th.

Opening Hours
As a rule most shops are open until at least 7pm, but some close for lunch (noon–2) and on Mondays. The major chains are open continuously Monday to Saturday 9:30–7, usually with late nights till 10pm on Thursdays. Sunday opening is limited by law, but some supermarkets and small shops may open for at least part of the day, especially in more touristy areas.

Top Markets
Marché Biologique Raspail (➤ 69) for organic fruits and vegetables.
Marché aux Fleurs (➤ 83) for all types of flowers.
Marché aux Puces de Saint-Ouen (➤ 163) seems to offer everything imaginable.
Marché du Livre (Parc George Brassens, open Sat and Sun 9:30–6; Metro: Porte de Vanves) for second-hand and antiquarian books.

Entertainment

The weekly *Pariscope* or *l'Officiel des Spectacles* magazines are essential listings guides to what's on in Paris, available at newsstands, www.paris nightlife.fr, gives information about concerts, clubs and bars.

Tickets

■ For tickets to all events, including sport, classical music, jazz and rock, apply to **FNAC** (136 Rue de Rennes, 75006; tel: 08 25 02 00 20; www. fnac.com; Metro: St-Placide – also eight other FNAC branches). Make sure to book at least two weeks in advance.

■ For discounted tickets on the day, be prepared to queue at **Kiosque Théâtre** (opposite 15 Place de la Madeleine, 75008; Tue–Sat 12:30–8, Sun until 4, closed Mon; Metro: Madeleine). Avoid the ticket agencies around the city.

Opera and Theatre

■ Paris has **two opera houses** and four of France's **five national theatres**. In the latter you'll find French-language productions of the classics, including Molière, Goethe and Shakespeare.

■ French theatre is very much geared towards **intellectual stimulation** rather than comedy and spectacle, the emphasis being on style and content of the spoken word rather than on action or characterization.

Cinema

■ Paris is the capital of the small **art-house cinema**, with more than 300 films a week being screened in more than 400 cinemas.

■ The large **UGC George V** (146 Avenue des Champs-Élysées, 75008; tel: 08 92 70 00 00; www.ugc.fr; Metro: George V) has two old-style cinemas, complete with balconies, and with multi-screens. Films shown in their original language are designated "VO" *(version originale)*.

■ Cinémathèque Française (51 Rue Bercy, 75012; tel: 01 71 19 33 33; www.cinemathequefrancaise.com; Metro: Bercy) shows classic films in their original language. La Pagode (➤ 70) is one of the world's most beautiful cinemas set in a 19th-century replica of a Japanese pagoda.

Cabarets and Clubs

■ Paris's cabarets and live shows are a spectacle of glitter, dance-hall and transvestite vignettes nowadays geared towards an international audience. The most famous is the Moulin Rouge (➤ 158).

■ The city's club scene begins around 1am, is expensive and geared towards the beautiful and **ultra-chic**. Bars are a good alternative and many have DJs or jazz. Closing time is usually around 2am.

Sport

There's plenty to entertain sports fans, from **Grand Slam tennis** at the Roland Garros tennis complex (2 Avenue Gordon Bennet, 75016; tel: 01 47 43 49 56; www.rolandgarros.com; Metro: Porte d'Auteuil) to **international football and rugby** at the Stade de France (St-Denis-la-Plaine, tel: 08 92 70 09 00; www.stadefrance.com, RER: La Plaine-Stade de France). Major **horse-racing** events take place at Longchamp racecourse (www.france-galop. com) in the Bois de Boulogne, and the celebrated **Tour de France** (www. letour.fr) concludes in late July on the Champs-Élysées.

Eiffel Tower to St-Germain-des-Prés

 **Little Treats**

Ice Skating above Paris

Strange but true: in winter, you can actually go **ice-skating** on the first floor of the Eiffel Tower, absolutely free (➤ 53).

A Glimpse through Time

One of the clocks in the **Musée d'Orsay** is transparent, giving a clear view of the Sacré-Cœur basilica in the distance (➤ 56).

Stroll through the Musée Rodin

If the sun is shining outside and you don't fancy going into a museum, just take a stroll through the **sculpture garden** (➤ 63).

Eiffel Tower to St-Germain-des-Prés

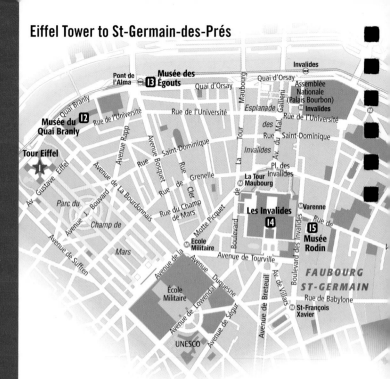

Getting Your Bearings

The Left Bank, or Rive Gauche, cradled by the Seine at the very heart of the city, oozes Parisian character and charm, with its bustling street markets, its long-aproned waiters in crowded cafés, its sophisticated shopping, and its tiny candle-lit bistros that look frozen in time with their cheery red-and-white checked tablecloths. It is hardly surprising that it is an eternal favourite for visitors and one of the most sought-after residential districts in Paris.

In this chapter, the Left Bank includes the area south of the Seine from the Eiffel Tower in the west to the Jardin du Luxembourg in the east, but not the Latin Quarter. It contains many of the city's best-known and most-loved attractions, including the extraordinary Musée d'Orsay (►56) – an Industrial Age railway station audaciously converted into the capital's main Impressionist gallery; the atmospheric St-Germain-des-Prés *quartier* – the traditional intellectual and literary heart of Paris and a veritable paradise for gourmets, shoppers and coffee drinkers; and, of course, Eiffel's famous tower, which sits astride the urban landscape like a gigantic piece of Meccano.

TOP 10

⭐ Tour Eiffel ➤ 53
9 Musée d'Orsay ➤ 56

Don't Miss

11 St-Germain-des-Prés ➤ 60

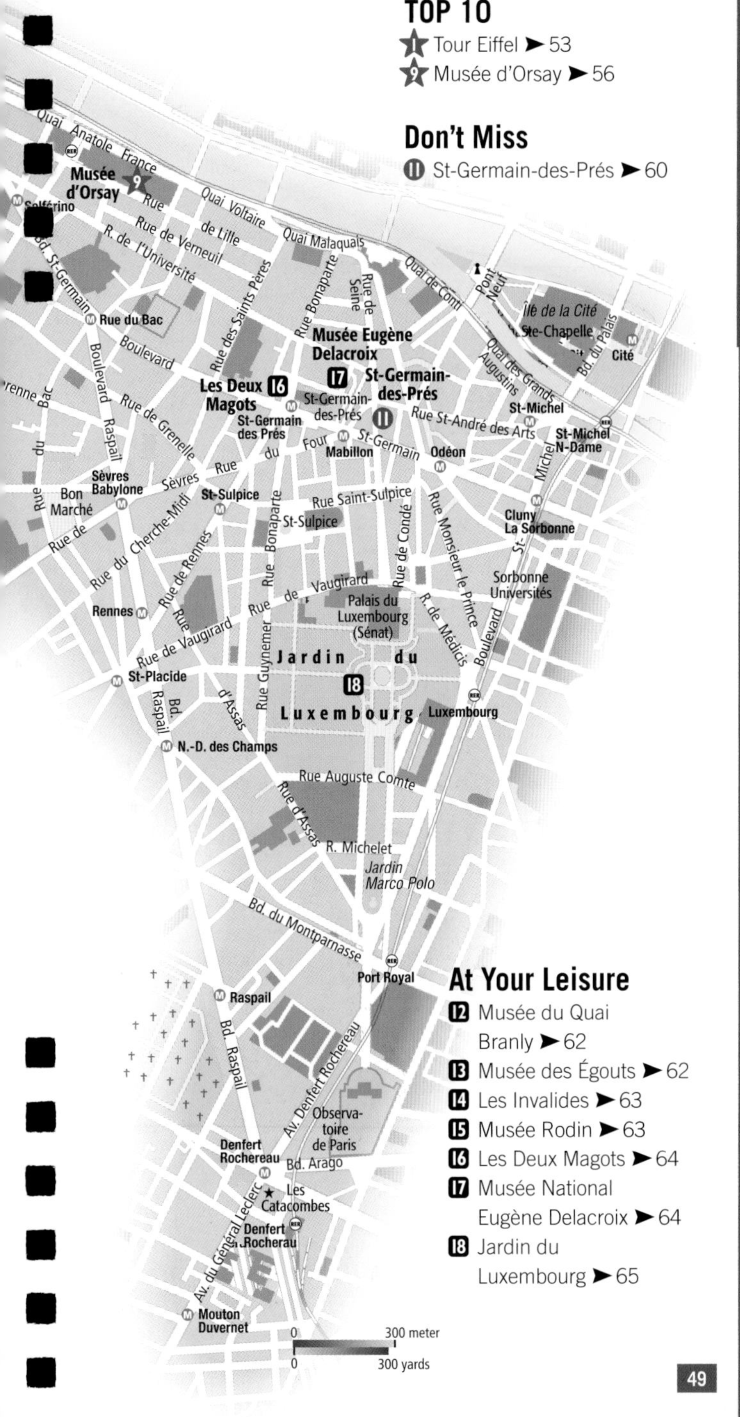

Quai Anatole France

Musée d'Orsay 9

Solférino

Quai Voltaire
Rue de Lille
Rue de Verneuil
R. de l'Université
Quai Malaquais
Quai de Conti
Pont Neuf

Quai Anatole France

Rue du Bac
Boulevard
Boulevard St-Germain
Rue des Saints Pères
Rue Bonaparte
Rue de Seine

Île de la Cité
Ste-Chapelle
Quai des Grands Augustins
Bd. du Palais
Cité

Musée Eugène Delacroix

17 **St-Germain-des-Prés**

Les Deux 16 **Magots**
St-Germain-des-Prés
St-Germain des Prés
Rue St-André des Arts
St-Michel

renne Bac
Boulevard Raspail
Rue de Grenelle
Rue du Four
St-Germain
Mabillon
Odéon
St-Michel N-Dâme

Sèvres Babylone
Bon Marché
Rue de Sèvres
Sèvres
Rue
St-Sulpice
St-Sulpice
Rue Saint-Sulpice
Rue de Condé
Cluny La Sorbonne

Rue du Cherche-Midi
Rue de Rennes
Rue Bonaparte
Rue Monsieur le Prince
Sorbonne Universités

Rennes
Rue de Vaugirard
Rue Guynemer
Rue de Vaugirard
de Vaugirard
Palais du Luxembourg (Sénat)
R. de Médicis
Boulevard

St-Placide
Bd. Raspail
d'Assas
J a r d i n   d u
18
L u x e m b o u r g Luxembourg

N.-D. des Champs

Rue Auguste Comte

Rue d'Assas
R. Michelet
Jardin Marco Polo

Bd. du Montparnasse

Port Royal

Raspail
Bd. Raspail
Av. Denfert Rochereau
Av. du Général Leclerc

Observatoire de Paris

Denfert Rochereau
Bd. Arago
★ **Les Catacombes**
Denfert Rochereau

Mouton Duvernet

0   300 meter
0   300 yards

At Your Leisure

12 Musée du Quai Branly ➤ 62
13 Musée des Égouts ➤ 62
14 Les Invalides ➤ 63
15 Musée Rodin ➤ 63
16 Les Deux Magots ➤ 64
17 Musée National Eugène Delacroix ➤ 64
18 Jardin du Luxembourg ➤ 65

Eiffel Tower to St-Germain-des-Prés

The Perfect Day

If you're not quite sure where to begin your travels, this itinerary recommends a practical and enjoyable day out exploring the Eiffel Tower to St-Germain area, taking in some of the best places to see. For more information see the main entries (➤ 52–65).

🕘 9:00am
Arrive early (9am June to August; 9:30 rest of year) at the ❶ **Tour Eiffel** (right, ➤ 53), beat the crowds and be among the first to reach the top for truly breathtaking views of the capital and the countryside beyond. On a clear day they say you can see as far as Chartres, more than 70km (45mi) away.

🕙 10:00am
Stroll down the Champ de Mars past *boules*-playing locals, children on ponies, lovers entwined on benches and camera-clicking tourists (the views from here of Eiffel's old Iron Lady are particularly photogenic). Continue on to ⓮ **Les Invalides** (right below, ➤ 63) – it's the last resting place of Napoleon Bonaparte, and it's also one of the world's most comprehensive museums of military history.

🕛 12:00 noon
Arrive at the famous ❾ **Musée d'Orsay** art gallery (➤ 56) in plenty of time for lunch at the museum's excellent Café des Hauteurs. Then, for dessert, feast on Manets, Monets and other Impressionist treasures.

🕞 3:30pm
Make your way westwards along the Seine to browse in the tattered, green wooden booths of second-hand books and prints that line the river, known as *les bouquinistes*.

13 Musée des Égouts

Assemblée Nationale

12 Musée du Quai Branly

★ Tour Eiffel

Parc du Champ de Mars

Les Invalides

9 Musée d'Orsay

14 **15** Musée Rodin

Musée National Eugène Delacroix

Les Deux Magots **16** **17**

11 St-Germain-des-Prés

UNESCO

Jardin du Luxembourg **18**

Les Catacombes

0   300 meter
0   300 yards

🕓 4:00pm

Explore the maze of streets south of *les bouquinistes* and you'll soon discover why **11** St-Germain-des-Prés (► 60), centred on its famous church, is considered a shoppers' paradise, with its myriad tiny galleries, antiques dealers, chic interior design shops and fashion boutiques.

🕕 6:00pm

If by now you've run out of energy on your shopping spree, recharge your batteries with a coffee (or a refreshing *citron pressé* on a hot day) at the famous but touristy café, **16** Les Deux Magots (► 64) on Boulevard St-Germain. If possible, find a table outside that overlooks the church of St-Germain-des-Prés. The bars and cafés of St-Germain have long been associated with Parisian intellectual life and, although the heydays of Ernest Hemingway and Jean-Paul Sartre are gone, Les Deux Magots still draws a fascinating crowd of would-be writers, actors and philosophers.

🕗 8:00pm

St-Germain really comes alive by night. Head south of Boulevard St-Germain and you'll be spoiled for choice of restaurants for dinner. Now, what do you fancy?

⭐Tour Eiffel

It's strange to think that Gustave Eiffel's famous tower, the universally beloved symbol of Paris, was considered a hideous eyesore when it was constructed more than 125 years ago. Since its inauguration in 1889, however, more than 200 million people have climbed the tower, and today the "Iron Lady" attracts around 6 million visitors annually, making it one of the best-loved tourist attractions in the world.

Above: Gustave Eiffel (bottom of steps) also designed the frame of the Statue of Liberty in New York

Left: The construction of the Eiffel tower still impresses today

The lacy wrought-ironwork of this masterpiece of engineering is amazing, and most visitors find soaring skywards in a double-decker glass lift both exciting and alarming. Writer Irwin Shaw saw it as a giant phallic symbol, while Hitler, passing through the city in 1940, was unimpressed: "Is that all it is? It's ugly." Whatever your reaction, no visit to Paris is complete without seeing this awesome 7,300-tonne structure of gleaming brown metal, and the views from the top on a clear day are unforgettable.

Competition Winner

In 1885, Paris held a competition to design a 300m (984-foot) tower as the centrepiece for the **World Fair** marking the centenary of the French Revolution in 1889. Gustave Eiffel, nicknamed the **"magician of iron"**, won the contest with his seemingly functionless tower, beating 107 other proposals, including one for a giant sprinkler and another for a commemorative guillotine.

It took **less than two years** to build the tower. Initially it grew at a rate of 10m (33 feet) a month, speeding up to nearly 30m (98 feet) a month as it neared the summit. Yet on the day it opened, none of the lifts worked. Eiffel and his 60-strong party of officials had to climb the 1,710 steps to place the French flag at the top. (There are now 1,665 steps to the top, but the staircase leading to the third level is closed to the public.)

For years the finished product remained a **world-record** breaker, twice the height of any other building (until New York's Chrysler building went up in 1930). For the first six months it drew a staggering 12,000 visitors a day. However, it was not without its **critics**, who slated it as "scrap metal".

Local residents objected to this "overpowering metal construction" that straddled their district, fearing it would

Eiffel Tower to St-Germain-des-Prés

sway and collapse, crushing their homes beneath it. Author Guy de Maupassant was a regular at the **second-floor restaurant**, swearing that it was the only spot in Paris from which you could not see the tower. Together with 300 other prominent members of the intelligentsia of the time (including Charles Garnier, Charles Gounod and Alexandre Dumas), he launched a petition against its erection, describing it as a "monstrous construction", a "skeleton", a "hollow candlestick" and a "bald umbrella", and condemning it as a "crime against history and against Paris". On a more positive note, the playwright Jean Cocteau described it as the **Queen of Paris**.

A view of the Champ de Mars and Tour Montparnasse from the tower

The tower was originally designed to stand for 20 years. Fortunately, its height was to be its salvation – the tall iron tower proved to be a marvellous **antenna**. The first news bulletin was broadcast from the Eiffel Tower in 1921, and the first television broadcast in 1935. It was also used to measure **atmospheric pressure** and, after being reclaimed from its German occupiers in 1944, to decipher German

INSIDER INFO

- 👫 Younger visitors to Paris will also have fun paying a visit to the gigantic tower.
- Visit early in the morning or late at night to avoid the worst of the crowds.
- **For the best views**, arrive one hour before sunset.
- The tower looks at its **best after dark** when every girder is illuminated.
- Get your postcards stamped with the famous **Eiffel Tower postmark** at the post office on level one (daily 10–7:30).
- The tower celebrated the **millennium** with a **sparkling show**. This lighting effect has now become a permanent feature; the **glittering lights** come on for the first 5 minutes of every hour, from nightfall until 2am in summer, 1am in winter.
- **Fast track** Climb the stairs to the first level (57m/187 feet; 5min.). Catch your breath in the *cineiffel* (a short film recounts the tower's history), then walk or take the lift to level two (115m/377 feet). Tickets for both stages from the ticket office at the bottom of the southern pillar (Pilier Sud.)

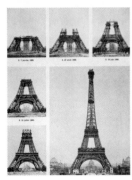

World War II radio codes. In 1937, it was the venue for a beauty contest, at which the minimum height required of contestants was 1.75m (5 feet 7 inches), as a token of respect for the tall Iron Lady!

Over the years, countless eccentrics have **jumped off** the tower with various home-built flying machines, hang gliders and parachuting kits. In 1977, a crazy but skilful American pilot flew between the legs of the tower and promptly lost his flying licence.

The stages of construction of the tower

TAKING A BREAK

Try the imaginative, well-priced set menus at **58 Tour Eiffel** (1st floor, tel: 01 72 76 18 46; daily noon–2:30, 7–11).

🕂 202 B2

✉ Champ de Mars, 75007 ☎ 01 44 11 23 23; www.tour-eiffel.fr

🕐 2 Sep to mid-June daily 9:30am–11:45pm; mid-June to 1 Sep 9am–12:45am. Last entrance 45 min before closing

🍴 Café (Level 1) €; 58 Tour Eiffel restaurant (Level 1) €€; Jules Verne restaurant (Level 2, ➤ 67) €€€€

🚇 Bir-Hakeim 🚉 RER Champ de Mars-Tour Eiffel

🎫 By elevator: 1st floor and 2nd floor €8.50; 3rd floor €14.50. On foot (1st and 2nd floors only): €5

⭐ Musée d'Orsay

If you visit only one art gallery during your stay, make it the Musée d'Orsay, a feast of 19th-century art and design, including a hugely popular collection of Impressionist paintings. The originality of this amazing museum lies in its presentation of a wide range of different art forms – painting, sculpture, decorative and graphic art – all under the lofty glass roof of a former Industrial Age railway station.

The museum occupies the former **Gare d'Orsay**, built by Victor Laloux on the site of the Palais d'Orsay, which was destroyed during the Paris Commune in 1871. The station was inaugurated in 1900 but ceased operating in 1939 with the dawn of electric trains, and remained empty for several decades. It was subsequently used as an auction room by Drouot-Richelieu, then as a theatre, and was saved from demolition by the skin of its teeth in 1973, thanks to the public outcry over the destruction of the historic pavilions at Les Halles food market (▶ 138). It was finally converted into a museum in 1986.

Musée d'Orsay – even the building itself is a work of art

Architectural Masterpiece
The Gare d'Orsay had always been an admirable piece of architecture. Even at its inauguration the monumental iron-and-glass edifice of cathedral-like proportions was considered so striking that painter Édouard Detaille suggested it should be converted into a museum or art gallery. Thankfully, much of the original architecture,

including its crowning glory, the **beautiful vaulted glass roof,** enhanced today by a statue-lined promenade, has been retained.

The station's **two massive clocks** have also been restored. One provides the backdrop for the **Café des Hauteurs** on the top floor. Watching its giant minute hand clunk round the hour ensures a swift lunch here! In its heyday, the Gare d'Orsay took great pride in its hotel. Its expansive belle époque dining-room has been preserved on the first floor, complete with gilded mirrors and candelabras, offering sensational views across the Seine to the Rive Droite.

Renoir's
*Bal du Moulin
de la Galette*
is among
the gallery's
collection

Seeing the Museum

The precious art collections span the years from 1848 to 1914, conveniently starting where the Louvre (➤ 102) leaves off and ending where the Centre Pompidou (➤ 133) begins. They are **organized chronologically on three levels,** with additional displays throughout clarifying the various contexts in which the art was created.

The skylit upper level houses the biggest crowd-puller – a dazzling collection of **Impressionist** and **post-Impressionist** treasures. It would be impossible to list all the star attractions, but favourites include Monet's *Coquelicots (Poppies)* and *La Rue Montorgueil – Fête du 30 juin 1878*, Renoir's *Danse à la ville (Town Dance)* and *Danse à la campagne (Country Dance)*, van Gogh's *La Chambre à Arles (The Room at Arles)* and Matisse's pointillist *Luxe, calme et volupté (Luxury, peace and pleasure)*. Montmartre fans will especially enjoy Renoir's *Bal du Moulin de la Galette*, Degas' *L'Absinthe* and Toulouse-Lautrec's *Danse au Moulin Rouge*, all inspired by local scenes.

The close juxtaposition of paintings and sculptures on the **ground floor** illustrates the huge stylistic variations in art from 1848 to the early 1870s (when Impressionism first made its name). Look out in particular for Courbet's *L'Origine du monde (Origin of the World)* and early Impressionist-style works such as Boudin's *La Plage de*

SCULPTURE

Throughout the museum you will find priceless sculptures at every turn, especially along the central aisle. The 26 caricature busts of members of parliament here by satirist **Honoré Daumier** are especially entertaining. The middle floor includes treasures by **Rodin**, including the plaster version of *La Porte de l'Enfer (Gateway to Hell)*, a vast bronze that occupied the last 37 years of his life but remained unfinished at his death. Many of the **Degas** bronzes on the top floor were cast from wax sculptures found in his studio after his death, but the beautiful and unique *Danseuse habillée (Clothed Dancer)* was exhibited during his lifetime.

Trouville (The Beach at Trouville) and Monet's *La Pie (The Magpie)*. Here, too, are the so-called opera rooms – devoted to architect Charles Garnier and his *pièce de résistance*, the Palais Garnier (Opéra de Paris; ➤ 113) – and a fantastic bookshop.

The **middle level** features *objets d'art* of the art nouveau movement, displaying the sinuous lines – epitomized here in furniture by Charles Rennie Mackintosh and jewellery and glassware by Lalique – that led the French to nickname the movement *style nouille* (noodle style).

Left: The central sculpture aisle in the museum

Below: The museum's Van Gogh Gallery

🏛 204 B2　✉ 1 Rue de la Légion d'Honneur, 75007
☎ 01 40 49 48 14; www.musee-orsay.fr
🕐 Tue–Sun 9:30–6 (Thu until 9:45). Last entrance 45 min before closing
🍴 Self-service cafeteria €; café €; restaurant €€
Ⓜ Solférino　🚆 RER Musée d'Orsay
🎫 €12. 18-25 year olds from EU member states go free.

INSIDER INFO

- Be sure to **pick up a plan of the museum** as the layout is not clearly signed and can be rather confusing.
- The half-dozen guides in the museum shop provide a succinct outline of the most important works of the collection. For a more comprehensive look at the collection, the beautifully illustrated *Guide to the Musée d'Orsay* is a must.
- If you are pressed for time, *ignore the lower floors* and head straight to the upper level to see the famous Impressionists on the river side of the gallery.

Insider Tip

TICKETS AND TOURS

- Tickets for the permanent exhibits are valid all day, so **you can leave and re-enter** the museum as you please.
- There are **separate fees** for temporary exhibitions. Prices vary depending on the exhibition. There are several ticket machines in the foyer. Those with a **museum pass** or a ticket purchased in advance can walk straight past the entrance queue.
- There are **tours in English**. Ask for a ticket at the information desk.
- **Audio guides** – audio tours (available in from just beyond the ticket booths on the right) steer you round the major works, many of which had a revolutionary impact on 19th-century art. Both these and the English-language tours are excellent.

⑪ St-Germain-des-Prés

Chic, lively and centrally located, St-Germain-des-Prés represents everyone's idea of the Left Bank. It bursts with cafés, restaurants, antiques shops, art galleries and fashion boutiques, and is peopled by students, arty types, the "*caviar gauche*" – the wealthy socialist intelligentsia – and the simply rich, who come here to sample the bohemian life.

St-Germain's eventful history dates back to the sixth century with the founding of the **Benedictine Abbey of St-Germain-des-Prés**, a powerful ecclesiastical complex throughout the Middle Ages. After the Revolution of 1789 only the church of St-Germain-des-Prés survived, a fine example of the Romanesque style and the oldest church in Paris. Its bell tower is a useful landmark for visitors.

Intellectual Haunt

The area around the church was first developed in the late 1600s, but today it is celebrated for its 19th-century charm. It gained its reputation as the intellectual and literary heart of Paris between the two world wars, when just about every notable Parisian artist, writer, philosopher and politician frequented three now-legendary cafés on Boulevard St-Germain – the **Café de Flore** (No 172, ➤ 29), **Brasserie Lipp** (No 151) and, most famous of all, **Les Deux Magots** (6 Place St-Germain, ➤ 29, 64). Later, in the 1950s, the area became the hot spot for the jazz generation.

The main artery of Boulevard St-Germain stretches east-west from the Latin Quarter to the staid government buildings and mansions of the Faubourg St-Germain. It also divides St-Germain-des-Prés neatly into two halves. To the north, you will find traditional cafés, hundreds of art galleries and antiques shops and the **École des Beaux-Arts**; to the south lie trendy bars, eateries and shopping streets containing such gems as **Le Bon Marché** (➤ 69), Paris's first department store.

Today, St-Germain is uncertain whether to cling to its pre-war intellectual days or to move with the times as part of the new, forward-looking capital. It is still the literary and artistic heart of Paris, with the École des Beaux-Arts and most publishing houses established here, and with countless antiques dealers still thriving on selling the past.

Busy tables outside Les Deux Magots café (above) and Café de Flore (right)

But the spotlight has been turned on to fashion, and the area is now considered a **luxury shopping district** with such designers as Giorgio Armani, Kenzo, Christian Lacroix, Yves Saint-Laurent and Sonia Rykiel moving in from the Rive Droite. Yet despite its *nouveau-glamour*, St-Germain still retains its arty atmosphere, a slower pace of life than the Rive Droite, and its popularity (see walk, ➤ 186).

➕ 204 B1 ✉ 75006
🚇 St-Germain-des-Prés

Left: A sign at the Place Sartre–Beauvoir remembers the philosophers and writers

INSIDER INFO

- Treat yourself to **picnic supplies** from the Rue de Buci market (mornings only) or the covered Marché St-Germain.
- Soak up the atmosphere of tiny, tranquil **Place Furstemberg**.
- **Window-shop** in the streets of the Carré Rive Gauche, the grid of streets around Rue de Beaune, famous for high-quality antiques.
- **People-watch** in one of the great literary cafés (➤ 28).
- Browse through *les bouquinistes*, the ramshackle old green booths of second-hand literary treasures that line the banks of the Seine.

At Your Leisure

12 🏛 Musée du Quai Branly

Designed by Jean Nouvel and surrounded by landscaped public gardens, this stunning ethnological museum devoted to the arts and civilizations of Africa, Asia, Oceania and the Americas offers visitors a new approach to non-Western cultures. What's more, the exhibition also boasts works of art

🚺 202 B2
✉ 27, 37 and 51 Quai Branly; 206 and 218 Rue de l'Université, 75007
☎ 01 56 61 70 00; www.quaibranly.fr
🕐 Tue–Wed, Sun 11–7, Thu–Sat 11–9. Last entrance 45 min before closing. Closed public hols
🍴 Café €, restaurant €€
Ⓜ Alma-Marceau ⓇⒺⓇ RER Pont de l'Alma
🎟 €8.50

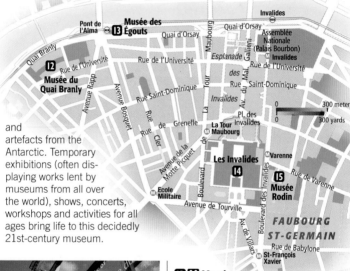

and artefacts from the Antarctic. Temporary exhibitions (often displaying works lent by museums from all over the world), shows, concerts, workshops and activities for all ages bring life to this decidedly 21st-century museum.

13 🏛 Musée des Égouts

Immortalized in *Les Misérables* as an escape route for Jean Valjean, and the location of the phantom's lair beneath the Opéra Garnier in the hit show *Phantom of the Opera*, the sewers of Paris form a sophisticated 2,100km (1,300mi) maze of subterranean tunnels, masterfully constructed by Baron Haussmann in the late 19th century. You, too, can discover the mysteries of underground Paris in what is undoubtedly the smelliest museum in the city.

The Musée du Quai Branly is one of Paris's newest museums

➕ 202 C3 ✉ Pont de l'Alma, rive gauche
(entrance in front of 93 Quai d'Orsay), 75007
☎ 01 53 68 27 81 🕐 May–Sep Sat–Wed 11–5;
Oct–April 11–4. Closed 2 weeks in Jan for
maintenance Ⓜ Alma-Marceau
🚆 RER Pont de l'Alma 🎟 €4.30

🔟4 Les Invalides

The imposing architectural ensemble of Les Invalides, constructed
around a grand church and hous-
ing several museums, is a must
for anyone interested in history.
It is best approached from Pont
Alexandre III, up the long grassy
esplanade, with its fountains carefully chosen by Napoleon to out-do
the fountains of Rome. The Hôtel
National des Invalides was originally built by Louis XIV as a convales-
cent home for wounded soldiers.
Its austere 195m (640-foot) long
slate and stone facade is a splendid example of 17th-century classical architecture. In its heyday, the
complex resembled a small town.

Though still home to war veter-
ans, Les Invalides stands today as
a memorial to the endless battles
and campaigns that have marked
French history, all vividly portrayed
in the **Musée de l'Armée** – one of the
most comprehensive museums of
its kind in the world. Of particular
interest is the **Museum of Relief Maps**
with its models of fortified towns,
illustrating the art of siege from
Louis XIV to Napoleon III, and the
exhibition spanning the two world
wars. Admission to the museum
also covers the **Musée de l'Ordre
de la Libération** and the **Église
du Dôme**. This masterpiece of
17th-century church architecture
rises high above the Hôtel des
Invalides. Inside, the centrepiece
is Napoleon's mausoleum: a
circular crypt containing his ashes
within a red porphyry sarcophagus.

Adjoining the Dôme, and origi-
nally a part of it, the **Soldiers Church**
is far more tasteful, decorated
only by a row of poignantly faded
tricolore pennants.

Les Invalides illuminated at night

➕ 203 E1 ✉ Esplanade des Invalides, 75007
☎ 01 44 42 38 77; www.invalides.org
🕐 Apr–Oct daily 10–6 (July–Aug Sun until
6:30); Nov–March 10–5; Dôme 10–7.
Closed 1st Mon of month
🍴 Café € Ⓜ La Tour-Maubourg/Varenne/
Invalides 🚆 RER Invalides
🎟 €9.50

🔟5 Musée Rodin

Nowhere is more pleasurable on
a sunny day than the sculpture-
studded gardens of the Musée
Rodin, an open-air museum dedicated to the best-known sculptor
of the modern age. Rodin lived
and worked in the adjoining elegant
mansion – Hôtel Biron – alongside
Cocteau and Matisse. Built in

NAPOLEON BONAPARTE

Napoleon is associated with this district
more than any other French ruler.
Here he celebrated his military suc-
cesses, staging grandiose parades on
the Champ de Mars. He used the esplanade outside Les Invalides to show
off his war spoils – guns captured in
Vienna in 1803 and a lion statue
plundered from St Mark's Square in
Venice – and he honoured his victorious armies in Les Invalides and the
nearby École Militaire, where he himself had trained as a young officer. His
passing-out report noted: "If the cir-
cumstances are right, he could go far."

The Chambre à Coucher in the Musée Delacroix

1730, the house was a dance hall, convent and school before becoming artists' studios. After Rodin's death, it became the Musée Rodin.

Inside are 500 Rodin sculptures, including such masterpieces as *The Kiss*, and *The Age of Bronze*, whose realism so startled the critics that they accused him of having imprisoned a live boy in the plaster.

You can see Rodin's most celebrated work, *The Thinker*, in deep contemplation in the garden he loved so much. Today it provides an intimate setting for such major works as the *Burghers of Calais*

CHAMBER OF HORRORS

If it's bones you want, visit Paris's eerie Catacombs – ancient Roman stone quarries filled in the 18th and 19th centuries with the overflow from the cemeteries. The sides of the underground route are constructed from the bones of some 6 million people, arranged from floor to ceiling, with spooky seams of skulls running through them. Not for those of a sensitive disposition or young children, but a visit will make a great adventure for teenagers! It is advisable to wear practical shoes.

✉ Avenue du Colonel Henri Rol-Tanguy, 75014 ☎ 01 43 22 47 63 🕙 Tue–Sun 10–5 (last entrance 1 hour before closing) 🎫 €8 🚇 Denfert-Rochereau

---

and *Balzac*, as well as sculptures by Camille Claudel, his one-time pupil, model and lover.

✚ 208 A5 ✉ 79 Rue de Varenne, 75007 ☎ 01 44 18 61 10; www.musee-rodin.fr 🕙 Tue–Sun 10–5:45, Wed until 8:45; Oct–March garden until 5 🍴 Café (April–Sep 9:30–5:30; Oct–March 9:30–4:30) €. Free 1st Sun of month 🚇 Varenne 🎫 €9, garden only €1

16 Les Deux Magots

Described by journalist Albert Thibaudet as "an intersection of roads, an intersection of professions, an intersection of ideas", Les Deux Magots was founded in 1881 and named after the wooden statues of two Chinese dignitaries (*magots*) who sit atop boxes of money on a pedestal inside the café. It was a particular favourite of Picasso and Hemingway, who would read his works aloud here. Jean-Paul Sartre and Simone de Beauvoir, however, preferred **Café de Flore** nearby in Boulevard St-Germain (No 172, ➤ 29), while Brasserie Lipp (No 151) was a favourite of St-Exupéry, Camus and President Mitterrand. Nowadays, the cafés are popular tourist haunts, but legends die hard and they still attract a surprising number of celebrities and members of the literary élite.

✚ 209 D5 ✉ 6 Place St-Germain-des-Prés, 75006 ☎ 01 45 48 55 25; www.lesdeuxmagots.fr 🚇 St-Germain-des-Prés

17 Musée National Eugène Delacroix

Hidden off the road in a charming cobbled courtyard, this tiny museum was the last home and studio of the great French Romantic painter, from 1857 until his death, at the age of 60, in 1863. Among the modest belongings on display are Delacroix's paint-boxes and palettes, some of his sketches, self-portraits and animal paintings and lots of letters. In many ways, his airy, generously windowed studio is an attraction in itself. As Delacroix himself wrote, "My lodgings are indeed charming. The sight of my small garden and the cheerfulness of my studio always give me pleasure."

🎭 PROUD AS PUNCH!

If you're with kids who might appreciate a Punch and Judy show, take them to see the **puppet shows** on the Champ de Mars (daily at 3:15 and 4:15 during school holidays).

Luxembourg, one of the oldest parks in Paris and its second largest. It was designed in the formal French style with precisely planted rows of trees, trim hedges, immaculate lawns, fountains, ponds and bench-lined gravel paths. The park remains a favourite rendezvous for students and residents of the Latin Quarter, although visitors from all the surrounding *quartiers* come to play chess or tennis, or simply to lounge on one of the park's benches. The *jardin* also makes a great destination for children thanks to its adventure playground, its street performers, its pony rides, the carrousel and the motorboats for hire.

The grand Palais du Luxembourg overlooking the gardens was built for Marie de Médicis, widow of Henri IV. It was completed in 1627, but she lived there for only five years before being expelled from France by Cardinal Richelieu. The palace remained a royal residence until the Revolution, when it was used as a prison.

Since 1879, it has been the seat of the French Senate, with a brief interlude during World War II, when the German occupying forces made it their headquarters.

✚ 209 D3   ✉ Boulevard St-Michel, 75006
☎ 01 42 34 23 89   🕐 Daily 7:30/8:15–dusk
🎟 Free   🚇 Odéon   🚆 RER Luxembourg

✚ 209 D5
✉ 6 Rue de Furstemberg, 75006
☎ 01 44 41 86 50;
www.musee-delacroix.fr
🕐 Wed–Mon 9:30–5;
June–Aug Sat–Sun until 5 (last entrance 30 min before closing)
🚇 St-Germain-des-Prés
🎟 €5. Free 1st Sun of month

18 🎭 Jardin du Luxembourg

Numerous artists, poets, writers and philosophers have paid tribute to the beautiful Jardin du

Where to...
Eat and Drink

Prices

Expect to pay per person for a meal, excluding drinks:

€ under €25   €€ €25–€50   €€€ €51–€100   €€€€ over €100

L'Affriolé €€

This intimate bistro's name comes from the Old French word for "to tempt", and the inventive brasserie-based cuisine conjured up by Alain Atibard does just that. Dishes burst with flavour and use seasonal produce: *magret de canard* (fillet of duck) with vegetable samosas, or a summer soup of rhubarb and strawberry. Lesser-known regions are featured on the extensive wine list. The laid-back bistro décor conjures up a genuinely Parisian ambience, much favoured on weekdays by politicians from the nearby Assemblée Nationale.

🚩 203 D2 ✉ 17 Rue Malar, 75007
☎ 01 44 18 31 33
🕐 Tue–Sat noon–2, 7:30–10:30. Closed Aug
🚇 Invalides

Aux vieux garcons €€

With its mosaic floors and the elegant stucco on the walls, this bistro has retained the charm it's had since 1902. Monkfish and scallops are served perfectly garnished with fine herbs under the watchful eye of managers from the Basque region. The meat dishes also bear witness to their meticulous preparation of the freshest ingredients. It goes without saying that all the side orders in this historic establishment are also homemade. The desserts are a real feast for the eyes. The lunch menu is particularly good value for money.

🚩 204 A1 ✉ 213 Boulevard Saint Germain, 75006 ☎ 01 42 22 06 57
🕐 Mon–Sat noon–10:30 🚇 Rue du Bac

L'Arpège €€€€

Located in a quiet street mainly of government offices, the restaurant interior is sombrely, yet stylishly, minimalist with its largely unadorned curved pearwood panelling. In this setting Alain Passard's three-Michelin-star cooking positively glows with originality. The lunch-time and evening tasting menus are the best ways to sample the award-winning, mostly vegetarian, fare on offer. Advance booking is a necessity.

🚩 208 A5 ✉ 84 Rue de Varenne, 75007
☎ 01 47 05 09 06; www.alain-passard.com
🕐 Mon–Fri noon–2, 6–10 🚇 Varenne

Le Bistrot du 7ème €

A little gem among the handful of great bistros just off Place Salvador Allende, where outdoor sun terraces and candlelit tables are the order of the day. The cuisine is traditional with a slight regional influence: foie gras and canard à l'orange, confit de canard (duck conserve), kidneys in mustard sauce. There is a choice of menus at very reasonable prices and a great selection of wines.

🚩 203 E2 ✉ 56 Boulevard de la Tour-Maubourg, 75007 ☎ 01 45 51 93 08
🕐 Mon–Fri noon–2:30, 7–10:30, Sat–Sun 7–10:30 🚇 La Tour-Maubourg

Les Bouquinistes €€

One of Guy Savoy's satellite restaurants, this trendy Left Bank bistro is named after the *bouquinistes* (booksellers) on the *Quai*. Décor is a blend of creamy hues with small colourful highlights gouged out of the plastered walls. The minimalist setting complements a short, modish menu. A blackboard lists a selection of the day's specials. Dishes are innovative and prepared with attention to detail, while service is pleasant and friendly.

✚ 209 E5 ✉ 53 Quai des Grands Augustins, 75006 ☎ 01 43 25 45 94; www.lesbouquinistes. com ⊙ Mon–Fri noon–2:30, 7–11, Sat 7–11:30 Ⓜ St-Michel

Le Cherche Midi €€

The ideal place to take refuge from chic shopping in the neighbourhood boutiques, this is a good old-fashioned cram-them-in and feed-them-well trattoria. The tasty menu holds no surprises – antipasti, pasta, grilled meats and veal escalopes – but servings are hearty, and the Montepulciano flows copiously. Meats are served with perfectly cooked vegetables as well as polenta. There's a small terrace for the summer months. The puddings belong to the familiar repertoire of Italian specials, including *panna cotta* and *tiramisù*, but you can also sample the famous Berthillon ice cream.

✚ 208 C4 ✉ 22 Rue du Cherche-Midi, 75006 ☎ 01 45 48 27 44; www.lecherchemidi.fr ⊙ Daily noon–3, 8–11:45 Ⓜ Sèvres-Babylone

Chez Germaine €

A place where St-Germain locals hunker down on shared tables with a newspaper and a *pichet* of wine. Like an exotic *grand-mère*'s kitchen, the cuisine is unfussy and hearty with the odd culinary twist: *faux-filet* and *magret de canard* are topped by touches of coriander or ginger. Bargain set menus are available for both lunch and dinner. **Insider Tip**

✚ 208 B4 ✉ 30 Rue Pierre Leroux, 75007 ☎ 01 42 73 28 34 ⊙ Mon–Sat noon–2:30, 7:30–10 Ⓜ Vaneau

Le Divellec €€€€

Jacques Le Divellec is one of Paris's prime exponents of contemporary fish cooking, the juxtaposition of raw fish and *foie gras* being his

creation. His lobster press is based on the Tour d'Argent's famous duck press (►94). The dining room overlooks the Esplanade des Invalides and the décor has a nautical theme, complementing the simple yet innovative cuisine. Elaborate sauces and unnecessary garnishes are shunned in favour of the quality and flavour.

✚ 203 E2 ✉ 107 Rue de l'Université, 75007 ☎ 01 45 51 91 34; www.chezgermaine. com ⊙ Mon–Fri noon–2, 7:30–10. Closed 1 week at Christmas Ⓜ Invalides

Le Jules Verne €€€€

You need to book online or by phone at least a month in advance to secure a table for a pricey dinner (one week ahead for a much less expensive lunch) in this stunning location on the second level of the Eiffel Tower, reached via a dedicated elevator. At 115m (375 feet) above the city, the superb views complement the highly imaginative and sophisticated cuisine of Alain Ducasse and his chef, Pascal Féraud. The black décor and artwork provide minimum distraction from the Parisian panorama.

✚ 202 B2 ✉ 2nd floor, Eiffel Tower, 75007 ☎ 01 45 55 61 44; www.lejulesverne-paris.com ⊙ Daily 12:15–1:30, 7:15–9:30 Ⓜ Bir Hakeim/Champ de Mars-Tour Eiffel.

Mariage Frères €

A chic and expensive tea shop which offers more than 460 teas from 20 countries. The colonial Indian atmosphere of the elegant upstairs dining room in the 17th-century building is the setting for an imaginative menu focused almost entirely on tea. While morning tea and cakes are available until 11:30, brunch comes in three varieties, all of which, including *Le Classique*, are served right up to 3pm – perfect for people who like a lie in.

✚ 209 E5 ✉ 13 Rue des Grands-Augustins, 75006 ☎ 01 40 51 82 50; www.mariagefreres. com ⊙ Daily 10:30–7:30 Ⓜ Odéon

Eiffel Tower to St-Germain-des-Prés

Le Petit St-Benoît €

To rub shoulders with the locals – signed photos testify to past visits from great writers and intellectuals – this is the place to come, but don't confuse it with nearby similarly named restaurants. Old-fashioned dishes like *petit salé aux lentilles (pork and lentils)* are mainstays of this refreshingly inexpensive place. Soups and terrines are made to centuries-old recipes, while main courses usually come with a heap of mashed potatoes or pasta. Good bread and fruity house wines are bonuses, as is the terrace for summer lunchtimes. No credit cards.

✚ 204 C1 ✉ 4 Rue St-Benoît, 75006
☎ 01 42 60 27 92; www.petit-st-benoit.com
🕐 Mon–Sat noon–2:30, 7–10:30. Closed Aug
Ⓜ St-Germain-des-Prés

Cigale Récamier €€

A favourite of politicians and publishers – Michelle Obama dined here with her two daughters in 2009 – this is a snug, comfortable restaurant with a fine line in hearty French classics such as *côte 'agneau*, refined soufflés, and a wonderful *bœuf bourguignon*. The wine list features claret, burgundy and Rhône wines from the 1950s.

✚ 208 C4 ✉ 4 Rue Récamier, 75007
☎ 01 45 48 86 58 🕐 Mon–Sat 12:30–2:30, 7:30–11 Ⓜ Sèvres-Babylone

La Rôtisserie d'en Face €€

Tucked away down a narrow street and across the road from his main eponymous restaurant at 14 Rue des Grands-Augustins (tel: 01 43 26 49 39), this is one of Jacques Cagna's cheaper dining options (the other is L'Espadon Bleu). A good selection of food is served in an informal, modern setting. The quality of such dishes as the Hereford roast beef, the spit-roasted *poulet fermier* and the poached pike is exquisite. Look for game in season; for dessert, opt for the fruit tart of the day.

✚ 209 E5 ✉ 2 Rue Christine, 75006
☎ 01 43 26 40 98; www.larotisseriedenface.com
🕐 Mon–Fri noon–2:30, 7–11, Fri–Sat 7–11:30
Ⓜ Odéon/St-Michel

Samiin €€

Not your average Korean restaurant. Instead, each perfectly presented dish has a French-gastro twist, from bite-sized egg pancakes to Korean-spiced *steak tartare*, alongside classics, such as *bibimbap* (baked rice topped with ground beef) and *kimchi* (pickled cabbage) soup. The calm yet attentive service is backed with soft Korean music.

✚ 207 F4 ✉ 74 Avenue de Breteuil, 75007
☎ 01 47 34 58 96 🕐 Tue–Sun noon–11
Ⓜ Sèvres-Lecourbe

Vagenende €/€€

This fine listed building, designed as a brewery at the turn of the 20th century, is now an elegant brasserie boasting a stunning art nouveau décor. The French cuisine is prepared with fresh market produce in true regional tradition: Provençal beef stew, duck with olives, traditional Alsace-style *choucroute (sauerkraut)*.Seafood is also a speciality, with a selection of oysters and shellfish.

✚ 209 E5 ✉ 142 Boulevard St-Germain, 75006 ☎ 01 43 26 68 18; www.vagenende.fr
🕐 Daily noon–1am Ⓜ Odéon

Le Violon d'Ingres €€€

Christian Constant, former head chef at Les Ambassadeurs in the Hôtel de Crillon, combines *haute cuisine* with a more down-to-earth rusticity at his comfortable and fashionable Left Bank bistro.
The same team put together the trendier – and less expensive – Les Cocottes bistro (same tel, closed Sun) next door. (For more info on Christian Constant, see ▶ 69.)

✚ 202 C2 ✉ 135 Rue St-Dominique, 75007
☎ 01 45 55 15 05; www.leviolondingres.com
🕐 Daily noon–2:30, 7–10:30.
Closed 3 weeks Aug Ⓜ École Militaire

Where to ...
Shop

The 6th is one of the most quintessentially Parisian of the *arrondissements*, famous for its shopping, and attracting designers such as Armani, Hermès, Lacroix and Kenzo, in the wake of Sonia Rykiel. Rue de Buci and its environs are a food shopper's paradise, with a daily market groaning under piles of cheese, fruit, meat and vegetables.

WHAT'S WHERE

Rue du Bac stretches from the 6th *arrondissement* to the Seine in the smart, largely residential 7th, where Rue du Pré-aux-Clercs and Rue Cler are worth investigating, but the main shopping streets are Rue de Grenelle and Rue St-Dominique.

DEPARTMENT STORE

Le Bon Marché (24 Rue de Sèvres, 75007; tel: 01 44 39 80 00; Metro: Sèvres-Babylone) is the best department store on the Left Bank with its Grande Épicerie food hall.

FOOD

Barthélemy (51 Rue de Grenelle, 75007; tel: 01 45 48 56 75; Metro: Rue du Bac) sells cheeses ripened to perfection, as does **Marie-Anne Cantin's** celebrated shop (12 Rue du Champ-de-Mars, 75007; tel: 01 45 50 43 94; Metro: École Militaire). For chocolate, try **Christian Constant** (37 Rue d'Assas, 75006; tel: 01 53 63 15 15; Metro: Notre-Dame-des-Champs/St-Placide) and **Debauve et Gallais** (30 Rue des Sts-Pères, 75007; tel: 01 45 48 54 67; Metro: St-Germain-des-Prés). **Oliviers & Co** (28 Rue de Buci, 75006; tel: 01 44 07 15 43; www.oliviers-co.com; Metro: St-Germain-des-Prés/Mabillon) sells olives and olive products. The **Marché Couvert St-Germain** (4 Rue Lobineau, 75006) has 20 high-end food stalls. On Sundays, a wonderful but expensive **organic market** (*marché biologique*) livens up the Boulevard Raspail near Rennes Metro station.

FASHION AND ACCESSORIES

Emporio Armani (149 Boulevard St-Germain, 75006; tel: 01 53 63 33 50; www.armani.com; Metro: St-Germain-des-Prés) also has a coffee shop (open Mon–Sat 12:30–midnight), not far from **Sonia Rykiel's** ready-to-wear fashion house, with its accessories and cosmetics (175 Boulevard St-Germain, 75006; tel: 01 49 54 60 60; www.soniarykiel.com; Metro: St-Germain-des-Prés). **Yves Saint-Laurent** for women is at 6 Place St-Sulpice, 75006 (tel: 01 43 29 43 00; www.ysl.com). The men's shop is at 12 Place St-Sulpice, 75006 (tel: 01 43 26 84 40; Metro: Mabillon). **Shu Uemura** (176 Blvd St-Germain, 75006; tel: 01 45 48 02 55; www.shuuemura.co.jp; Metro: St-Germain-des-Prés) is the outlet of a top make-up artist.

GIFTS

Find a vintage title at **Tea & Tattered Pages** (24 Rue Mayet, 75006; tel: 01 40 65 94 35; Metro: Duroc) or a coffee-table book from **La Maison Rustique** (26 Rue Jacob, 75006, tel: 01 42 34 96 60; Metro: St-Germain-des-Prés). **Emilio Robba** (63 Rue du Bac, 75007; tel: 01 45 44 44 03; www.emiliorobba.fr; Metro: Rue du Bac) specializes in exquisite artificial flowers. Visit **Souleiado** (78 Rue de Seine, 75006; tel: 01 43 54 62 25; www.souleiado.com; Metro: Mabillon/Odéon) for table and bed linen.

Where to ...
Go Out

This part of the city's Left Bank is virtually the world centre for alternative cinema, with a fantastic choice of films on offer. These art-house cinemas, mostly located in the 5th and 6th *arrondissements* (► 96) are all conveniently close to each other. Although a few venues may have seen better days, it is worth checking the listings pages in the Cinema section of *Pariscope* for the most diverse choice of programmes on offer anywhere in the world, and www.paris.angloinfo.com lists every original-language film playing each evening. Theatre and nightclubs are far thinner on the ground in these parts, but there are one or two notable exceptions.

CINEMA

At any one time you'll find classics such as *Metropolis* and *Easy Rider* alongside masterpieces such as the late Stanley Kubrick's *A Clockwork Orange*. Following the outcry when it was released, Kubrick forbade its screening, but Paris was one of the few cities where the film could be seen in its entirety. More recent cult films are also shown. Entry prices are thankfully a fair bit less than one would find in the city's larger, more commercial, cinemas.

Insider Tip
La Pagode (57 bis Rue de Babylone, 75007; tel: 01 45 55 48 48; Metro: St-François Xavier) is probably the city's most charming cinema: shipped over in sections from Japan, it is wonderfully exotic, with velvet seats, painted screens and a Japanese garden. Cult classics and recent arty releases are shown in the original language on

two screens. The following cinemas are also worth investigating:
Cinéma Christine (4 Rue Christine, 75006; tel: 01 43 25 85 78; Metro: Odéon).
L'Arlequin (76 Rue de Rennes, 75006; tel: 01 45 44 28 80; Metro: St-Sulpice).
Les Trois Luxembourg (67 Rue Monsieur-le-Prince, 75006; tel: 08 92 68 93 25; Metro: Cluny-La Sorbonne, RER: Luxembourg).

THEATRE AND CONCERTS

The **Théâtre du Vieux Colombier** (21 Rue du Vieux Colombier, 75006; tel: 01 44 58 15 15; www.vieux.colombier.free.fr; Metro: St-Sulpice) offers both classical and contemporary theatre by the world-famous Comédie-Française troupe (www.comedie-francaise.fr).
Odéon, Théâtre de l'Europe (1 Place Paul Claudel, 75006; tel: 01 44 85 40 00; www.theatre-odeon.fr; Metro: Odéon), stages classical and contemporary theatre from all over Europe, often in languages other than French.
The **American Church in Paris** (65 Quai d'Orsay, 75007; tel: 01 40 62 05 00; www.acparis.org; Metro: Invalides) holds free classical concerts.
Concerts range from gospel to classical recitals at the **church of St-Germain-des-Prés** (3 Place St-Germain-des-Prés, 75006; tel: 01 55 42 81 33; Metro: St-Germain-des-Prés), whose acoustics and setting are superb.

NIGHTLIFE

Le Don Camilo (10 Rue des Saints-Pères, 75007; tel: 01 42 60 82 84; Metro: St-Germain-des-Prés) offers dinner shows in French.
L'Echelle de Jacob (12 Rue Jacob, 75006; tel: 01 46 34 00 29; Metro: St-Germain-des-Prés) is a smart, gay-friendly nightspot open until 5am.

The Latin Quarter and the Islands

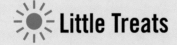 **Little Treats**

Read Traces of the Middle Ages

You can still see medieval street names carved into the stone of the **large square in front of Notre-Dame** (➤ 76) today.

The Best Ice Cream in the City

You'll find the city's best ice cream on the Île St-Louis. Enjoy it on **the small bridge leading to the Île de la Cité** (➤ 89).

Dancing by the Seine

After a **visit to the sculpture garden** (➤ 92), round off your evening with a boogie on the banks of the Seine.

Getting Your Bearings

The Latin Quarter has been the centre of learning in Paris for more than 700 years, home to prestigious schools and universities all clustered around their doyenne, the Sorbonne. The area's name derives from the academic tradition of studying and speaking in Latin, but nowadays in this multi-ethnic district, this is just about the only tongue you're guaranteed not to hear.

Today, despite the ever-increasing number of tourist shops and fast-food joints, the area is still a lively student district. It's a warren of cobbled medieval streets, overflowing with innumerable cafés, bookstores, cheap restaurants, quirky boutiques, cinemas, jazz clubs and smoky bars that stay open until late, preserving the quarter's legendary bohemian feel. Of the two river islands beside the Latin Quarter, the Île de la Cité is the more historic – home to the earliest inhabitants of Paris, the Gallic tribe of the Parisii (hence the city's name) – and it also boasts such awe-inspiring sights as the jewel-like Sainte-Chapelle and Notre-Dame. By contrast, the more intimate Île St-Louis provides a tranquil retreat from the hustle and bustle of the city.

Sainte-Chapelle – one of the city's most dazzling landmarks

At Your Leisure

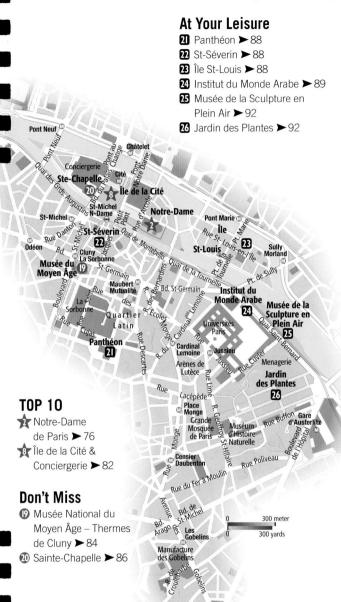

TOP 10

Don't Miss

The Perfect Day

If you're not quite sure where to begin your travels, this itinerary recommends a practical and enjoyable day out exploring the Latin Quarter and Islands, taking in some of the best places to see. For more information see the main entries (►76).

🕘 9:15am

Start your day gently at the most serene museum in Paris, the ⑲ **Musée National du Moyen Âge** (right, ►84), whose medieval treasures are among the greatest collections from this era. You will find them displayed in a beautiful Gothic mansion, built on the ruins of an ancient Roman bathhouse.

🕚 11:00am

Stroll northwards towards the river, stopping off for morning coffee and a croissant in one of many student bars nestling in the lively tangle of streets behind the church of ㉒ **St-Séverin** (►88).

🕛 12:00 noon

Cross the Petit Pont on to the ⑧ ★**Île de la Cité** (►82) to visit the mighty cathedral of ★**Notre-Dame** (►76). Quasimodo had a fantastic view from the towers: it's a long, long climb to the top, but if the weather's fine it's well worth every step.

Ste-Chapelle ⑳
Île de la Cité ⑧
St-Séverin ㉒ ⑦ **Notre-Dame**
Île ㉓ **St-Louis**
Musée Nat. du **Institut du**
Moyen Âge ⑲ **Monde Arabe** ㉔
Musée de la ㉕
㉑ **Sculpture en**
Panthéon **Plein Air**
㉖
Jardin
des Plantes

0   300 meter
0   300 yards

Manufacture
des Gobelins

🕐 1:00pm

Have lunch at **Au Vieux Paris** (►93), around the corner from **Notre-Dame**, or cross over to ㉓ Île **St-Louis** (►88) for lunch at **Wadja** (►95). For dessert join the locals waiting outside Berthillon (►89) for a taste of the most heavenly ice cream in Paris.

🕒 3:00pm

Return to the Île de la Cité, past the quaint **flower market** (top right, ►83) in

Place Louis-Lépine, and on to the ⭐**8 Conciergerie** (➤ 82), a museum full of gory tales from the days of the guillotine, then the stunning stained-glass windows of the **36 Sainte-Chapelle** (➤ 86).

🕔 5:30pm

Relax awhile in the peaceful, green **square du Vert-Galant** (➤ 180) at the westernmost end of the island, and watch the barges plying the river past the Louvre. Then why not hop aboard a **Vedettes du Pont Neuf** tour boat for a sightseeing cruise (bottom, ➤ 180) as the sun sets over the city?

🕗 8:00pm

The abundance of fresh air is bound to have given you a hearty appetite. Treat yourself to panoramic views and a sumptuous meal at **La Tour d'Argent** (➤ 94), followed by a nightcap in a nearby café.

★2 Notre-Dame de Paris

Despite the inevitable crowds of tourists, the grandeur of this landmark cathedral, with its impressive sculpture-encrusted facade, its distinctive flying buttresses and its soaring nave, never fails to inspire.

Holy Site

In the early 12th century, as the population of Paris continued to expand, the Bishop of Paris decided to build one **immense cathedral** here at the very heart of Paris to replace two old ones – the former Notre-Dame and the neighbouring St-Etienne, both of which were in a state of disrepair. The resulting church was erected as an expression of profound religious faith on a site considered holy for many centuries: the Romans had earlier built a temple to Jupiter here. It took more than 150 years to complete (1163–1345) and has undergone many alterations. During the Revolution,

The lofty interior near the altar

A detail of the rich interior

the **statues of the Kings of Judaea** on the facade were decapitated by the mob in the belief that they represented French monarchs. The originals, in the Musée National du Moyen Âge – Thermes de Cluny (➤ 84), have been replaced with replicas.

Viollet-le-Duc

The cathedral has fulfilled many roles: as a place of worship and as a community hall as well as the setting for banquets and amateur theatrical productions. At one point it was abandoned but, thanks largely to the success of Victor Hugo's *Hunchback of Notre-Dame*, it was finally saved by architect Viollet-le-Duc, who in the mid-19th century carried out extensive renovations, all in keeping with the original style.

Statue of the Virgin and Child above the entrance to the cathedral

Today we can enjoy one of the world's most beautiful examples of early Gothic architecture. **The façade is** remarkable. It seems perfectly proportioned, with its two towers narrower at the top than at the base, giving them the illusion of great height. Look closer and you will notice

DID YOU KNOW?
- The interior is 128m (420ft) long, 48m (157ft) wide and 35m (115ft) high.
- 402 spiral steps lead to the top of the 70m (230-foot) high south tower.
- 13 million people visit each year (as many as 50,000 on peak days).
- The main bell, the "Emmanuel" (13t), rang in 1944 to celebrate the liberation of France.

Insider Tip

SQUARE JEAN XXIII

Every year pairs of kestrels nest in the towers of Notre-Dame, and some years, around late June, local ornithologists set up a public hide in the delightful park behind the cathedral, with telescopes and even a video camera transmitting detailed shots of the birds. The park also offers striking views of the cathedral's flying buttresses.

the north (left) tower is wider than the south tower and that each of the three main entrances is slightly different in shape. If you 👫 **climb one of the towers**, you'll be rewarded with a bird's-eye view of the heart of the city and a glimpse of the grotesque gargoyles. An unforgettable experience that kids will love, too!

Try to visit Notre-Dame on a sunny day, when **the soaring nave** is bathed in multi-coloured lights, filtered through the stained-glass windows: **the rose windows** are particularly celebrated. In the transept, the window on the north side (left as you face the altar) depicts scenes from the Old Testament, while the one on the south (right) side shows Christ surrounded by virgins, saints and the apostles. The stunning red and blue west window (in the main facade) portrays the Virgin and Child.

➕ 205 E1 ✉ 6 Place du Parvis Notre-Dame, 75004
☎ 01 42 34 56 10; www.notredamedeparis.fr
🕐 Mon–Fri 8–6:45, Sat–Sun 8–7:15. Treasury: Mon–Fri 9:30–6,
Sat 9:30–6:30, Sun 1:30–6:30. Closed some religious feast days
Ⓜ Cité ⓇRER St-Michel–Notre-Dame
✋ Sacristy: €5. Tower: €8.50

The west facade of Notre-Dame

INSIDER INFO

- **Visit early in the morning**, when the cathedral is least crowded.
- If you plan to climb the towers, **wear sensible shoes** and **be prepared to queue** (April–Sep daily 10–6:30; June–Aug Sat–Sun until 11pm); April–May, Sep 10–6; Oct–March 10–5:30. Last entrance 45 min before closing; closed 1 Jan, 1 May, 25 Dec). The north tower entrance is on Rue du Cloître Notre-Dame (turn right out of the main door and round the corner of the facade). The entrance is on the left-hand side of the facade.
- You can get information about the **guided tours in English** when you arrive.
- Try to attend a **free organ concert** on Sunday, except during Lent, at 4:30, or one of the opera concerts every Thursday and Saturday at 9:15pm.
- Notre-Dame's southern wing contains the **cathedral treasury**, a collection of ornate amulets, rings and chalices.

In more depth In the **side chapels**, note the **series of religious canvases** by Charles Le Brun known as the *May* paintings; during the 17th and 18th centuries the Paris guilds presented a painting to the cathedral each May Day.

- Against a pillar near the modern high altar stands a beautiful 14th-century **statue of the Virgin and Child** – *Notre-Dame de Paris (Our Lady of Paris)*.
- Beside the high altar is a **kneeling statue of Louis XIII**, who, after many years of childless marriage, pledged to erect a high altar if an heir was born to him – but although the future Louis XIV was born soon after, the altar was not built for another 60 years.

The Grand Old Lady of Paris

This world-famous cathedral on the Île de la Cité is regarded as a Gothic masterpiece. The grand old lady has been part of the history of France and its capital city for more than 800 years.

❶Gallery of Kings: The decapitated ensemble, created after 1220 and unique in terms of its number and size, has been replaced with copies today.

❷Arcade Gallery: The filigree arcades that conceal the foundations of the tower and the nave gable with columns just 20cm thick were added around 1230.

❸Organ: With its 8,500 pipes and 113 stops on five keyboards, the cathedral's mighty-sounding organ, built by François Thierrys at the start of the 19th century and expanded between 1863 and 1868 by Aristide Cavaillé-Coll, is one of the largest in the land. The free organ concerts that are held every Sunday at 4.30pm are a real treat.

❹Notre-Dame de Paris: A highly revered slender statue of the cathedral's patron saint from 1330 has stood at the south easternmost crossing pier since 1855.

❺Choir Screens: The choir screens bear 23 reliefs depicting the life of Christ right through to the Passion. They were carved in stone, painted and partly gilded by Jehan Ravy and his nephew Jehan de Bouteiller from 1319 to 1351.

❻Treasury: The "Grand Relics" – a thorn from the Crown of Thorns and a piece of wood and a nail from the True Cross of Christ – are housed in the Trésor to the right of the Choir. Louis IX originally built Sainte-Chapelle as a repository for the Crown of Thorns, which was acquired in Constantinople in 1237. The crown is presented at the "Vénération de la Sainte Couronne d'Épines" at around 3pm on the first Friday of every month. You can also look at precious manuscripts and monstrances.

❼South Tower: If you've got a head for heights, you can climb the 70m high tower for €8.50. After scaling just just 387 steps, you'll have the whole of Paris at your feet. You can also admire the demonic gargoyles and grotesques. Entrance: Rue du Cloître Notre-Dame – there isn't an elevator!

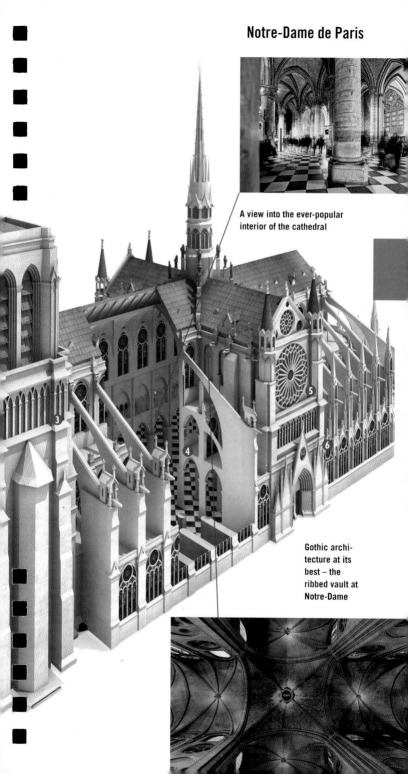

Notre-Dame de Paris

A view into the ever-popular interior of the cathedral

Gothic architecture at its best – the ribbed vault at Notre-Dame

★8 Île de la Cité & the Conciergerie

The history of this small, boat-shaped island in the Seine is the history of Paris. Here, in around 300BC, the earliest inhabitants of Paris (the Parisii tribe) settled, and it was here, two centuries later, that the Romans built the town of Lutetia, meaning "settlement surrounded by water". This was to become the seat of the ancient kings of France and the centre of political power, and in medieval times it also became the home of the church and the law.

For such a small island, the Île de la Cité boasts a remarkably high number of key sights, including the Cathedral of Notre-Dame (➤ 76), Sainte-Chapelle (➤ 86), and the **Conciergerie**.

The Gothic architecture of the Conciergerie reflected in the Seine

The Buildings

The imposing cluster of buildings which stretch the entire width of the island at its western end were once the seat of royal power, and today house the **Palais de Justice**, the city's law courts. The 🏛 **Conciergerie** occupies part of the lower floor of the complex and a couple of towers on the north bank of the island. Originally the residence of the governor of the king's palace – hence the name – it became a prison in 1391 (when the

PLACE DU PARVIS NOTRE-DAME

Not only is the Île de la Cité the heart of Paris, but it is also the heart of France. Set into the ground on the square outside the main portal of Notre-Dame, a bronze star marks the *point zéro des routes de France*, the point from which all distances are measured to and from Paris throughout France.

concierge became the chief gaoler) and remained so until 1914.

Condemned

Lovers of lurid history will be in their element here. Starting in the impressive church-like **Salle des Gens d'Armes** (Hall of the Men-at-Arms), you continue along the "Rue de Paris" (sinisterly named after the executioner, Monsieur de Paris), to the **Salle de la Toilette** or "preparation room". Here prisoners handed over their possessions and were prepared for the guillotine – their hands tied behind their backs, their heads shaved to the nape of the neck and their collars ripped apart. They were then escorted to the May courtyard, where they waited for the dreaded tumbrels (carts) to deliver them to the guillotine in Place de la Révolution (today's Place de la Concorde, ➤114).

Among pre-Revolution prisoners who awaited death here were Ravaillac, the assassin of Henri IV; Marquise de Brinvilliers, a mass poisoner who killed off the majority of her family; and Cartouche, the French equivalent of Robin Hood, who terrorized the streets of Paris.

During the Revolution, 2,780 people were guillotined between March 1793 and May 1795 – peasants, politicians, artists, nobles – including **Marie-Antoinette**, who spent 76 days in a cell here before losing her head in 1793. A visit to the Conciergerie is an exciting trip into the past – it's also good for (older) kids.

TAKING A BREAK

For French country cooking at great prices try **Au Vieux Paris d'Arcole** (➤93) on Rue Chanoinesse, on the eastern end of the Île de la Cité.

✚ 205 E1 🚇 Cité

Conciergerie
✉ 2 Boulevard du Palais, Île de la Cité, 75001
☎ 01 53 40 60 93; www.conciergerie.monuments-nationaux.fr
🕐 Mar–Oct daily 9:30–6; Nov–Feb 9–5 🚇 Cité 🚆 RER Châtelet
💶 €8.50; combined Conciergerie/Sainte-Chapelle ticket: €12.50

INSIDER INFO

The colourful flower market – **Marché aux Fleurs** – which on Sundays becomes a bird market (Marché aux Oiseaux), and the busy staging post for the *bateaux-mouches* that ply the Seine (Place Louis-Lépine, 75004, Mon–Sat 8–7, Sun 9–7; Metro: Cité).

Insider Tip

⑲ Musée National du Moyen Âge – Thermes de Cluny

Even if you're not a particular fan of medieval art and history, the National Museum of the Middle Ages, with its exhibits spanning fifteen centuries of Parisian history, is is an absolute must – if only for the remarkable building, which in itself is the architectural embodiment of this period.

The collections are housed in two adjoining buildings – the remains of Gallo-Roman baths and the late 15th-century Hôtel de Cluny, the mansion of the abbots of Cluny and a masterpiece of flamboyant Gothic style.

Roman Baths

Around AD200, the wealthy guild of Paris boatmen built a complex of Roman baths here, only to have them destroyed by barbarians less than a century later. The unearthed remains of the well-preserved "frigidarium" (the cold section of the bathhouse) form a kind of basement gallery in the museum, exhibiting various Roman bits and bobs, including fragments of **mosaics** and **frescoes** from the bathhouse.

The carved staircase inside the museum

Abbot's Mansion

Centuries later, the monks of the abbey of Cluny in Burgundy built a mansion – the Hôtel de Cluny – on this spot as a residence for visiting abbots. As a contemporary saying justly claimed: "Wherever the wind blows, the abbey of Cluny holds riches." Today, with its ornate turrets, gargoyles and **cloistered courtyard** (to which admission is free), it represents the finest remaining example of medieval civil architecture in Paris.

The many treasures in the museum reflect the richness and diversity of life in the Middle Ages, including furnishings, stained glass, jewellery, statuary, carvings, illuminated manuscripts, paintings and, most famous of all, the *Dame à la Licorne (Lady and the Unicorn)* **tapestries**. This exquisite series of six panels portraying a lady flanked by a lion and a unicorn, set against a pink flower-strewn background, provides a delightful reflection of the chivalrous world of courtly love. Each panel symbolizes one of the five senses: (from left to right) taste,

Medieval tapestries count among the many priceless treasures here

hearing, sight, smell and touch. In the sixth and largest panel, entitled *À mon seul désir*, the lady returns the necklace depicted in the other five tapestries to its jewel casket, refusing to capitulate to the passions aroused by the senses.

TAKING A BREAK

Have lunch at **La Gueuze** (➤ 94), close to the Jardin du Luxembourg.

⊞ 209 F4 ✉ 6 Place Paul Painlevé, 75005
☎ 01 53 73 78 00; www.musee-moyenage.fr 🕐 Wed–Mon 9:15–5:45
Ⓜ Cluny-La Sorbonne 🚆 RER B, C St-Michel–Cluny-Sorbonne
💷 €8. Free 1st Sun of month

INSIDER INFO

- Even if you don't have time to visit the museum, step inside the courtyard to admire its **ornate turrets, gargoyles and friezes**.
- You don't have to pay the price of a museum ticket to see the Roman remains: just **peer through the iron fence** from the Boulevard St-Michel.
- Pick up a leaflet at the ticket desk which **details the key sights** and provides a plan of the floors of the museum. Once inside, it's easy to find your way round as each room is clearly marked.
- Don't miss the **colourful stained-glass windows** from Sainte-Chapelle and Rouen Cathedral in room 6 on the ground floor.
- The museum also boasts the **statues of the Kings of Judea** (ground floor, room 8). They originally formed part of the facade of Notre-Dame.
- The **Roman Baths** are equally worth a visit (basement, room 9).
- The world-renowned *Lady and the Unicorn* tapestry hangs in room 13 on the 1st floor.
- Don't leave without seeing the **Chapel of the Monks of Cluny**, built in a late-Gothic style (1st floor, room 20).
- Also on display: Gallic jewellery; 15th-century illuminated **Book of Hours**; 16th-century **Averbode altarpiece**, depicting three carved scenes including the Last Supper; 14th-century **winklepickers; medieval-style gardens** inspired by the museum's collections.

⑳ Sainte-Chapelle

Sainte-Chapelle has to be seen to be believed. It is surely Paris's most beautiful church – a veritable sonata of shimmering stained glass – and a fusion of art and religion, although it is not always rated as one of the top sights.

It was built next door to the royal palace in 1248 by Louis IX – a king so devout that he came to be known as St Louis – to house a fragment of the Holy Cross and the entire Crown of Thorns. Louis had paid the outrageous sum of 1.3 million francs (the chapel itself only cost 400,000 francs) for these relics. He wanted the edifice to have the light, lacy aspect of a reliquary, and the result, which took only five years to build, was this bejewelled **masterpiece of Gothic architecture**.

Chapel Layout
The chapel is split into two levels. The **lower chapel**, dedicated to the Virgin Mary, was for the palace staff, while the **upper chapel** was originally linked to the palace by an outside walkway, so that the king could enter it directly. The most striking feature of the upper chapel is its transparency. It seems as though there are no walls – only

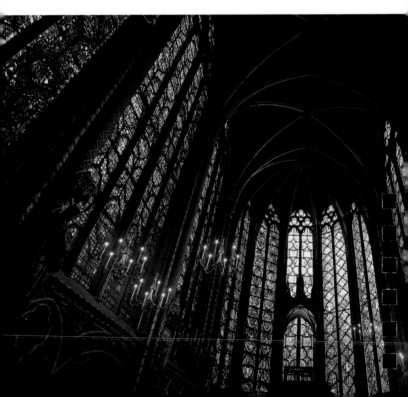

INSIDER INFO

- Try to visit when the **sun is shining**, flooding the interior with rich red, green, blue and gold rays of light.
- For a truly magical experience, attend one of the regularly held **candlelit chamber music and opera concerts**. Ask for details at either the ticket office, at the tourist information office or call the ticket reservation hotline on 01 42 77 65 65.
- To avoid the crowds, plan your visit for a weekday morning.

glowing stained-glass windows and clusters of slender columns rising to the vaulted ceiling. The verticality of the design is accentuated externally by the tall spire. The angel on the roof once revolved so that its cross could be seen everywhere in Paris.

Survival

It is a miracle that Sainte-Chapelle is still here. During the Revolution, its chapel was neglected and its relics removed to Notre-Dame. Thereafter, it was used to store flour, then as a depot for the court archives. It became so dilapidated that, in 1837, it was sold. Purchased by the State, it was restored and given a new spire. In 1871, the Communards poured petrol over the chapel, failing to set it on fire only for lack of time.

Sainte-Chapelle's *pièce de résistance* is undoubtedly its **stained-glass windows** – a pictorial Bible illustrating 1,134 scenes from both the Old and New Testaments. The most famous, and best seen at sunset, is the gigantic rose window, which depicts the Apocalypse in 86 multicoloured glass panels.

TAKING A BREAK

Make your way over to Île St-Louis for lunch at **Wadja** (▶ 95), working up your appetite by admiring the mouth-watering displays in many of the shops near by.

✚ 205 E1
✉ 4 Boulevard du Palais, 75001
☎ 01 53 40 60 80; sainte-chapelle.monuments-nationaux.fr
🕐 Daily March–Oct 9:30–12:30, 2:15–6; Nov–Feb 9–12:30, 2:15–5. Last entrance 30 min before closing
🚇 Cité/St-Michel
🚆 RER Châtelet-Les Halles/St-Michel–Notre-Dame
🎫 €8.50; combined Sainte-Chapelle/ Conciergerie ticket: €12.50

Glowing stained glass in the chapel

At Your Leisure

🔢 Panthéon

Originally commissioned around 1750 as a church by Louis XV in thanks following his remarkable recovery from a grave illness, it remained unfinished until 1789 owing to lack of finance (➤ 90). Two years later, all Christian references were removed and it was converted into a secular mausoleum for the *"grands hommes de l'époque de la liberté française"* (great men of the age of French liberty). Since then, Voltaire, Rousseau, Hugo, the Resistance leader Jean Moulin, Braille (inventor of the reading system for the visually impaired) and other great figures have been buried here. Nobel Prize-winner Marie Curie, the first woman to be interred in the Panthéon for her own achievements, was reburied here in 1995. There's not as much to

Fountains in the street in front of the Panthéon

see as you'd expect inside this massive, highly visible structure – the simplicity of the building with its many sculptures and column-filled hall nevertheless serves its purpose effectively.

🕂 209 F3 ✉ Place du Panthéon, 75005
☎ 01 44 32 18 00;
pantheon.monuments-nationaux.fr
🕐 Apr–Sep daily 10–6:30; Oct–March 10–6.
Last entrance 45 min before closing
🚇 Place Monge/Cardinal Lemoine
🚉 RER Luxembourg 🎟 €7.50

🔢 St-Séverin

Not only is St-Séverin one of the most beautiful churches in the capital, with one of the finest organs (upcoming concerts are listed outside), but it is also one of its best-kept secrets. It has a delightful blend of flamboyant Gothic architecture and contemporary stained glass (depicting the Seven Sacraments), with one of the oldest bells in Paris, and an intimate garden enclosed by a cloister, all constructed on the site of the Left Bank's former parish church and graveyard. St Séverin, a sixth-century hermit, was closely associated with St Martin, patron saint of travellers, so parishioners would hang horseshoes here as a token of thanks on their safe return from a journey.

The old cobbled streets surrounding St-Séverin, popular with students and tourists alike, are full of cafés, shops and cheap eateries.

🕂 209 F4
✉ 1 Rue des Prêtres-St-Séverin, 75005
☎ 01 42 34 93 50; www.saint-severin.com
🕐 Mon–Sat 11–7:30; Sun 9–8:30 🚇 St-Michel

🔢 Île St-Louis

When you tire of urban life, head for the Île St-Louis – an oasis of tranquillity at the heart of the city.

Insider Tip

The smaller of Paris's two islands, it has a village-like atmosphere, with tree-lined quays, matchless views of Notre-Dame and peaceful streets of elegant grey stone mansions, built in the 17th century as an annex to the fashionable Marais district. Little has changed since the writer Louis-Sébastien Mercier observed two centuries ago, "the island seems to have escaped the great corruption of the city, which has not reached here yet".

One of the attractions of the island is its main street, Rue St-Louis-en-l'Île, with its luxury shops, including the legendary **Maison Berthillon**. There's always a queue outside, and for good reason; an ice cream bought here will be a highlight of your day.

Berthillon

✚ 210 B4

✉ 29–31 Rue St-Louis-en-l'Île, 75004

☎ 01 43 54 31 61; www.berthillon.fr

🕐 Wed–Sun 10–8. Closed Aug 🚇 Pont Marie

24 Institut du Monde Arabe

The architecture of the Institut du Monde Arabe (Arab World Institute) must be seen to be believed. The main (south) facade of this striking 1988 glass-and-steel edifice by French designer Jean Nouvel

consists of 240 mechanized metal panels that act like the aperture of a camera, opening and closing to let in just the correct amount of natural light, while at the same time creating a beautiful pattern reminiscent of *moucharabieh* (traditional Arab latticework). Inside, the museum houses historic artefacts from a score of Islamic

The banks of the Seine on the Île St-Louis

🚣 MESSING ABOUT IN BOATS

A **river cruise** from the Île de la Cité (► 182) on one of the Vedettes du Pont Neuf tour boats is a fun way to combine sightseeing with a relaxing trip down the river.

Temple of the Greats

You can see the mighty dome that sits atop the Montagne Sainte-Geneviève from far and wide. The earthly remains of such great Frenchmen as Voltaire, Rousseau and Zola were interred here shortly after the French Revolution. Alexandre Dumas' coffin was moved here in 2002, adding the 70th famous name to the temple of glory.

❶ Portico and Triangular Pediment: With his design, Soufflot wanted to set himself apart from his role model, Sir Christopher Wren, architect of St Paul's Cathedral in London. To this end, Soufflot built a protruding portico on the main facade that draws the viewer's gaze up to the dome, making it look as if the structure is floating above the rest of the building below.

Sat atop 18 Corinthian columns, the pediment bears the inscription "to the great men – the grateful fatherland". It also boasts David d'Angers' relief of the history of the French nation: such figures as Mirabeau, Voltaire and Rousseau appear on the left while Napoleon and his Generals stand on the right.

❷ Supporting Pillars: Clarity was key to Soufflot's design for the interior. To free up more space, he built a long row of columns instead of the then-usual thick supporting pillars round the four arms of a cruciform structure. He added a second colonnade of massive pilasters behind this first row of load-bearing columns.

❸ Barrel Vault with Lunettes: Each cupola is set on top of a square, the sides of which are formed by barrel vaults. These vaults are fitted with openings called "lunettes", a design which allows the building's structural loads to be optimally redirected onto specific intersections supported by columns.

❹ Windows: As the windows were walled up during the French Revolution, the upper windows near the opening of the central dome provide the only source of light today. As with the flying buttresses, they are not visible from outside the building.

❺ Tambour: The special feature of this cylindrical structure supporting the dome is its double row of widely spaced columns.

❻ Central Dome: The three overlapping sections of the dome – all of which were made entirely from stone – were a bold innovation for the time. Napoleon I, under whose rule the Panthéon temporarily served as a church, had the dome decorated with a fresco of "The Apotheosis of Saint Genevieve" in 1811. If you climb up the dome, you'll get some magnificent views of Paris from the colonnade!

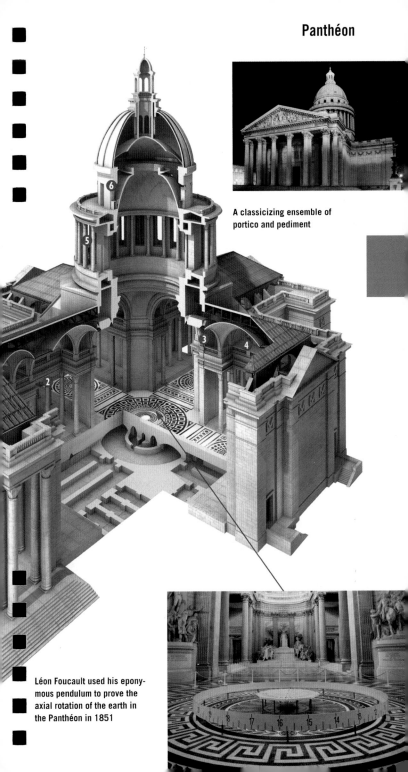

Panthéon

A classicizing ensemble of portico and pediment

Léon Foucault used his eponymous pendulum to prove the axial rotation of the earth in the Panthéon in 1851

nations from Morocco to Iran. The restaurant on the ninth floor has one of the finest views in Paris.

➕ B4

✉ 1 Rue des Fossés-St-Bernard, 75005

☎ 01 40 51 38 38; www.imarabe.org

🕐 Tue–Sun 10–6

🚇 Cardinal Lemoine/Jussieu 💷 €8

25 Musée de la Sculpture en Plein Air

This modern, imaginatively land-scaped riverside promenade, running along Quai St-Bernard from the Gare d'Austerlitz to the Institut du Monde Arabe, is dotted with more than 40 avant-garde sculptures by Brancusi, César and Zadkine among others. With col-ourful barges often moored along the waterside, and views of Île St-Louis opposite, this is one of the most enjoyable stretches of the river for a daytime stroll, and a great picnic spot too.

➕ 210 C3

✉ Quai St-Bernard, 75005

🚇 Gare d'Austerlitz

26 Jardin des Plantes

Louis XIII's "Garden of Medicinal Herbs", established by two physi-cians in 1626, was first opened to

Behind the steel-and-glass facade of the Institut du Monde Arabe

the public in 1640. Today it is the city's botanical garden. As well as magnificent walkways flanked by flowers, ancient trees and statues, it has a stunning alpine garden with more than 2,000 species of plants from all over the world, a small zoo (set up during the Revolution to house survivors from the Ménagerie at Versailles), and the Musée National d'Histoire Naturelle.

The natural history and anthro-pology collections here are among the world's largest. Of particular interest is the palaeontology gallery with its reconstructed skeletons of prehistoric mammals. The late 19th-century Grande Galerie de l'Évolution, with its glass roof, and palaeobotany and mineralogy gallery, telling the story of plants since their first appearance on Earth, are also worth a visit.

Insider Tip

➕ 210 C3 ✉ Garden and Ménagerie: 57 Rue Cuvier, 75005. Museum: 2 Rue Buffon, 75005

☎ Ménagerie: 01 40 79 37 94. Museum: 01 40 79 30 00 (recorded information). Grande Galerie: 01 40 79 54 79; www.mnhn.fr

🕐 Garden: April–Aug daily 7:30am–8pm; Sep 8–7:30; Oct 8–7; Nov–Jan 8–5:30; Feb 7:30–6, March 7:30–7.
Ménagerie: Mon–Sat 9–6; Sun 9–6:30.
Museum: Wed–Mon 10–5 (10–6 in summer).
Grande Galerie: Wed–Mon 10–6

🚇 Jussieu/Gare d'Austerlitz

💷 Ménagerie: €11; Museum: €9; Garden: free

Where to…
Eat and Drink

Prices
Expect to pay per person for a meal, excluding drinks:
€ under €25   €€ €25–€50   €€€ €51–€100   €€€€ over €100

L'Atelier de Maître Albert €€€
Tucked away in a narrow street, this rotisserie, owned by Guy Savoy, has an elegant décor blending the traditional and new. Although light and modern, the cuisine is deeply rooted in French tradition, with a choice of spit-roasted meats and poultry: spit-roasted French beef sirloin with béarnaise sauce and potato gratin, skewered monkfish with braised carrots and onions savoured with hazelnut juice. Lively atmosphere and a warm welcome.

➕ 210 A4 ✉ 1 Rue Maître Albert, 75005
☎ 01 56 81 30 01; www.ateliermaitrealbert.com
🕐 Daily noon–2:30, 6:30–11:30
(Thu–Sat until 1am). Closed Sat–Sun lunch, and 1st 2 weeks of Aug
🚇 Maubert-Mutualité

Insider Tip Au Vieux Paris d'Arcole €€
Few would have thought that gastronomic French country dining would be possible at this location, just minutes away from Notre-Dame, let alone at honest prices. But chef and proprietor Odette (motto: Wild Woman, Wild Food) sources all-organic stock for her stunning rural French recipes. Dishes go unlisted on the more expensive seven-course "surprise d'Odette" prix-fixe menu. The dining rooms are furnished with theatre-esque fittings.

➕ 210 A5
✉ 24 Rue Chanoinesse, Île de la Cité, 75004
☎ 01 40 51 78 52; www.auvieuxparis.fr
🕐 Daily noon–2:30, 7:30–10. Closed Sat lunch
🚇 Cité

Le Bar à Huîtres €€
One of a group of three oyster bars serving, among other dishes, wonderful shellfish and enormous seafood platters. The other branches are on Boulevard Beaumarchais and Boulevard Montparnasse. Staff won't bat an eyelid if you just call in for a half-dozen oysters and a glass of white wine, although the excellent set menus do, if necessary, make this an inexpensive treat

➕ 209 F4 ✉ 33 Rue St-Jacques, 75005
☎ 01 44 07 27 37; www.lebarahuitres.com
🕐 Daily noon–1am 🚇 Cluny-La Sorbonne

Brasserie Balzar €€
Located at the heart of the University district, this lively brasserie is the rendezvous of professors and students, of writers and publishers, of intellectuals and artists who flock here to have a meal in typically Parisian 1930s décor. The cuisine has been modernized but remains traditional: steak au poivre, calf's liver and choucroute garnie (meat and pickled cabbage) are among the favourite dishes.

➕ 209 E4 ✉ 49 Rue des Écoles, 75005
☎ 01 43 54 13 67; www.brasseriebalzar.com
🕐 Daily noon–2:30, 6:30–midnight
🚇 Cluny-La Sorbonne

Le Buisson Ardent €€
This sumptuous restaurant in a leafy locale specializes in fine pan-French cuisine, with a good list of wines from around the country to match. There is caramelized tête de veau (calf's head) from the Languedoc or rockfish soup from southern France and a pièce du

The Latin Quarter and the Islands

boucher (butcher's cut) for two sharing, guaranteed to floor the most insistent of carnivores.

➕ 210 B3 ✉ 25 Rue Jussieu, 75005 ☎ 01 43 54 93 02; www.lebuissonardent.fr 🕐 Mon–Fri noon–2, 7:30–10; Sat 7:30–10:30; Sun noon–3 🚇 Jussieu/Cardinal Lemoine

Chieng Maï €€

Amid a sea of other fine Asian restaurants, this ranks among the city's best for Thai cooking, so it is always necessary to book in advance. The menu is true to its classic roots, though spicing is a little less fiery than is traditional. Pork satay, fish steamed in a banana leaf, and sautéed beef with basil are perennial favourites.

➕ 210 A4 ✉ 12 Rue Frédéric Sauton, 75005 ☎ 01 43 25 45 45 🕐 Mon–Sat noon–2:30, 7–11:30. Closed Aug 🚇 Maubert-Mutualité

La Gueuze €

Only a few steps from the Jardin du Luxembourg, the speciality here is the vast selection of some 150 beers from around the world. The menu features Belgian staples served in generous portions, such as *moules marinières* (mussels in white wine) and *carbonnade flamande* (the Belgian national dish of beef in beer).

➕ 209 E3 ✉ 19 Rue Soufflot, 75005 ☎ 01 43 54 63 00 🕐 Mon–Sat 11am–1am, Sun 11–11 🚇 Cluny-La Sorbonne 🚈 RER Luxembourg

Mavrommatis €€/€€€

A far cry from the tourist-touting tavernas on nearby Rue Mouffetard, this classy Greek restaurant adds a sophisticated touch to traditional dishes like *tzatziki* and *stifado* (rabbit casserole). The subtly balanced menu includes preserved lamb and yoghurt with honey, vine leaves and moussaka. The desserts are clever adaptions of French dishes, including *nougat glacé* with fresh figs, chestnut and vanilla mousse, and *baklava*. Greek wines are the perfect accompaniment.

➕ 210 A4 ✉ 42 Rue Daubenton, 75005 ☎ 01 43 31 17 17; www.mavrommatis.fr 🕐 Fri–Sat noon–2:15, 7–11, Sun noon–2:15, Tue–Thu 7–11 🚇 Censier-Daubenton

Le Pré Verre €/€€

The lunch menu at this small, modern *bistrot à vins* near the Musée Cluny is especially good value and includes a glass of wine and coffee. Following five years training in Asia, chef Philippe Delacourcelle is considered a master of spices, conjuring up such subtle flavour combinations as tuna with celery and sesame, and veal with ginger and polenta. Dishes include crispy Asian pork with beetroot chutney. Each month features different well-priced house wines.

➕ 209 F4 ✉ 8 Rue Thenard, 75005 ☎ 01 43 54 59 47; www.lepreverre.com 🕐 Tue–Sat noon–2, 7:30–10:30 🚇 Cluny-La Sorbonne/Maubert-Mutualité

La Rôtisserie du Beaujolais €€€

Under the same ownership as La Tour d'Argent across the road, this waterfront bistro enjoys a view of Notre-Dame from its covered terrace. Typical dishes featured on the menu include *pigeon rôti, coq au vin* and pigs' trotters. The spit-roasted meats are wonderful, especially the duck.

➕ 210 B4 ✉ 19 Quai de la Tournelle, 75005 ☎ 01 43 54 17 47; www.larotisseriedu beaujolais.com 🕐 Daily noon–2:15, 7–10:30 🚇 Maubert-Mutualité/Pont Marie

La Tour d'Argent €€€€

Established in 1582, La Tour d'Argent (one Michelin star) is the second-oldest restaurant in Paris, and one of the oldest in the world. Commanding spectacular views of the Seine, Notre-Dame and Île St-Louis, it is an absolute must for any once-in-a-lifetime visit to Paris – for those with deep pockets. The menu is traditional, with modern influences subtly incorporated. The speciality is duck, especially *canard à la presse*, which has been on the menu for more than 100 years. (Do note that it is served on the rare side.) Other renowned dishes include lobster quenelles and *pêches flambées à l'eau de vie de framboise* (peaches in raspberry liqueur). The wine cellar is superb and includes a museum.

➕ 210 B4
✉ 6th floor, 15–17 Quai de la Tournelle, 75005
☎ 01 43 54 23 31; www.latourdargent.com
🕐 Tue–Sat 12:30–2:30, 7:30–9:30.
Closed last 2 weeks Feb, and Aug
Ⓜ Maubert-Mutualité/Pont Marie

Wadja €€

You'll get a warm welcome at this small, eastern-influenced, family-run restaurant. They often only serve one set menu at lunchtimes. The simple eatery's old-fashioned atmosphere goes hand in hand with their traditional methods of preparation. Great emphasis is placed on using organic produce.

➕ 208 C2
✉ 10 Rue de la Grande-Chaumiére, 75004
☎ 09 60 54 07 68
🕐 Mon–Sat noon–2, 7:30–10 Ⓜ Vavin

Where to ...
Shop

The Latin Quarter remains the bohemian domain of students and is a paradise for book lovers. Other shops are a little down-market, with the exception of Les Comptoirs de la Tour d'Argent. Even if you can't dine at its famous restaurant, you can buy from a splendid selection of gourmet produce and tableware. Shoppers can find all manner of goodies on Rue St-Louis-en-l'Île.

MUSIC

Paris Jazz Corner (5 Rue de Navarre, 75005; tel: 01 43 36 78 92; Tue–Sat; Metro: Place Monge) is the place to head for a great selection of second-hand jazz recordings.

FOOD

Dalloyau (2 Place Edmond Rostand, 75006; tel: 01 43 29 31 10; daily 9–8:30; Metro: Cluny-La Sorbonne), once suppliers to Louis XIV, sells delicacies (e.g. *foie gras*, truffles, chocolates and macaroons).
   La Ferme St-Aubin (76 Rue St-Louis-en-l'Île, 75004; tel: 01 43 54 74 54; Tue–Sun; Metro: Pont Marie) has some 200 cheeses (French and European varieties), all in luscious, peak condition.

GIFTS & CRAFTS

Diptyque (34 Boulevard St-Germain, 75005; tel: 01 43 26 77 44; www.diptypeparis.com; Mon–Sat 10–7; Metro: Maubert-Mutualité) sells subtly scented candles, soaps, body lotions and eaux de toilette.
   La Tuile à Loup (35 Rue Daubenton, 75005; tel: 01 47 07 28 90; Tue–Sat 10:30–6, Mon 1–6; Metro: Censier-Daubenton) sells traditional French provincial arts and crafts.

BOOKS

Librairie Ulysse (26 Rue St-Louis-en-l'Île, 75004; tel: 01 43 25 17 35; Tue–Fri 2–8; Metro: Sully-Morland) stocks a wealth of travel information, including books (new and used), maps and magazines.
   Gibert Jeune (5 Place St-Michel, 75005; tel: 01 56 81 22 22; www.gibertjeune.fr; Mon– Sat 9:30–7:30; Metro: St-Michel) is one of the largest bookshops in Paris.
   Shakespeare & Co (37 Rue de la Bûcherie, 75005; tel: 01 43 25 40 93; www.shakespeareandcompany.com; Mon–Fri 10–11, Sat 11–11; Metro: St-Michel) is a mine of English-language books.

Where to...
Go Out

A stroll along Rue Mouffetard, running north – south almost parallel to Rue Monge, through the centre of the Latin Quarter, is almost an entertainment in itself. It is packed with diverse little gift and food shops, while numerous restaurants also beckon with mouth-watering window displays, soft candlelight, and often live music within.

CONCERTS AND CABARET

The church of **St-Julien-le-Pauvre** (79 Rue Galande, 75005; tel: 01 43 54 52 16; Metro: St-Michel), facing the Seine, stages regular concert recitals; arrive about 30 minutes early in order to ensure good seats.

At **Paradis Latin** (28 Rue du Cardinal Lemoine, 75005; tel: 01 43 25 28 28; www.paradislatin.com; Wed–Mon 8pm–midnight; Metro: Cardinal Lemoine/Jussieu) the classically risqué live cabaret show can be preceded by dinner.

JAZZ

Established in 1946, the **Caveau de la Huchette** is always crowded (and particularly so at weekends) with people who want to listen and dance to swing, boogie and rock (5 Rue de la Huchette, 75005; tel: 01 43 26 65 05; www.caveau delahuchette.fr; Sun–Wed 9:30pm–2:30am, Thu–Sat 9:30–4am; Metro: St-Michel). The ancient vaulted cellar provides the perfect setting for the top-class jazz and blues performers who play here.

Le Petit Journal (71 Boulevard St-Michel, 75005; tel: 01 43 26 28 59; Mon–Sat 6pm–2am, closed Aug, RER: Luxembourg) offers a programme of trad jazz from mostly French performers.

Les Trois Maillets (56 Rue Galande, 75005; tel: 01 43 54 42 94; daily 5pm–dawn; Metro: St-Michel) is a terrific jazz café in the narrow streets between the Seine and Boulevard St-Germain.

Les Caveau des Oubliettes (52 Rue Galande, 75005; tel: 01 46 34 23 09; daily 5pm–4am; Metro: St-Michel) has five live jam sessions each week, with blues on Sundays and funk Thursdays.

Insider Tip

CINEMAS

Among the cluster of art-house cinemas, **Studio Galande** (42 Rue Galande, 75005; tel: 01 43 54 72 71; Metro: Cluny-La Sorbonne) shows independent and cult films. It's also famed for showing *The Rocky Horror Picture Show* every Friday and Saturday night. **Le Cinéma du Panthéon** (13 Rue Victor-Cousin, 75005; tel: 01 40 46 01 21; Metro: Cluny-La Sorbonne/Odéon, RER: Luxembourg) is the city's oldest remaining cinema.

Others include **Action Écoles- "Le Desperado"** (23 Rue des Écoles, 75005; tel: 01 43 25 72 07; Metro: Maubert-Mutualité), **Le Champollion** (51 Rue des Écoles, 75005; tel: 01 43 54 51 60; Metro: St-Michel), **Grand Action** (5 Rue des Écoles, 75005; tel: 01 43 54 47 62; Metro: Cardinal Lemoine/Jussieu) and **Studio des Ursulines** (10 Rue des Ursulines, 75005; tel: 01 56 81 15 20, RER: Luxembourg). Check the weekly *Pariscope* for current screenings, or visit www.paris.angloinfo.com for a list of every original-language film.

CLUB

Le Saint (7 Rue St-Séverin, 75005; tel: 01 40 20 43 23; www.lesaint disco.com; Tue–Sun 11pm–6am; Metro: St-Michel), not far from Place St-Michel, is a small dance club playing a wide range of music, including salsa and R&B.

The Louvre to the Arc de Triomphe

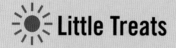 **Little Treats**

A coffee break in the Jardin des Tuileries

It's a lot of fun to settle down in one of the terrace cafés in the park (► 110) and enjoy the scenery with a cup of coffee.

A sea of lights around the Arc de Triomphe

The view in the evenings is particularly impressive when the headlights of passing cars shine along the boulevards (► 108).

Floating above the roofs of Paris

You can enjoy fantastic views from the **ferris wheel** (► 114) at the Place de la Concorde from December to February.

Getting Your Bearings

From the Louvre to the Arc de Triomphe, this area of western Paris is not noted for its charm but rather for its grandeur. It is the plutocratic plethora of luxury hotels, elegant squares, formal gardens and fashion emporia that lends this part of the city its special character.

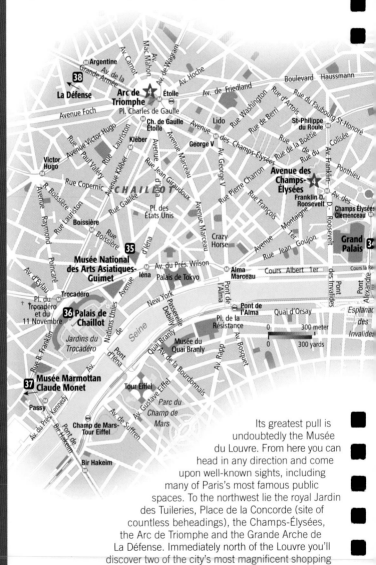

Its greatest pull is undoubtedly the Musée du Louvre. From here you can head in any direction and come upon well-known sights, including many of Paris's most famous public spaces. To the northwest lie the royal Jardin des Tuileries, Place de la Concorde (site of countless beheadings), the Champs-Élysées, the Arc de Triomphe and the Grande Arche de La Défense. Immediately north of the Louvre you'll discover two of the city's most magnificent shopping

At Your Leisure

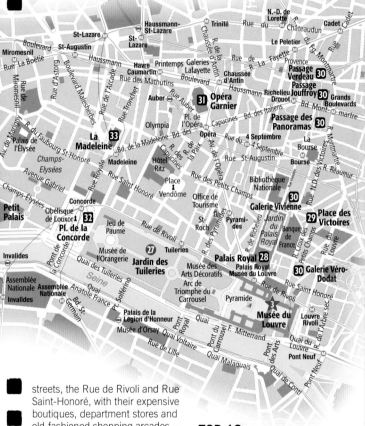

streets, the Rue de Rivoli and Rue Saint-Honoré, with their expensive boutiques, department stores and old-fashioned shopping arcades – a veritable shoppers' paradise. In the evenings, there's fine dining, sophisticated nightclubs, the Paris Opéra or the world-renowned Comédie-Française, not to mention some of the city's most romantic night-time promenades and viewpoints.

TOP 10

Don't Miss

The Perfect Day

If you're not quite sure where to begin your travels, this itinerary recommends a practical and enjoyable day out around the Louvre and the Arc de Triomphe, taking in some of the best places to see. For more information see the main entries (➤ 102–118).

🕤 9:00am

Make sure you arrive at the ⭐Louvre (above, ➤ 102) really early (preferably before the doors open at 9) to get a head start on the average 25,000–30,000 visitors who traipse through the galleries daily. Once inside, take your time and be selective.

🕛 12:00 noon

If your stomach's started rumbling and you're feeling extravagant, have a light lunch at the stylish **Café Marly** (right, ➤ 28) in the courtyard of the Louvre overlooking the glass Pyramid. Alternatively, try **Bistrot Richelieu**, a tiny, great-value bistro (45, Rue de Richelieu, 75001; tel: 01 42 60 19 16; www. bistrotrichelieu.fr; Metro: Palais Royal; closed Sat lunch and Sun).

🕑 2:00pm

Where better to walk off your lunch (or take an afternoon siesta) than the delightful and typically French statue-studded **㉗Jardin des Tuileries** ➤ 110). If you have not yet had your fill of art for the day, take your pick from the

Musée de l'Orangerie (▶ 111), which houses Claude Monet's crowning glory, the water-lily series, or the **Jeu de Paume** (left, ▶ 111) featuring contemporary art exhibitions inside a former Real Tennis court.

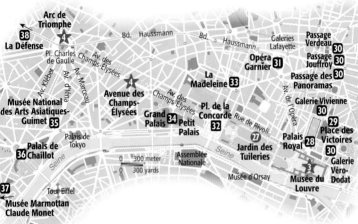

⊛ 3:00pm
Cross the majestic **32 Place de la Concorde** (▶ 114) and head up the the famous Avenue des ⭐ **Champs-Élysées** (▶ 108) – once an aristocratic pleasure park, now thoroughly commercialized. Nevertheless, there is still a certain thrill associated with sauntering up one of the world's most famous streets. If you'd rather not stroll, you can take the Metro from Tuileries or Concorde to Charles de Gaulle-Étoile.

⊛ 5:00pm
High atop the ⭐ **Arc de Triomphe** (below, ▶ 108) is undoubtedly the best place to be during rush hour, 50m (165 feet) above the noise and traffic of the 12 major avenues that radiate from the largest triumphal arch in the world. You'll be astonished by the volume of traffic navigating round the triumphal arch – and the views are quite simply unforgettable.

⊛ 7:00pm
If all the day's sightseeing has given you an appetite, why not treat yourself to dinner at **Le Fouquet's** (▶ 120).

⭐3 Musée du Louvre

The old Musée du Louvre contains one of the most important art collections in the world. Whether you find your visit here breathtaking, overwhelming, frustrating or simply exhausting, one thing's for sure – you would need a lifetime to see everything. Defeated in advance, some visitors to Paris skip it altogether. The key to a successful visit is to pace yourself, be selective and enjoy: there's nothing to stop you returning tomorrow for more.

The museum took its name, according to one theory, from the Latin word *luperia* ("wolf lodge" or "hunting lodge"), when the 12th-century king Philippe Auguste built a lodge here and, fearing a Viking invasion while he was away fighting in the Crusades, ordered it to be surrounded by fortified walls. (The massive walls of the twin towers and drawbridge support of this fortress can be seen today, impressively floodlit, in the excavated basement of the Sully Wing.) After the Hundred Years' War, the fortress became a royal residence.

Statues in one of the galleries

The Collection Begins

Throughout the following four centuries, a succession of kings and emperors all attempted to improve on or enlarge the palace complex. François I replaced the imposing keep with a Renaissance-style building and also started the Louvre's collections with 12 stolen Italian works of art, including the *Mona Lisa*. Henri IV ordered the construction of the **Grande Galerie** to link the palace with the Tuileries.

The Louvre's artistic heyday arrived in the 17th century under Louis XIV, a great patron of the arts, who considerably enhanced the collections, adding works by Leonardo da Vinci, Raphael and Titian. Napoleon I, too, although notorious for having the most deplorable taste of any leader in the history of France, filled the palace with artworks looted

Inside the pyramid in the courtyard

HENRI IV

Much to the annoyance of his wife Marie de Médicis, Henri accommodated his many mistresses and their children at the Louvre until his decadent life came to an abrupt end in 1610. Stabbed by an assassin in the streets, he was rushed back inside the Louvre, where he became the only king to die within its walls.

THE PYRAMID
The Chinese-American architect Ieoh Ming Pei designed the extraordinarily modern glass pyramid in the Louvre's main courtyard, which now forms the main entrance to the museum. Made of glass in order to be "transparent and reflect the sky", this now much-loved landmark is 21.6m (71 feet) high and contains 793 panes of glass. It even boasts its own robot, designed especially for the weekly cleaning.

during his victorious years. The Louvre's collections were first opened to the public after the Revolution, in 1793.

Modern Additions
More recent architectural additions to the Louvre include the controversial pyramid entrance (1989) and the stunning renovation of the Richelieu wing, with its two modern glass-covered courtyards (1993). The latest addition was opened in 2012, however, and takes the form of a golden "flying" carpet spun from glass and metal thread that seems to float over the Cour Visconti. An enormous collection of Islamic Art is housed under the structure's glass roof.

Tackling the Louvre
Rule number one – be patient: there are more than 35,000 works of art displayed in an enormous exhibition space, which today covers 60,600m² (652,300ft²).

Allow at least **half a day**. Even then, by the time you've queued for a ticket, queued at the information desk for a map, and left your coats in the cloakroom, you'll probably only have a couple of hours left for the galleries themselves.

STAR ATTRACTIONS

- Leonardo da Vinci's **Portrait of Mona Lisa**, also called *La Joconde, La Gioconda* or *Portrait of Lisa Gherardini* (1503–06, Denon, first floor, room 6).
- Théodore Géricault's moving shipwreck, **The Raft of the Medusa** (1819, Denon, first floor, room 77).
- **The Lacemaker** by Jan Vermeer (1670–71, Richelieu, second floor, room 38), an exquisite portrayal of everyday domestic life in Holland.
- Michelangelo's **Dying Slave** (1513–20, Denon, ground floor, room 4), sculpted for the tomb of Pope Julius II in Rome.
- The unrivalled **Venus de Milo** (second century BC, Sully, ground floor, room 12), found in 1820 on the Greek island of Milos.
- The **Winged Victory of Samothrace** (*c.*190BC, between Sully and Denon, first floor), probably once a ship's figurehead and poised for flight at the head of a staircase.
- The wild **Marly Horses** by Guillaume Coustou (1743–45, Richelieu, Cour Marly).
- The **Apollo Gallery** (Denon, first floor, room 66) served as a model for the celebrated Hall of Mirrors at Versailles (➤ 172).

One saving grace is that the galleries are clearly marked (each room bears a number), and it is hard to get lost. If you don't want to tackle the museum on your own, ask at the information desk under the pyramid about the daily tours (in English and French) or rent an audio guide (moderate: available in six languages at the access to any of the wings).

It's easy to spend hours exploring the cavernous galleries

In such a huge museum, it is impossible to see everything. If this is your first visit to the Louvre, look out for *Louvre: The Visitor's Guide*, published by the museum itself, which steers you round some of the main attractions.

The Louvre to the Arc de Triomphe

THE *MONA LISA*

If you are going to the Louvre solely to see the small portrait, painted between 1503 and 1506, of a Florentine noblewoman known as the *Mona Lisa* or *La Giaconda* (as many visitors do), you may be disappointed to find her enigmatic smile encased behind bullet-proof glass and surrounded by masses of tourists – all eagerly taking snapshots as souvenirs. Every art thief must dream of stealing this Leonardo da Vinci masterpiece and, in 1911, a former museum worker named Vincenzo Perugia succeeded. Unsure how to sell the most famous painting in the world, he hid it in a hotel room in Florence, until it was discovered two years later and safely returned to the Louvre.

You may prefer to concentrate on a particular period in greater depth: among the most dazzling collections are the **Greek, Etruscan and Roman antiquities** (Denon, ground floor, rooms 5–30); **16th- to 17th-century Italian paintings** (Denon, first floor); **French sculpture from the early Middle Ages to the 19th century** (Richelieu, ground floor, Cour Puget and Cour Marly separated by the Passage Richelieu); **18th- to 19th-century French School of painting** (Sully second floor, rooms 36–73). The **arts of Africa, Asia, Oceania and the Americas**, once temporarily in the Louvre, are now displayed in the **Musée du Quai Branly** (▶62).

For a comprehensive catalogue, try the weighty, well-illustrated *Louvre: The Collections* (available in the bookshop under the pyramid).

Art appreciation in the Louvre

PUTTING HIS FOOT IN IT

According to his mistress Françoise Gilot, Picasso once stepped on what he took to be an old canvas protecting the floor in a Louvre storage room – only to realize it was a priceless 10m by 6m (33 by 20 foot) Delacroix ceiling painting, which was destined for one of the galleries.

The Wings – Finding Your Way Around
The Collections are divided between three main wings – the **Sully** (named after Henri IV's Chancellor of the Exchequer); the **Richelieu** (eminent Cardinal and minister to Louis XIII); and the **Denon** (first director of the Central Arts Museum under Napoleon). Each wing has four levels, on which are arranged nine departments, each represented by a colour: yellow for Oriental Antiquities; dark green for Arts of Islam; light green for Egyptian Antiquities; blue for Greek, Roman and Etruscan Antiquities; red for Paintings; pink for Prints and Drawings; purple for Decorative Arts; light brown for Sculpture; dark brown stripes for Medieval Louvre.

TAKING A BREAK
Café Marly makes a pleasant lunch stop (➤ 28).

✚ 205 D2 ✉ 34 Quai du Louvre, 75001
☎ 01 40 20 53 17 (information desk); www.louvre.fr
🕐 Wed–Mon 9–6 (Wed and Fri until 9:45pm). Closed public hols
🍴 Cafés €; restaurant €€
Ⓜ Palais Royal-Musée du Louvre/Louvre Rivoli
💶 €12 (reduced rate Wed and Fri after 6pm). Free 1st Sun of month

INSIDER INFO

- Pick up a **plan of the museum from the information desk** before you get stuck in and tackle any of the galleries. There's a special map available for visitors with disabilities, as well as documentation in Braille, a dedicated tactile gallery and monthly guided visits in French (and sometimes British) sign language. For more information: tel: 01 40 20 59 90.
- **The museum shop is a great source** of books, souvenirs and museum gifts.
- Consider hiring an **audio guide** (charge: moderate) with commentaries on around 1,000 artworks, or take a a guided, English-language **"Discovery Visit"** (for an inexpensive supplement to the entrance fee) at 11am and 2pm daily, except on the first Sunday of the month.
- There are four entrances – via the pyramid, via the Richelieu passage (off the Rue de Rivoli), via the Porte des Lions (closed Friday) by the Seine, or via the Carrousel du Louvre shopping complex.
- Visit **early in the morning**, 9am, or Wednesday or Friday evening. Avoid Sunday, when the museum is at its most crowded.
- If you have a Museum Pass (➤ 38) or purchase your ticket in advance on the website or from FNAC or a Virgin Megastore (the nearest is in Carrousel du Louvre), you can **use the priority entry** at the Richelieu entrance.
- If, like most people, you don't already have a ticket or a Museum Pass, go in by the **Carrousel entrance**: the queues are usually shorter here. Once inside the Louvre's lofty foyer, seek out the rows of self-ticketing machines. They accept both cash and credit cards, and the queues tend to be fast-moving.
- Once inside, your ticket will get you into any of the wings **as many times as you like** during one day.
- **Wear comfortable shoes** (you will have probably walked several kilometres by the end of your visit) and set yourself a few viewing priorities.

⭐4 Avenue des Champs-Élysées & Arc de Triomphe

The Arc de Triomphe rises majestically at the head of the city's most famous avenue, the Champs-Élysées. Planned by Emperor Napoleon I as a monument to his military prowess, the colossal arch was not finished until 15 years after his death, in 1836.

Two hundred and eighty-four steps up a narrow spiral staircase will lead you to the 50m (165-foot) high terrace. Here, the breathtaking view highlights the city's unmistakable design – the Voie Triomphale from the Louvre to La Défense, and the 12 avenues radiating out from the arch itself like the points of a star. Beneath the vault of the archway, the **flame of remembrance** has burned daily since 11 November 1923; time your visit in the evening, and you can catch the 6:30 relighting ceremony, which takes place every day.

It is hard to believe that the broad and busy thoroughfare of the **Champs-Élysées** was just an empty field before

INSIDER INFO

- The best times to visit the Arc de Triomphe are early in the day, when the **morning light emphasizes the details** of the sculptures, late afternoon as the sun sets over the rooftops, or in the evening as lights map out the city.
- **Don't try to cross the road** to reach the arch. Access is via a subway at the top of the Champs-Élysées.
- Be sure to take your camera as the views are stupendous. An orientation table at the top of the arch makes spotting the key landmarks easy.

Hidden gem The 🏛 museum at the top of the Triumphal Arch is also worth a visit. Older children in particular will find it exciting, thanks to the large collection of interactive exhibits and scale models on display.

The Arc de Triomphe: Planned by Napoleon

Le Nôtre converted it into parkland as an extension of the Tuileries (➤ 110). For centuries it was a popular strolling ground, reaching its zenith in the mid-1800s, when a constant flow of horse-drawn carriages paraded up the street in order to allow ladies to show off their finest fashions. Today, with its brash shops, cinemas and fast-food joints, the avenue that was once the "most beautiful street in the world" has lost much of its magic, glamour and prestige, yet it still retains an aloof grandeur and unique appeal.

TAKING A BREAK

Have lunch or dinner at **Le Fouquet's** (➤ 120).

Arc de Triomphe
🔲 202 B5 ⊠ Place Charles-de-Gaulle-Étoile, 75008
☎ 01 55 37 73 77; www.arc-de-triomphe.monuments-nationaux.fr
🕐 April–Sep daily 10am–11pm; Oct–March 10am–10.30pm
Ⓜ Charles de Gaulle-Étoile 🎫 €9.50

Champs-Élysées
⊠ 193 E4 Ⓜ Charles de Gaulle-Étoile/George V/Franklin D Roosevelt

STREET CELEBRATIONS

The Champs-Élysées has always been associated with grand parades and parties. In 1810 Napoleon organized a lavish procession here (complete with life-size mock-up of the Arc de Triomphe, then under construction) to celebrate his marriage to his second wife, Marie Louise. The avenue's patriotic status was confirmed by the World War I victory parade of 14 July 1919. Twenty-five years later, Charles de Gaulle followed the same triumphal route at the end of World War II.

It remains the venue for national celebrations – the last leg of the Tour de France cycle race every July ends here, and it is the scene of great pomp on Bastille Day (14 July) and Armistice Day (11 November).

27 Jardin des Tuileries

When you've had your fill of museums and monuments, take a relaxing stroll through the Tuileries gardens, one of the oldest and most beautiful public gardens in Paris. Stretching along the right bank of the Seine, it offers unforgettable views embracing the Louvre, Place de la Concorde, Arc de Triomphe and, across the river, the Musée d'Orsay and the Eiffel Tower.

The garden was first created in the 16th century by Catherine de Médicis as an adornment in the Italian style to her pleasure palace, the Palais des Tuileries (once adjoining the Louvre but burned down during the Commune of 1871). The location of concerts and other entertainments, it also proved a useful spot for introducing to the French the Florentine fashion for horse-drawn carriages.

André Le Notre

In the 17th century, the garden was transformed by Louis XIV's architect, André Le Nôtre (of Versailles fame, ➤ 171) into a *jardin à la française* – a formal and symmetrical garden, studded with **ornamental statues**, and embellished with carefully manicured lawns, orderly box-edged flower beds, topiarized trees and gravel walkways. Le Nôtre also laid out a long, straight path leading from the palace, through the middle of the gardens and way beyond to the west. This later became the Champs-Élysées and the first section of the city's famous Voie Triomphale, or Triumphal Way, which today stretches from the Louvre (➤ 102) to La Défense (➤ 118), 9km (5.5mi) away.

A hedged avenue leads to the Louvre from the Jardin des Tuileries

Jardin des Tuileries

Public Garden

Le Nôtre's gardens were the first in France to open to the public. Instantly popular as a place to see and be seen, they soon became the model for public gardens throughout Europe, and still remain a firm favourite with locals and tourists alike. Children especially love the pony rides and the large pond towards the eastern end of the garden, where they can sail old-fashioned toy boats

The garden is a pleasant place to while away (which can be rented from a nearby kiosk). Once a Real Tennis court, the **Jeu de Paume** (on the Rue de Rivoli side) housed the city's Impressionist collection until it was moved to the **Musée d'Orsay** (► 56) in 1986. Along with its satellite premises just south of Place des Vosges (► 130), it now stages temporary exhibitions of contemporary visual arts, photography and multimedia. The **Orangerie** museum (on the river side) provides an intimate setting for a small collection of **Impressionist paintings**, including Claude Monet's lovely and unmissable water-lily series.

Insider Tip

TAKING A BREAK

Try **Lescure** (7 Rue de Mondovi, 75001; tel: 01 42 60 18 91; www.lescure1919.fr; Mon–Fri noon–2:15, 7–10:15, closed Aug) for traditional home cooking in a rustic restaurant, family-run since 1919.

➕ 204 B3 ✉ 75001 ☎ 01 40 20 90 43
🕐 Jul–Aug daily 7:30am–11:45pm; April–June, Sep 7:30am–9pm; Oct–March 7:30–7:30 🚇 Tuileries/Concorde

Musée de l'Orangerie
➕ 204 A3 ☎ 01 44 77 80 07; www.musee-orangerie.fr
🕐 Wed–Mon 9–5:45 🚇 Tuileries/Concorde 💶 €10. Free 1st Sun of month

INSIDER INFO

- Enter the gardens either through the Arc de Triomphe du Carrousel at the end nearest the Louvre or **through the grand golden gates** that stand on the edge of Place de la Concorde.
- From late June to late August, the annual **Fête Foraine du Jardin des Tuileries** attracts thousands of families with its funfair and amusement park.
- The **Jeu de Paume** (tel: 01 47 03 12 50; www.jeudepaume.org, moderate) is open Tue noon–9, Wed–Fri noon–7, Sat–Sun 10–7.

Hidden gem Look out for the **fine series of bronze figures** by 20th-century sculptor Aristide Maillol, which decorate the pathways.

At Your Leisure

28 Palais Royal

Tired of sightseeing? Step through the gates of the Palais Royal into a haven of peace, and leave the noise and bustle of the city behind. The buildings of this 17th-century palace, commissioned by Cardinal Richelieu, Louis XIII's minister, today house the French Ministry of Culture and are closed to the public. However, the lovely arcaded gardens, where on 12 July 1789 a revolutionary named Camille Desmoulins made the fiery speech that kick-started the city's revolt, are always open. The south end of this beautiful park, which once belonged to Cardinal Richelieu's estate, is today filled with modern art in the form of Daniel Buren's grey and white striped columns. These are accompanied by with shining silver sculptural fountains.

➕ 204 C3 ✉ Place du Palais Royal, 75001
☎ www.palais-royal.monuments-nationaux.fr
🕐 April–May daily 7am–10:15pm; June–Aug 7am–11pm; Sep 7am–9:30pm; Oct–March 7am–8.30pm
🚇 Palais Royal-Musée du Louvre

29 Place des Victoires

Anyone who enjoys window-shopping should visit the graceful, circular Place des Victoires. Designed by Versailles architect Jules Hardouin-Mansart (► 171), it is more famous today for its designer shops than for the victories of Louis XIV that it commemorates, but the Sun King does feature in an equestrian statue at the centre of the square. The harmony and symmetry of the surrounding architecture now create a showcase for popular names in fashion, such as Kenzo.
➕ 205 D3 ✉ 75002 🚇 Sentier/Bourse

Steel fountain by Pol Bury in the courtyard of the Palais Royal

This mosaic floor is in the elegant Galerie Vivienne

30 Les Galeries

As Paris has always been at the forefront of chic shopping, it comes as no surprise to discover that shopping arcades are a Parisian invention. The trend began in 1785, when the Duke of Orléans, in need of money, decided to sell the arcades he had constructed in his garden at the Palais Royal. A variety of merchants set up shop and the arcade instantly became a commercial success. You can still find several of these early 19th-century *galeries* dotted around the district, with their high glass roofs and ornate cast-iron structures forming covered passageways from one street to the next. In the 19th century they fell into disuse, but many were dramatically revived in the 1970s, once again becoming a popular rendezvous for journalists, designers and couturiers. Among the most charming are Galerie Véro-Dodat (antiques, bookshops and galleries), Passage des Panoramas, lit with fairy lights (cafés, boutiques), Passage Verdeau (drawings, engravings, old books and postcards), Passage Jouffroy (speciality shops – dolls' houses, cinema posters, toys and books) and, most sophisticated of all, **Galerie Vivienne** (fashion, interior design and an excellent *salon de thé*, A Priori Thé).

Insider Tip

Galerie Véro-Dodat
🔲 205 D3
✉ 19 Rue Jean-Jacques Rousseau, 75001
🚇 Louvre-Rivoli/Palais Royal-Musée du Louvre

Passage des Panoramas
🔲 205 D4 ✉ 11 Boulevard Montmartre/
10 Rue St-Marc, 75002
🚇 Richelieu-Drouot/Grands boulevards

Passage Verdeau
🔲 205 D5 ✉ 31 bis Rue du Faubourg
Montmartre, 75009 🚇 Le Peletier

Passage Jouffroy
🔲 205 D5 ✉ 10 Boulevard Montmartre, 75009
🚇 Richelieu-Drouot/Grands boulevards

Galerie Vivienne
🔲 205 D3 ✉ 4 Rue des Petits-Champs, 75002
🚇 Bourse

31 Opéra Garnier

From the outside, the Opéra Garnier looks more like a wedding cake than a world-renowned opera house. Designed by Charles Garnier to showcase the splendour of Napoleon III's France, its exuberant design represents the climax of 19th-century classical and baroque architecture in Paris,

The Louvre to the Arc de Triomphe

and one of the crowning glories of the urban redevelopment plans of Baron Haussmann (➤ 30).

The extravagance continues inside, with the Grand Foyer (freshly re-opened in 2009 after almost two years of renovations) and staircase illuminated by chandeliers, and the ceiling of the intimate red-and-gold auditorium painted by Marc Chagall with scenes from operas and ballets.

Following an attempt on Napoleon III's life in 1858, Garnier added a pavilion equipped with a curved ramp so that the emperor could step from his carriage straight into the rooms adjoining the royal box. The Palais Garnier was inaugurated in 1875, five years after the fall of the Empire. It contains a small museum that tells the story of opera through an extensive collection of musical memorabilia, including scores, manuscripts, sets and photographs. Tarot cards and ballet slippers of the Russian dancer Nijinsky are also here. The museum ticket includes a visit to the opera house, unless a rehearsal or performance is in progress.

🚹 204 B4
✉ Place de l'Opéra, 75009
☎ Opera house information and box office: 01 71 25 24 23, or 08 92 89 90 90 (within France); www.opera-de-paris.fr

🕐 Box office (on the corner of Rue Scribe and Rue Auber): Mon–Sat 1:30–6.30. Museum: daily 10–5; tours: 01 41 10 08 10 for details. No performances in Aug
🚇 Opéra

32 Place de la Concorde

This spacious cobbled square was laid out between 1755 and 1775, with a giant 3,300-year-old pink granite obelisk as its centrepiece (originally brought from the Temple of Ramses at Luxor, Egypt) and eight female statues, representing France's largest cities, adorning its four corners. The north side is lined by the Hôtel de la Marine (headquarters of the French Navy) and Hôtel de Crillon (➤ 40), one of the city's most exclusive hotels. In 1793, the square – renamed Place de la Révolution – was the scene of the execution of Louis XVI (➤ 10), and during the following two years a further 1,343 "enemies of the Revolution" were guillotined here, including Marie-Antoinette and, six months later, revolutionary leaders Danton and Robespierre. At the end of this "Reign of Terror", the square was given its present name evoking peace – ironically now, as it's one of the city's busiest squares.

🚹 204 A3   ✉ 75001   🚇 Concorde

The Opéra Garnier illuminated at night

33 La Madeleine

This immense neoclassical church is one of Paris's great landmarks. Construction began in 1764, and the finished church was dedicated to Mary Magdalene in 1845. In between came numerous attempts to convert it into a bank, parliament buildings and a Temple of Glory to the armies of Napoleon (hence its resemblance to a Greek temple, surrounded by giant columns supporting a sculpted frieze).

PLACE DE LA MADELEINE

Place de la Madeleine is always the first port of call for foodies in Paris, for the caviar, champagne and handmade chocolates sold in the specialist shops surrounding the Madeleine church. Pride of place goes to Fauchon (▶123), which earns epithets such as "the Harrods Food Hall of Paris" and "millionaire's supermarket", with its mouth-watering showcase of French food. Just opposite Fauchon is a small flower market (Mon–Sat).

As you enter the lavish marble and gilt interior, topped with three skylit cupolas, note the bas-reliefs depicting the Ten Commandments on the bronze doors. As you leave, admire the striking vista down Rue Royale to Place de la Concorde across to its architectural counterpoint, the Palais-Bourbon (home of the Assemblée Nationale, the French parliament) on the far side of the Seine.

🔂 204 A4 ✉ Place de la Madeleine, 75008
☎ 01 44 51 69 00; www.eglise-lamadeleine.com
🕓 Daily 9–7 🚇 Madeleine

34 Grand Palais & Petit Palais

These two attractive art nouveau-style buildings were constructed as temporary galleries for the

Fountain on the Place de la Concorde

The Louvre to the Arc de Triomphe

The Palais de Chaillot

World Fair of 1900. A century later, they are still two of Paris's major exhibition spaces. The most striking feature of the Grand Palais is its curved glass roof; at night it glows with the interior lighting. The eastern side of the palace hosts art exhibitions, while the western side has a science museum called the Palais de la Découverte.

The Petit Palais houses the Musée des Beaux-Arts de la Ville.
➕ 203 E3 ✉ Avenue Winston-Churchill, 75008 ☎ Grand Palais: 01 44 13 17 17; www.grandpalais.fr. Petit Palais: 01 53 43 40 00; www.petitpalais.paris.fr ◔ Grand Palais: Wed–Mon 10–8 (Wed until 10). Petit Palais: Tue–Sun 10–6 (Thu until 8 during temporary exhibitions only) Ⓜ Champs-Élysées-Clemenceau

35 Musée National des Arts Asiatiques-Guimet

Following renovation work, this museum is considered among the world's foremost on Asiatic art. Opened in 1889, it was the brainchild of Emile Guimet (1836–1918), a Lyons industrialist and fine arts fanatic. Its dazzling collection of 45,000 rare religious and secular items spans more than 3,000 years. The free 90-minute audio guide steers you round Cambodian Khmer Buddhist sculptures from Angkhor Wat, Afghanistan's Begram Treasures, and the Calmann and Grandidier collections of Chinese porcelain.
➕ 202 B3 ✉ 6 Place d'Iéna, 75016 ☎ 01 56 52 53 00; www.museeguimet.fr ◔ Wed–Mon 10–6 (last entrance 5.30) Ⓜ Iéna, Trocadéro/Boissière 🎫 €7.50

36 Palais de Chaillot

Built for the 1937 Paris exhibition, the two curved wings of this art deco cultural centre house a theatre and three museums.

The **Musée de l'Homme** – which tracks human evolution – is under renovation until 2015, while the **Musée de la Marine** (tel: 01 53 65 81 32; www.musee-marine.fr; Mon, Wed–Thu 11–6, Fri 11–9:30, Sat–Sun 11–7) portrays the history of the French navy through model ships and other nautical paraphernalia. In the

Opposite: The Arc de Triomphe

east wing is the Cité de l'Architecture et du Patrimoine (tel: 01 58 51 52 00; www.citechaillot.fr; Mon–Wed Fri–Sun 11–7, Thu 11–9; €8), an architecture and heritage museum as huge as it is impressive.

The biggest crowd-puller here, however, is the magnificent view across the Seine to the Eiffel Tower.

Just down the road, the Palais de Tokyo (Tues–Sun noon–9; €8) has been recently refurbished. **Insider Tip** A showcase for contemporary art, its exhibitions, shows and performances have earned it a daringly avant-garde reputation.

➕ 202 A2 ✉ 17 Place du Trocadéro, 75016 🚇 Trocadéro

37 Musée Marmottan Monet

If you have visited the Musée d'Orsay (➤ 56) and Musée de l'Orangerie (➤ 111) and still thirst for more Impressionist art, this museum is for you. Set in an elegant 19th-century mansion near the Bois de Boulogne, it contains the world's largest collection of Monets, including *Impression, soleil levant* (the work that gave the Impressionist movement its name, ➤ 22) and such celebrated series as *Cathédrale à Rouen* and *Parlement à Londres*, as well as paintings by Gauguin and Renoir.

➕ 202 off A2
✉ 2 Rue Louis-Boilly, 75016
☎ 01 44 96 50 33; www.marmottan.com
🕐 Tue–Wed, Fri–Sun 10–6; Thu 10–8
🚇 La Muette 💰 €10

38 La Défense

This modern skyscraper district on the western outskirts of Paris bristles with around 60 ultra-modern high-rise buildings, which create an atmosphere so different from the rest of the city that it's worth a brief visit. Most of the buildings are occupied by the offices of more than 1,200 companies, including the headquarters of more than half of France's 20 largest corporations.

The *pièce de résistance*, designed by Danish architect Otto von Spreckelsen, is the Grande Arche de La Défense – a hollow cube of white marble and glass symbolizing a window open to the world and measuring 112m (368 feet) on each side. The Tour First (225m), completed in 2011, is considered the tallest building in France.

La Grande Arche
➕ 202 off A5 ✉ Parvis de La Défense
☎ 01 49 07 27 27; www.grandearche.com
🕐 Currently closed to the public until further notice; check website
🚇 Grande Arche de La Défense
🚈 RER La Défense

🎭 GRÉVIN

Paris's answer to Madame Tussaud's (10 Boulevard Montmartre, 75009; tel: 01 47 70 85 05; www. grevin.com; Mon–Fri 10–6:30, Sat–Sun 10–7).

Modern sculpture and architecture at the esplanade de La Défense

Where to ...
Eat and Drink

Prices

Expect to pay per person for a meal, excluding drinks:

€ under €25   €€ €25–€50   €€€ €51–€100   €€€€ over €100

Alain Ducasse €€€€

Having achieved the highest critical acclaim for his Louis XV restaurant in Monaco, Alain Ducasse has done virtually the same at the Hôtel Plaza Athénée. He has reinterpreted some classics of French *haute cuisine*, instilling into them a lighter influence that has been gleaned from the simpler cooking of the provinces. His choice of ingredients is first class, and is perhaps best illustrated in the fabulous stuffed pigeon, chicken with *cèpes* and two kinds of pasta. The service is superb.

1203 D3 ☒ Hôtel Plaza Athénée, 25 Avenue Montaigne, 75008 ☎ 01 53 67 65 00; www.alain-ducasse.com ⏰ Thu–Fri 12:45–2:15, 7:45–10:15, Mon–Wed 7:45–10:15. Closed mid-July to mid-Aug, 2 weeks Dec ⓜ Alma-Marceau

L'Angle du Faubourg €€€

Located near the Place Charles-de-Gaulle-Étoile, this one-Michelin-star restaurant is decidedly contemporary: the décor is simple yet elegant. The constantly updated menu includes such dishes as chilled cream of chanterelle soup, jellied oysters, grilled langoustines served with artichokes *à l'orange*, roast lamb with braised fennel and, for dessert, roast figs with blackcurrant and vanilla, and delicious soft macaroons with pineapple. Those on a budget should drop by at lunchtime for the very reasonable, three-course *menu du jour*.

202 C5
☒ 195 Rue du Faubourg-St-Honoré, 75008
☎ 01 40 74 20 20; www.angledufaubourg.com
⏰ Mon–Fri 12:30–2:30, 7:30–10:30. Closed Aug
ⓜ Charles de Gaulle-Étoile/Ternes

Bistrot du Sommelier €€€

The owner has won awards for the best *sommelier* (wine waiter) both in France and in the world. The wine list here is phenomenal. There is also a fabulous variety available by the glass. Wine is the theme of the décor too, and though food almost takes second place, it is nevertheless good. The menu is short and modish, with the chance to sample different wines with each course.

203 F5 ☒ 97 Boulevard Haussmann, 75008 ☎ 01 42 65 24 85; www.bistrotdusommelier.com ⏰ Mon–Fri noon–2:30, 7:30–10:30. Closed 3 weeks Aug, 1 week Christmas ⓜ St-Augustin/Miromesnil

Café de la Paix €

Famous customers have included Oscar Wilde, Maurice Chevalier, Josephine Baker, Maria Callas and Plácido Domingo. The interior was designed by the Opéra's architect, Charles Garnier, and the walls are decorated with fine Second Empire frescoes. Forget the fairly uninteresting restaurant and grab a terrace table (shielded by glass in the colder months) and indulge in the impeccable *pâtisseries* and ice-cream sundaes. Enormous baguette sandwiches filled with pâté, ham or salami should fuel your shopping sprees, while the coffee is also top quality, but expect to pay for the view of the opera house and to observe the continuous flow of Parisian passers-by.

Insider Tip

204 B4 ☒ 5 Place de l'Opéra, 75009 ☎ 01 40 07 36 36; www.cafedelapaix.fr ⏰ Restaurant: 7am–12:30am (lunch from 12); terrace 9am–12:30am ⓜ Opéra

The Louvre to the Arc de Triomphe

Carré des Feuillants €€€€

Pearwood-panelled walls and Murano crystal chandeliers help to create an elegant setting just off the Rue Rivoli for Alain Dutournier, the city's foremost exponent of the cooking of his beloved native Gascony. Utilizing the wonderful produce of the region, including Chalosse beef and chicken, he has taken traditional recipes and reworked them into two-star Michelin cuisine, yet he manages to retain much of their original character and flavour.

🔢 204 B3 ✉ 14 Rue de Castiglione, 75001
☎ 01 42 86 82 82; www.carredesfeuillants.fr
🕐 Mon–Fri 12:15–2, 7:30–9:45, Sat 7:30–9:45.
Closed Aug 🚇 Tuileries

Chez Jean €€/€€€

This formal but friendly restaurant, run by two alumni of Taillevent (one of the city's top restaurants, ➤ 121), specializes in classic dishes with a refreshingly modern twist. Try the *foie gras* with rhubarb and caviar, followed by slow-cooked farmhouse pork with a chutney of apricots, preserved lemons and sage. The cuisine is refined, the presentation exquisite, and the service second to none.

🔢 200 C1 ✉ 8 Rue Saint-Lazare, 75009
☎ 01 48 78 62 73; www.restaurantjean.fr
🕐 Mon–Fri noon–2:30, 8–10:30
🚇 Notre-Dame-de-Lorette/Trinité

La Fontaine Gaillon €€€

The elegant Fontaine Gaillon, owned by French actor Gérard Depardieu, sits neatly between Opéra Garnier and the Paris stock exchange; its understated elegance makes it equally popular with both crowds. Patrons dine on fresh seasonal cuisine, dished up on the discreet terrace hugging the 18th-century Fontaine d'Antin, or in one of the five private salons.

🔢 204 C4
✉ 1 Rue Gaillon, 75002 ☎ 01 42 65 87 04;
www.restaurant-la-fontaine-gaillon.com
🕐 Mon–Fri noon–2:30, 7–11:30 🚇 Opéra

Le Fouquet's €€€

A real Paris institution that's listed as a historic building. It is very much a place in which to see and be seen: particularly famous faces head to the veranda. The menu is that of a *brasserie de luxe*, offering a selection of generally well-prepared classics such as *foie gras* terrine and *hachis parmentier* (Gallic shepherd's pie). A snack menu is available all day in the bar or on the terrace 11–11.

🔢 202 C4
✉ 99 Avenue des Champs-Élysées, 75008
☎ 01 40 69 60 50; www.lucienbarriere.com
🕐 Daily noon–3, 7–midnight 🚇 George V

Harry's New York Bar €

A legendary bar just off the Avenue de l'Opéra, Harry's is said to be where the Bloody Mary was first concocted in the 1920s. With its English-speaking bartenders, it can make for a welcome refuge if your French is limited. Cocktails are the reason to come here, and some argue that the dry martinis are the best in the city. Snack lunches (sandwiches, salads or croques-monsieur) are served during the daytime, but at night you won't be allowed in unless you're smartly dressed (live music on some evenings). It may not be a typical French bistro but it's such an institution it's worth at least one visit during your stay.

🔢 204 B4 ✉ 5 Rue Daunou, 75002
☎ 01 42 61 71 14; www.harrys-bar.fr
🕐 Daily noon–4am 🚇 Opéra

Ledoyen €€€€

This is one of the city's most historic restaurants, which in the past was patronized by Robespierre, painted by Tissot and written about by Maupassant. It opened in 1792 in a pavilion near the Petit Palais in the Jardin des Champs-Élysées, and the elegant first-floor dining-room looks out over the gardens. Modern dishes, described without undue elaboration, are prepared with painstaking attention to detail.

🗺 203 F3 ✉ 1 Avenue Dutuit, 75008
☎ 01 53 05 10 01; www.ledoyen.com
🕐 Tue–Fri 12:30–1:45, 8–9:45, Mon 8–9:45
🚇 Champs-Élysées-Clemenceau

Pierre Gagnaire €€€€

Hailed by many in the know as one of the most creative chefs in France, Pierre Gagnaire's extra-ordinarily inventive cooking combines unparalleled culinary skills with consummate artistry on the plate. His imagination appears to be limitless, but there is nothing in any of his dishes that is not perfectly harmonious. Menus range from vegetarian to five courses paired with vintages of Dom Pérignon: be prepared for a magical assault on your tastebuds. Demand is very high at this three-Michelin-star restaurant; book well in advance.

🗺 202 C5 ✉ 6 Rue de Balzac, 75008
☎ 01 58 36 12 50; www.pierre-gagnaire.com
🕐 Mon–Fri noon–3:30, 7:30–9:30, Sun 7:30–9:30. Closed Aug 🚇 George V

Restaurant Palais Royal €€

Located in the northeast corner of the Jardins du Palais Royal, the terrace of this modern Mediterranean restaurant spills out into the enchanting gardens themselves. Order platters of *tapenade* and *gazpacho* to share, or opt for chef Bruno Hees' fish and chips – *chic, très chic*.

🗺 205 D3 ✉ 110 Galerie de Valois, 75001
☎ 01 40 20 00 27; www.restaurantdupalais royal.com 🕐 Mon–Sat noon–2:30, 7:30–10 🚇 Palais Royal-Musée du Louvre

Taillevent €€€€

The city's most enduring "grand" restaurant, whose panelled walls and discreet service help to create a civilized and refined ambience favoured by the great and the good of the city's establishment, has been owned and managed by the Vrinat family since 1946. There is a wonderfully old-fashioned and classic basis to the cooking, with only a few modern trends. Specialities include *foie gras*, lobster and truffles. The white truffle sorbet with chocolate *croquant* (crunch) will round off your meal in style.

🗺 202 C5 ✉ 15 Rue Lamennais, 75008
☎ 01 44 95 15 01; www.taillevent.com
🕐 Mon–Fri 12:15–2, 7:15–9.30. Closed Aug, public hols 🚇 George V

Terminus Nord €€

Eurostar passengers rightly see this venerable institution as a real godsend – it's conveniently opposite the Gare du Nord, open all hours and it's a bastion of delicious French cooking. The whole country is represented, from Alsace's *choucroute garnie* (a mountain of subtle sauerkraut garlanded with sausages and pork) to Mediterranean *bouillabaisse*, a fish stew flavoured with saffron. True to the brasserie tradition, the draught beer, shellfish and wine list are superb. A sumptuous 1920s decor and white-aproned, stern waiters reinforce your first (or last) taste of Paris.

🗺 201 E2 ✉ 23 Rue de Dunkerque, 75010
☎ 01 42 85 05 15; www.terminusnord.com
🕐 Daily 8am–1am 🚇 Gare du Nord

Willi's Wine Bar €€

Englishman Mark Williamson's splendid bistro/wine bar is not far from Place des Victoires. On offer is a wonderful selection of Côtes du Rhône and Bordeaux wines in particular. Choose between eating in the chic bar, which does excellent wines by the glass, or in the dining room, where the walls are decorated with annual takes on the locale's signature "bottle art" images and where a short, daily-changing menu favours seasonal dishes.

🗺 204 C3 ✉ 13 Rue des Petits-Champs, 75001
☎ 01 42 61 05 09; www.williswinebar.com
🕐 Mon–Sat noon–2:30, 7:30–11 (bar open noon–midnight) 🚇 Bourse

Where to...
Shop

This is the area for gifts or perfumes, or perhaps a little designer number, from the city that is the epicentre of the world of high fashion. The *crème de la crème* of *haute couture* and one of the most exclusive shopping streets anywhere, is Rue St-Honoré in the 1st *arrondissement* (which becomes Rue du Faubourg St-Honoré in the 8th). A stroll west from Palais Royal reveals a roll-call of designer names.

HOME FURNISHINGS

Colette (213 Rue St-Honoré, 75001; tel: 01 55 35 33 90; www.colette.fr; Mon–Sat 11–7; Metro: Palais Royal-Musée du Louvre/Tuileries/Pyramides) is the place to go for leading designs in both fashion and home furnishings – from Alexander McQueen to Tom Dixon and the latest from Sony. The "Water Bar" in the basement, with more than 100 brands of water, also does snacks.

ACCESSORIES

Hermès, 24 Rue du Faubourg St-Honoré, 75008; tel: 01 40 17 47 09; www.hermes.com; Mon–Sat 10:30-6:30, closed Sun; Metro: Concorde) is the place for handbags and accessories. It's easy to spot **Louis Vuitton's** store on the Champs-Élysées (22 Avenue des Champs-Élysées, 75008; tel: 08 10 81 00 10; www.louisvuitton.com; daily; Metro: George V) by the queues outside.

FASHION

Niçois brand **Façonnable** (9 Rue du Faubourg St-Honoré, 75008; tel: 01 47 42 72 60; www.faconnable. com; Metro: Concorde) offers men's

co-ordinated separates. **Lanvin** (22 (Women), 15 (Men) Rue du Faubourg St-Honoré, 75008; tel: 01 44 71 31 73 (Women), 01 44 71 31 25 (Men), www.lanvin.fr; Metro: Concorde) features classic designs. Rue Cambon, crossing Rue St-Honoré, is where **Chanel** (31 Rue Cambon, 75001; tel: 01 42 86 26 00; www.chanel.com; Metro: Concorde/Madeleine) is based – not the place for bargains, though the accessories are more affordable.

Avenue Montaigne is a street of immense chic, lined by the likes of **Christian Dior** (30 Avenue Montaigne, 75008; tel: 01 47 20 00 60; www. dior.com; Metro: Alma-Marceau), **Dolce e Gabbana** (54 Avenue Montaigne, 75008; tel: 01 42 25 68 78; www.dolcegabbana.com; Metro: Alma-Marceau), **Céline** (36 Avenue Montaigne, 75008; tel: 01 56 89 07 92; www.celine.fr; Metro: Franklin D Roosevelt), **Nina Ricci** (39 Avenue Montaigne, 75008; tel: 01 40 88 64 51; www.ninaricci.com; Metro: Alma-Marceau) and **Valentino** (17–19 Avenue Montaigne, 75008; tel: 01 47 23 64 61; www.valentino.com; Metro: Alma-Marceau). **Givenchy** (3 Avenue George V, 75008; tel: 01 44 31 51 25; www.givenchy.com; Metro: Alma-Marceau) is fairly near.

Another small enclave of superior boutiques is located around Place des Victoires, which joins Rue des Petits-Champs and Rue Étienne-Marcel. A branch of **Jean-Paul Gaultier's** is in Galerie Vivienne (6 Rue Vivienne, 75002; tel: 01 42 86 05 05; www.jeanpaulgaultier.com; Metro: Bourse/Palais Royal-Musée du Louvre). Gaultier offers bespoke fashion and dazzling ready-to-wear. His flagship store is at 44 Rue George V.

HAIR AND BEAUTY

Carita (11 Rue du Faubourg St-Honoré, 75008; tel: 01 44 94 11 11; www.carita.fr; Metro: Concorde) is one of the city's best ladies' hair stylists. They also offer facials.

Annick Goutal (14 Rue de Castiglione, 75001; tel: 01 42 60 52 82; www.annickgoutal.com; Metro: Tuileries/Concorde), whose products are favoured by exclusive outlets including the Hôtel de Crillon, is a tiny and exquisite perfume salon.

At the **Salons du Palais Royal Shiseido** (142 Galerie de Valois, Jardin du Palais-Royal, 25 Rue de Valois, 75001; tel: 01 49 27 09 09; www.salons-shiseido.com; Mon–Sat; Metro: Palais Royal-Musée du Louvre), make-up artist Serge Lutens offers exclusive perfumes and cosmetics.

Guerlain (68 Avenue des Champs-Élysées, 75008; tel: 01 45 62 26 57; www.guerlain.fr; Metro: Franklin D Roosevelt), the French perfumer, has a beauty salon on Avenue des Champs-Élysées.

JEWELLERY

In Place Vendôme is **Cartier** (23 Place Vendôme, 75001; tel: 01 44 55 32 20; www.cartier.com; Mon–Sat; Metro: Opéra/Tuileries) with its top-quality jewellery.

Guerlain Le Spa (68 Avenue des Champs-Élysées, 75008; tel: 01 45 62 11 21; www.guerlain.fr; Metro: Franklin D Roosevelt): The French parfumier has a beauty salon located right on the Champs-Élysées.

GIFTS

Musée des Arts Décoratifs (107 Rue de Rivoli, 75001; tel: 01 44 55 57 50; www.lesartsdecoratifs.fr, closed Mon; Metro: Palais Royal), in the Louvre's northwest wing, has a bookshop and gift shop offering selections of unusual fine gifts. On the same street, **Nature et Découvertes** (99 Rue de Rivoli, 75001; tel: 01 47 03 47 43; www.natureetdecouvertes.com; closed Aug; Metro: Palais Royal-Musée du Louvre) is a unique shop: its sells almost everything, from

Insider Tip

camping equipment to cosmetics and health products.

DEPARTMENT STORES

No serious shopping trip would be complete without a visit to at least one of the department stores. **Galeries Lafayette** (40 Boulevard Haussmann, 75009; tel: 01 42 82 34 56; www.galerieslafayette.com; Metro: Chaussée d'Antin) and **Au Printemps** (64 Boulevard Haussmann, 75009; tel: 01 42 82 50 00; www.printemps.com; Metro: Havre-Caumartin) are glamorous neighbours offering perfumes, jewellery and ready-to-wear fashion.

FOOD & DRINK

On Rue Coquillière, just north of the domed Bourse du Commerce, the remarkable **E Dehillerin** (18 Rue Coquillière, 75001; tel: 01 42 36 53 13; www.e-dehillerin.fr; Metro: Les Halles) has supplied cookware of all shapes and sizes to the great chefs since 1820.

Alléosse (13 Rue Poncelet, 75017; tel: 01 46 22 50 45; www. fromage-alleosse.com, closed Sun pm, Mon; Metro: Ternes) off Avenue des Ternes, is one of Paris's finest cheese shops.

Les Caves Augé (116 Boulevard Haussmann, 75008; tel: 01 45 22 16 97; www.cavesauge.com; Metro: St-Augustin) on Boulevard Haussmann, is the oldest wine shop in Paris. Jean-Paul Hévin's eponymous **Hévin** is *the* place for chocolates (231 Rue Saint-Honoré, 75001; tel: 01 55 35 35 96; www. jphevin.com; Metro: Concorde).

Insider Tip

Place de la Madeleine is home to two of the greatest gourmet emporia, **Fauchon** (24–26 Place de la Madeleine, 75008; tel: 01 70 39 38 00; www.fauchon.fr, closed Sun; Metro: Madeleine) and **Hédiard** (21 Place de la Madeleine, 75008; tel: 01 43 12 88 88; www.hediard.fr; Metro: Madeleine).

Where to ...
Go Out

The capital's greatest diversity of entertainment venues is within this area on the Right Bank.

CINEMAS

Le Balzac (1 Rue Balzac, 75008; tel: 01 45 61 10 60; www.cinem-abalzac.com; Metro: George V/ Charles de Gaulle-Étoile) and **Le Lincoln** (14 Rue Lincoln, 75008; tel: 01 42 25, 45 80; www.lelincoln.com; Metro: George V/ Franklin D Roosevelt), both on streets off the Champs-Élysées, are excellent and popular art-house cinemas.

CLASSICAL MUSIC

The Orchestre Nationale de France – known as the best orchestra in Paris – is based at **Maison de Radio-France** (116 Avenue du Président-Kennedy, www.radiofrance.fr; Metro: Ranelagh), close to the Seine, which also offers free classical concerts and operas throughout the year, as well as radio shows open to the public.

Elegant **Théâtre des Champs-Élysées** (15 Avenue Montaigne, www.theatredeschampselysees.com, closed July–Aug; Metro: Alma-Marceau/Franklin D Roosevelt) hosts opera, ballet, classical and chamber music orchestras.

The **Opéra National de Paris-Palais Garnier** (➤ 113; Place de l'Opéra, tel: 08 92 89 90 90; www.opera-de-paris.fr, closed Aug; Metro: Opéra) is one of central Paris's most imposing buildings, and it enjoys near-perfect acoustics for operas and ballets.

The **Salle Gaveau** (45 Rue La Boétie, tel: 01 49 53 05 07; www.sallegaveau.com, closed July–Aug; Metro: Miromesnil) is a favoured venue for chamber music and recitals, while the **Salle Pleyel** (www.sallepleyel.fr) is the home of the Orchestre de Paris (252 Rue du Faubourg St-Honoré, tel: 01 42 56 13 13; www.orchestredeparis.com; Metro: Ternes).

THEATRE

The **Comédie-Française** (1 Place Colette, tel 08 25 10 16 80; www.comedie-francaise.fr, closed July–Sep; Metro: Palais Royal) presents high-quality productions.

NIGHTCLUBS

A stylish nude revue takes place at the **Crazy Horse Saloon** (12 Avenue George V, tel: 01 47 23 32 32; www.lecrazyhorseparis.com, shows Sun–Fri 8:15pm, 10:45pm, Sat 7pm, 9:30pm, 11:45pm; Metro: Alma-Marceau), while the **Lido de Paris** (116 bis Avenue des Champs-Élysées, tel: 01 40 76 56 10; www.lido.fr, shows 9:30, 11:30pm; Metro: George V) offers an optional dinner preceding a spectacular show featuring the Bluebell Girls.

Queen Club (102 Avenue des Champs-Élysées, tel: 01 45 63 16 87; www.queen.fr; daily midnight–dawn; Metro: George V) is a gay club and the haunt of outrageous drag queens, while remaining straight-friendly.

La Scala (188 bis Rue de Rivoli; www.la-scala.abcsalles.com; Wed–Sun 11pm–dawn; Metro:Palais Royal/Tuileries) offers funk, dance, deep house and R&B.

At the **Rex** (5 Boulevard Poissonnière, tel: 01 42 36 10 96; www.rexclub.com; Thu–Sat 11pm–6am, some Weds, Suns, closed Aug; Metro: Bonne Nouvelle), the best DJs spin house and techno.

Le Marais & Bastille

 Little Treats

Falafel in the Jewish Quarter
Numerous stands in the **Rue des Rosiers** (► 132) sell the tastiest falafel in the whole of Paris.

Chatting, surfing, chilling
The **Place des Vosges** (► 130) boasts excellent WiFi coverage, making it a real hotspot for people with laptops and tablets.

Garden Tranquillity
The elegant garden at the **Musée Carnavalet** (► 138) is a great place to take a break from the bustling quarter outside.

Le Marais & Bastille

Getting Your Bearings

The ancient, maze-like Marais ("swamp") quarter, once an uninhabitable stretch of marshy ground used for market gardening, is now one of Paris's most historic and sought-after residential districts – home to chic Parisians, the city's oldest Jewish community and a vibrant gay community.

The pace of life in the Marais is slow and laid-back compared with the rest of the city. This gives you time to appreciate its narrow cobbled streets, studded with small squares and gardens, and to enjoy the modish boutiques, art galleries, intimate restaurants, bars and cafés – not to mention such museums as the Musée Picasso (re-opening after renovation expected for beginning 2014) and Musée Carnavalet that are housed in some of the magnificent Renaissance mansions characteristic of the neighbourhood.

The central Chatelet Les Halles metro station – the largest in the city – is currently sitting in the shadow of a major construction site. The plan is to modernise the 30 year-old Forum des Halles shopping centre with such features as a curved glass roof the size of a football pitch. Further east is the Centre Pompidou and the trendy Bastille district, once famed for the prison that was stormed so notoriously on 14 July 1789, and known today for its plethora of ethnic restaurants, its hip bars and clubs and the prestigious Opéra Bastille.

Shoppers in Le Marais

At Your Leisure

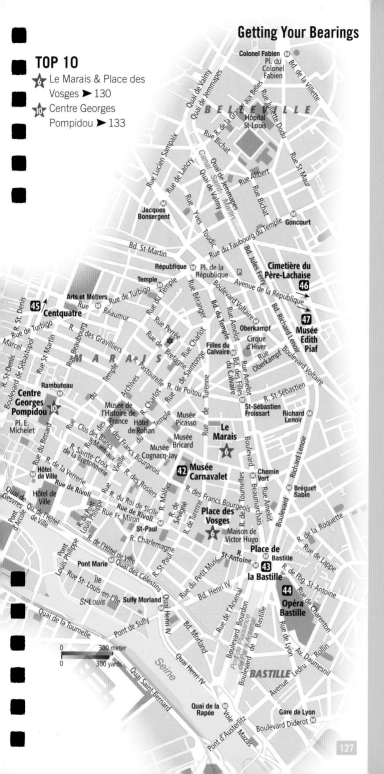

TOP 10

☆ 6 Le Marais & Place des Vosges ➤ 130
☆ 10 Centre Georges Pompidou ➤ 133

Colonel Fabien Ⓜ
Pl. du Colonel Fabien
Bd. de la Villette

Quai de Valmy
Quai de Jemmapes
Rue de la Grange aux Belles
Rue Juliette Dodu

B E L L E V I L L E

Hôpital St-Louis

Rue St-Maur

Rue Bichat

Rue Lucien Sampaix
Rue de Lancry
Canal Saint-Martin
Quai de Jemmapes
Quai de Valmy
Rue Alibert
Rue Bichat

Jacques Bonsergent Ⓜ

Rue Yves Toudic

Goncourt Ⓜ

Rue du Faubourg du Temple

Bd. St-Martin

République Ⓜ
Pl. de la République
Bd. Jules Ferry
P

Cimetière du Père-Lachaise
46 →

Temple Ⓜ

Arts et Métiers Ⓜ
45 ↗ **Centquatre**
Rue Réaumur
Rue de Turbigo
Rue du Temple
Rue Béranger
Bd. du Temple
Boulevard Voltaire
Rue Amelot
Avenue de la République

Oberkampf Ⓜ
Cirque d'Hiver
Rue Oberkampf
Bd. Richard Lenoir
Boulevard Voltaire

47
Musée Edith Piaf

R. St-Denis
Rue de Turbigo
R. Beaubourg
Rue St-Martin
Rue des Gravilliers
R. de Bretagne
Rue Perrée
Rue Charlot
Rue de Saintonge
Filles du Calvaire Ⓜ
Bd. des Filles du Calvaire
Rue Amelot

Marcel Ⓜ
Boulevard de Sébastopol
R. St-Denis
Temple
Pastourelle
Rue Charlot
R. de Poitou
Rue de Turenne
St-Sébastien Froissart Ⓜ
R. St-Sébastien
Richard Lenoir Ⓜ

M A R A I S
Archives

Rambuteau Ⓜ
Centre Georges Pompidou Ⓜ 10
Pl. E. Michelet

Musée de l'Histoire de France
Hôtel de Rohan
Rue des Francs Bourgeois
Musée Picasso
Musée Bricard
Musée Cognacq-Jay

Le Marais ☆ 6

Chemin Vert Ⓜ
Bréguet Sabin Ⓜ

R. du Renard
Clos des Blancs
Manteaux
R. Sainte-Croix de la Bretonnerie
R. Vieille du Temple
Rue de Turenne
Boulevard Beaumarchais
Boulevard Richard Lenoir

Hôtel de Ville
Rue de la Verrerie
Hôtel de Ville Ⓜ
Rue de Rivoli
R. des Rosiers
R. Malher
R. de Sévigné
42 **Musée Carnavalet**
R. des Francs Bourgeois

R. de la Roquette

Quai de Gesvres
Pont d'Arcole
Qu. de l'Hôtel de Ville
Île de Ville
R. du Roi de Sicile
Rue de Rivoli
Rue Fr. Miron
St-Paul Ⓜ
R. Charlemagne
R. St-Antoine
Rue de Turenne

Place des Vosges ☆ 6
Maison de Victor Hugo

Place de la Bastille 43
Bastille Ⓜ
R. de Fbg. St-Antoine
Rue de Lappe

Pont Louis Philippe
Pont Marie
Rue St-Louis-en-l'Île
Pont Marie Ⓜ
Qu. de l'Hôtel de Ville
Qu. des Célestins
Rue du Petit Musc
Bd. Henri IV

44 **Opéra Bastille**
Rue de Charenton
Rue de Lyon

Île St-Louis Ⓜ
Sully Morland Ⓜ
Quai Henri IV
Pont de Sully

Rue de l'Arsenal
Boulevard Bourdon
Pont de Sully
Rue Morland
Bd. Morland
Boulevard de la Bastille

Av. Daumesnil
Avenue Ledru Rollin

Quai de la Tournelle

Seine

BASTILLE

0 ——— 300 meter
0 ——— 300 yards

Quai Saint-Bernard
Quai de la Rapée Ⓜ
Voie Express
Pont d'Austerlitz
Quai Henri IV
Mazas

Gare de Lyon Ⓜ
Boulevard Diderot Ⓜ

Perfect Days in...

The Perfect Day

If you're not quite sure where to begin your travels, this itinerary recommends a practical and enjoyable day out exploring Le Marais and Bastille, taking in some of the best places to see. For more information see the main entries (► 130–143).

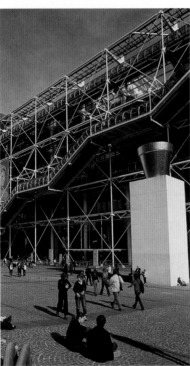

🕘 9:00am

Start the day with leisurely coffee and croissants at the legendary designer **Café Beaubourg** (► 145) overlooking the ☆**Centre Georges Pompidou** (left, ► 133). Pause awhile in the spacious square to watch the buskers, mime artists, fire-eaters and jugglers; sit and write those postcards beside the brightly coloured mechanical pop-art fountains in **Place Igor Stravinsky** (► 135) – or, for a fun souvenir, why not have your portrait sketched by a street caricaturist?

🕚 11:00am

Spend a few moments admiring the remarkable transparent architecture of the Centre Georges Pompidou, before stepping inside to enjoy one of the world's most exhilarating and controversial museums of modern art.

🕐 1:00pm

Head eastwards along Rue Rambuteau into the heart of the intriguing ☆**Marais quarter** (► 130). Either follow our suggested route (► 183) or stroll at random past its many fine aristocratic residences. Window-shop in the trendy boutiques and galleries on Rue des Francs-Bourgeois. Be sure to try some Jewish specialities in the kosher delis and bakeries along Rue des Rosiers as an hors-d'œuvre before lunch, in one of the countless cosy bistros in the surrounding streets.

🕒 3:00pm

Steep yourself in Parisian history at the **㊷ Musée Carnavalet** (► 138). Spread throughout the Hôtel Carnavalet and the Hôtel le Peletier (built during the 16th and 17th centuries), the collection documents major events and daily life in the capital over the past 500 years.

🕐 5:30pm

Wind your way through the Marais, down Rue de Sévigné and along Rue des Francs-Bourgeois to ⭐ **Place des Vosges** (above, ► 130), a gracious square of symmetrical brick houses with steeply pitched slate roofs and ground-floor arcades, mainly occupied by art galleries and antiques shops. At **Ma Bourgogne** café on the corner, the waiters sport traditional black jackets and long white aprons. Where better to enjoy an aperitif?

🕐 7:30pm

If you're lucky, you may be able to get tickets to attend an opera at the ㊹ **Opéra Bastille** (left, ► 140). If not, the gleaming glass edifice is still well worth admiring (especially after dark when floodlit) before ending your day with dinner at **Bofinger** (► 145).

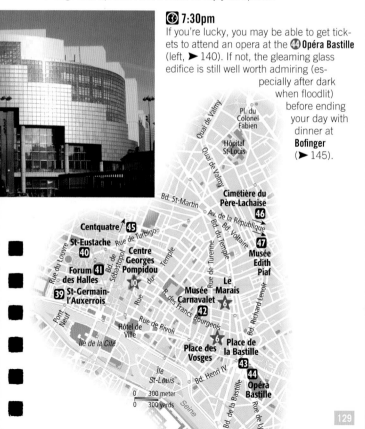

⭐6 Le Marais & Place des Vosges

The history of the Marais dates back to the 14th century and Charles V, who moved the royal court here from the Île de la Cité. But it was not until the 17th century, when Henri IV laid out the Place des Vosges, that the Marais became the place to live, and moneyed classes, keen to be associated with the monarchy, started to build the grand and sumptuous *hôtels particuliers* (mansions) that dot the neighbourhood today.

Le Marais

This magnificent quarter, which managed to escape the attentions of one Baron Haussmann, is regarded as one of the oldest districts in Paris. It was close to being torn down, but the extensive renovation of the "Hôtels particuliers" (private mansions) in the 1960s gave the area a new lease of life. It has since become one of the most lively, fashionable and atmospheric *quartiers* of central Paris, a magnet for elegant shops, fine restaurants and bars. The district is especially busy on Sunday afternoons, when many of its trendy boutiques defy Sunday opening laws.

A number of its mansions have been restored and now house museums. As well as the **Musée Picasso**, **Musée**

Elegant mansions surround Place des Vosges

Carnavalet (► 138) and **Musée Cognacq-Jay** (► 184), they are: the **Musée de la Chasse et de la Nature** (Hunting and Nature Museum, 62 Rue des Archives, 75003; tel: 01 53 01 92 40; www. chassenature.org; Tue–Sun 11–6) in the former residence of Louis XIV's Secretary of State; and the **Maison Européenne de la Photographie** (5–7 Rue de Fourcy, 75004; tel: 01 44 78 75 00; www.mep-fr.org; Wed–Sun 11–8), with exhibitions of contemporary photography.

Shoppers stroll along Rue des Rosiers in Le Marais

Elegant Square

The Marais's *pièce de résistance* is undoubtedly the **Place des Vosges**, the oldest square in Paris and, in many people's view, its most gracious. Originally called Place Royale, the square received its present name in 1800 in honour of the Vosges *département,* the first in France to pay taxes. Its stately 17th-century town houses, laid out by Henri IV for his courtiers and built in alternate brick and stone with steeply pitched slate roofs, are arranged symmetrically around an immaculate park, once a popular venue for duels. Madame de Sévigné, famous for her letters, was

Le Marais & Bastille

born at No 1 in 1626. Victor Hugo lived at No 6 from 1832 to 1848, before going into exile. It is now a small museum dedicated to his memory (tel: 01 42 72 10 16; www.musee-hugo.paris.fr; Tue–Sun 10–6). Otherwise, the graceful arcades nowadays house a variety of stylish galleries, antiques shops and elegant *salons de thé*. See pages 175–177 for an overview of the area and a walk.

TAKING A BREAK

Au Pied de Cochon is open all day and is a characterful and convivial brasserie (➤ 144).

Le Marais ✚ 206 B3
Place de Vosges ✚ 197 E3
🚇 St-Paul/Bastille/Chemin Vert

Musée Carnavalet is housed in a large mansion

INSIDER INFO

- The **Hôtel de Sens** is one of the city's few surviving medieval buildings, where Queen Margot, Henri IV's former wife, led a life of debauchery and scandal. Her life story was immortalised in Alexandre Dumas' novel that bears her name (1 Rue du Figuier, 75004).

- The **Hôtel de Sully** is a beautiful and meticulously restored 17th-century aristocratic mansion (62 Rue St-Antoine, 75004, ➤ 184). Between the courtyard and the grounds of the house – today home to the Centre for National Monuments – you'll find a bookshop with wooden beams painted in the 17th century that stocks the most sought-after literature on the city.

- For seven centuries the Marais has had a vibrant Jewish community, focused around **Rue des Rosiers** and **Rue des Écouffes**, which are lined with kosher shops and restaurants. Admire the synagogue (10 Rue Pavée, 75004), renowned for its art nouveau architecture by Hector Guimard, designer of the famous Metro entrances, and visit the Jewish Art and History museum (Musée d'Art et d'Histoire du Judaïsme, Hôtel de St-Aignan, 71 Rue de Temple, 75003; tel: 01 53 01 86 60; www.mahj.org; Mon–Fri 11–6, Sun 10–6; €8).

⭐ 10 Centre Georges Pompidou

Known to Parisians as "Beaubourg" (the name of the surrounding area), the avant-garde Centre Georges Pompidou is one of the world's most extraordinary museums and one of the city's most distinctive landmarks. An X-ray-style extravaganza of steel and glass, striped by brightly coloured pipes and snake-like escalators, it looks as if someone has turned the whole building inside out. What's more, it contains one of the largest collections of modern art in the world.

The futuristic architecture of the Centre Georges Pompidou

It was in 1969 that French President Georges Pompidou declared "I passionately want Paris to have a cultural centre that would be at once a museum and a centre of creation". The building caused an outcry when it was opened in 1977, in the heart of the then run-down Beaubourg district, and it has been the subject of great controversy ever since, but it is generally acknowledged as one of the city's most distinctive landmarks – a lovable

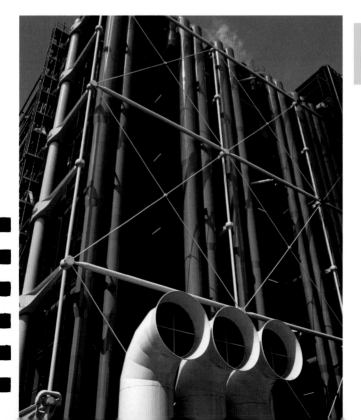

oddity, and far more popular as a gallery than anyone could ever have anticipated.

As a result, the building had to be closed for two years of major renovation work, reopening, appropriately, on New Year's Eve 1999 with an exhibition spanning the art of the 20th century.

Escalators inside the Centre

Exterior Style

Before you venture inside, pause to admire the centre's unique external structure, designed by world-famous architects Richard Rogers and Renzo Piano. Glass predominates, giving the entire edifice a transparency that abolishes the usual barriers between the street and the centre. To avoid using conventional upright columns, a riot of steel beams that are cross-strutted and hinged over the length and width of the entire building form an intriguing external skeleton. Inside, walls can be taken down or put up at will, enabling the various *espaces d'art* to change shape in order to accommodate various different displays.

On the outside, the building reveals all its workings by way of **multicoloured tubes, ducts and piping** in the "high-tech" style that was briefly popular in the 1970s but but that had fallen out of fashion by the time the building was completed. Far from being merely decorative, they are colour-coded: green for water, blue for air conditioning, yellow for electricity and red for the circulation of visitors. To complete the pattern, people zigzag up and down on red escalators that are also situated on the building's façade. Once inside, you will find that there is so much **natural light** that it's almost like walking around an open-air gallery.

Musée National d'Art Moderne

The Centre Pompidou's main attraction is the Musée National d'Art Moderne – more than 60,000 works of contemporary art (of which about 2,000 are on display at any one time), starting from the early 20th century, roughly where the Musée d'Orsay leaves off. Such modern schools as **fauvism, cubism and surrealism** are represented with works by Matisse, Derain, Chagall, Braque and Picasso. The collection also covers the futurists and minimalists – you name it, it's here, and you will be pleased to hear that there are thoughtfully placed clusters of chairs throughout for you to collapse in en route. The displays change annually, so if there's a particular piece you're eager to view, visit the website to check that it's on show.

In particular, look out for 1960s American pop art and the eccentric works of French New Realists Klein, César, Arman and Ben, many of which involved smashing, tearing, burning or distorting mundane objects in a spoof on society and the world of highbrow art.

The Centre boasts a 🎎 **Galerie des Enfants** (children's workshop). It doesn't really matter that the instructions are in French – both the art and craft workshops and the pantomime and puppet shows are focussed more on hands-on activities anyway (www.centrepompidou.fr).

Surrounding Sights

The area around the Centre Georges Pompidou is a great place to while away an hour or two, mingling with the 🎎 mime artists, musicians, magicians, fire-eaters and jugglers who perform on the spacious sloping plaza immediately outside the gallery, or wandering beside Paris's most remarkable contemporary fountain, the 🎎 **Stravinsky Fountain** (to the south in Place Igor Stravinsky). This consists of a wacky assortment of sculptures, including a dragon, a treble clef, a rotund woman and a pair of red pouting lips, each named after one of the great composer's works and all spinning and jetting

---

FINDING YOUR WAY AROUND

The centre consists of eight main floors:

- The **1st, 2nd and 3rd floors** house an information library, an exhibition area and a cinema.
- The **4th and 5th floors** house the permanent collections of the Musée National d'Art Moderne (MNAM). Works from 1905 to 1960 – the Collection Historique – are on the 5th; the 4th contains the Collection Contemporaine (1960–present) and a video room for viewing video-art. (To reach the 5th floor, enter the museum on the 4th floor.)
- The **1st and 6th floors** are used for temporary exhibitions.
- The **basement** (level –1) is used for all types of shows, films, meetings and documentation.
- On **level 0** there is a 🎎 children's gallery, a bookshop and a Printemps design boutique.

Le Marais & Bastille

streams of water in every direction, with the Gothic church of St-Merri as a backdrop.

Beside the fountain, the Institut de Recherche et Coordination de l'Acoustique et de la Musique (**IRCAM**) is one of the world's leading centres of experimental music.

Down Rue Brantôme to the north of the Pompidou Centre is the modern Quartier de l'Horloge. Here you will find the city's most ominous public clock, an impressive brass-and-steel mechanical sculpture under an archway called ★ *Le Défenseur du Temps*. France's answer to the German glockenspiel, it was designed by Jacques Monastier. The "defender" battles hourly (from 9am to 10pm) with the elements of air, water and earth in the form of savage beasts. At noon, 6pm and 10pm there are particularly lively combats, when all three are successfully defeated.

A superb city view can be seen from the top floor

TAKING A BREAK

Café Mezzanine is on the first floor and the ultra-cool **Restaurant Georges** (tel: 01 44 78 47 99), with sweeping views over the roof-tops of Beaubourg, is on the sixth floor.

🔁 205 F2 ✉ Place Georges-Pompidou, 75004
☎ 01 44 78 12 33; www.centrepompidou.fr
🕐 Wed–Mon 11–10 (MNAM and exhibitions until 9). Last entrance at 8
🚇 Rambuteau 💶 €13 Euro, free under 26

INSIDER INFO

- The **Museum and Exhibitions ticket** gives visitors admission to all current exhibitions. If you'd rather just check out the magnificent skyline over the city, opt instead for the **Panorama ticket** (€3), which allows direct access to the 6th-floor roof terrace only.
- Check the centre's **website** before visiting: all upcoming events are listed on the online agenda.
- *Mobile sur deux plans* by sculptor Alexander Calder (1898–1976) is an elegant example of the mobile (hanging sculpture) – a form that he invented.

If you are limited by time stick to the **fourth floor**: the exhibits here tend to be more frivolous, outrageous and highly entertaining. The level's extensive New Media Collection is also home to startling video-artworks by the likes of Nam June Paik and Bruce Nauman.

At Your Leisure

39 St-Germain l'Auxerrois

From the 14th century until the Revolution, when the adjacent Louvre was still a palace, St-Germain l'Auxerrois was the French royal family's parish church, and it still contains their pew.

One of its most fascinating aspects today is its eclectic architectural style: predominantly Gothic and Renaissance, it has been greatly altered over the centuries. At one point after the Revolution, it was used as a barn to store fodder.

The square tower rising beside the south transept contains the bell that was tolled to signal the start of the Saint Bartholomew's Day Massacre on 24 August 1572, one of the bloodiest pages of French history. On the eve of the royal marriage of Henri de Navarre (► 102) to Marguerite de Valois, thousands of Huguenots who assembled in Paris for the wedding were slaughtered in a brutal massacre instigated by the ruthlessly ambitious Catherine de Médicis and the Catholic Guise family.

✚ 205 D2
✉ 2 Place du Louvre, 75001
☎ 01 42 60 13 96;
www.saintgermainauxerrois.cef.fr
🕐 Early July–early Sep Mon 2–7, Tue–Sat 9:30–7:30, Sun 9–8; mid-Sep to June Mon–Sat 8–7, Sun 9–8; no visits during services
Ⓜ Louvre-Rivoli/Pont Neuf

40 St-Eustache

This huge and imposing church, the second largest in Paris after Notre-Dame, was built for the congregation of Les Halles. Modelled on Notre-Dame, the church took 105 years to construct, and now stands as a gem of Renaissance architecture.

One of the stained-glass windows in St-Germain l'Auxerrois church

Many illustrious names have been associated with St-Eustache over the years: Cardinal Richelieu was baptized here; Louis XIV celebrated his first communion here; the composer Jean-Baptiste Lully was married here; both the marriage and the funeral service for Mozart's mother Anna Maria were held here; and the playwright Molière was buried within its walls, later to be moved to the cemetery of Père-Lachaise (► 34, 141).

Blessed with remarkable acoustics, St-Eustache boasts a long musical tradition. Here, Berlioz's *Te Deum* and Liszt's *Grand Mass* were first performed. In the mid-19th century the choir was directed by composer Charles Gounod, whose most outstanding chorister was an artistic child

named Pierre-Auguste Renoir. The gargantuan organ, installed in 1989, is the biggest double-transmission organ in the world, making it especially suitable for the performance of 20th-century music. It is sometimes played weekdays from 5:30 to 6, before evening Mass. The resounding organ also accompanies masses on Saturdays at 6, and on Sundays at 11 and 6. Click on "cultures" on the church's website to find a list of all the concert dates.

✚ 205 E3
✉ 2 impasse St-Eustache, 75001
☎ 01 42 36 31 05; www.st-eustache.org
🕔 Mon–Fri 9:30–7, Sat 10–7, Sun 9–7
Ⓜ Les Halles
🚊 RER Châtelet-Les Halles

⓬ 👬 Forum des Halles

This was the hub of Parisian daily life, and the city's main market-place – vividly described by Émile Zola as "the belly of Paris" – for nearly 800 years, until consumerism pushed aside centuries of local tradition in a trend the French today call *McDonaldisation*.

The market was removed to a modern, concrete complex in the suburb of Rungis near Orly

St-Eustache is the second-largest church in Paris

Airport, and the elegant 19th-century iron-and-glass pavilions that had covered the stalls were bulldozed in 1969. They were replaced by the Forum des Halles – an ugly glass-and-chrome multi-level underground shopping centre, built around an open courtyard. Such structural issues as the gradual sinking of the area around Les Halles prompted the city to start a gigantic programme of reconstruction. The work, which has already devoured over a billion euros, should be finished in 2016. Within the Jardin des Halles, the 👬 **Jardin des Enfants** is a free adventure playground for 7 to 11-year-olds (one hour's timed play).

✚ 205 E2   ✉ 101 Porte Berger, 75001
☎ 01 44 76 96 56; www.forumdeshalles.com
🕔 Mon–Sat 10–8   Ⓜ Les Halles
🚊 RER Châtelet-Les Halles

⓭ Musée Carnavalet

It takes two vast Marais mansions to house the Musée de l'Histoire de Paris –17th-century Hôtel le Peletier de St-Fargeau and the

16th-century Renaissance-style Hôtel Carnavalet (former home of Madame de Sévigné, whose prolific and witty letters to her daughter give a vivid insider's view of Louis XIV's court).

Together these two *hôtels particuliers* provide a magnificent setting for the extensive collections of historic paintings, sculptures, decorative art, documents, maps and costumes, which together provide a real taste of Parisian life over the centuries. Be warned, however – it's easy to get lost once inside. Essentially, the Hôtel Carnavalet covers the history of Paris from the Middle Ages to 1789, while the Hôtel le Peletier traces the history of the capital from the Revolution to the present. The Orangery houses archaeological finds.

Musée Carnavalet's formal gardens

Highlights include keys to the Bastille, Napoleon I's death mask, an art nouveau jewellery shop moved intact from Rue Royale, Proust's cork-lined bedroom from his apartment, and the country's most important collection of memorabilia from the French Revolution. Allow at least two hours in this museum; a grasp of the city's colourful history will make walks around Paris more rewarding.

Insider Tip

✚ 206 B2

✉ 16 Rue de Francs-Burgeois, 75003

☎ 01 44 59 58 58; www.carnavalet. paris.fr

🕐 Tue–Sun 10–6

Ⓜ St-Paul 🎟 Free

🔢 Place de la Bastille

The Bastille, built in the 14th century as a fortress to defend the eastern entrance to the city and

Le Marais & Bastille

transformed into a prison for political offend- ers, is the most famous monu- ment in Paris that you cannot visit. It was demolished shortly after being stormed on 14 July 1789 (➤ 10), which came to symbolize the start of the French Revolution. Its site is marked by the Colonne de Juillet (July Column), a 50m (164-foot) high bronze shaft surmounted by a statue of the Spirit of Liberty, which commemorates those who died in two later uprisings, in 1830 and 1848. It stands on a hectic roundabout, with roads leading to other squares with equally evocative names – Place de la Nation and Place de la République. The Bastille area was smartened up in celebration of the bicentennial of the Revolution, and it is now one of Paris's trendiest *quartiers*, full of boutiques and galleries by day and lively bars, cafés and clubs by night.

Insider Tip

🔲 206 C1 ✉ Place de la Bastille, 75004 🚇 Bastille

44 Opéra Bastille

The austere glass and grey marble geometrical facade of the Bastille Opera towers over the Place de la Bastille. It is one of Paris's most contro- versial yet undeniably prestigious buildings.

Its construction was overseen by President Mitterrand in what was then a rather run-down district of Paris. The Opéra opened on 14 July 1989 (the bicentenary of the French Revolution) as an affordable, accessible "opera of the people". However, tickets are still pricey and you should book well in advance to guarantee a seat in the grey granite and oak 2,700-seat auditorium.

🔲 206 C1
✉ 120 Rue de Lyon, 2–6 Place de la Bastille, 75012 (box office: 130 Rue de Lyon)
☎ 01 71 25 24 23 (information and reservations from abroad); 08 92 89 90 90 (information and reservations within France); www.operadeparis.fr
🕐 Box office: Mon–Sat 10:30–6:30. Tours: phone 01 40 01 19 70 for schedule and details
🚇 Bastille 🎫 €12

The Spirit of Liberty sits atop the Colonne de Juillet in Place de la Bastille

Centquatre: 39,000m² (420,000ft²) packed with art and more

45 Centquatre

Formerly the city's central funeral parlour, the buildings that now house Centquatre were built by the Catholic Church during the late 19th century. In 1905, the Paris municipality set up a government-run funeral service (the SMPF), and its headquarters were established at 104 Rue d'Aubervilliers. Coffins and hearses were churned out by the thousand; on-site stables sheltered the SMPF's fleet of carriage horses, and the service had a monopoly on the funeral system until 1993. The Centquatre, inaugurated in late 2008 on the same site, continues to encourage artisans, but of a slightly different ilk: the complex is dedicated instead to the development and cultivation of contemporary art.

Two vast courtyards hold temporary exhibitions, including video installations. Le Cinq – three floors of *ateliers*, open to the public, that house budding artists from the 18th and 19th *arrondissements* – is located in the compound's southeast corner. There's an excellent bookstore across the courtyard, which also sells unique postcards and handmade toys. Check the centre's website for its schedule of films, concerts and children's activities, all of which inject a much-needed dose of edgy vitality into the city's art scene.

🚇 206 off 15
✉ 104 Rue d'Aubervilliers/5 Rue Curial, 75019
☎ 01 53 35 50 01; www.104.fr
🕐 Centquatre: Tue–Sun 11–8; later evening opening for concerts and films. Le Cinq: Wed–Fri noon–10, Sat–Sun noon–8. Closed 3 weeks Aug
🚇 Marx Dormoy/Stalingrad/Crimée/Riquet
🎟 Free

46 Cimetière du Père-Lachaise

This must be the world's most fascinating cemetery – a silent village with countless occupants in higgledy-piggledy tombs, and the final resting place of the city's most prestigious names: painters Corot, Delacroix, Pissarro and Ernst; composers Bizet and Chopin; writers Apollinaire, Daudet, Balzac and Molière; singers Maria Callas and Edith Piaf and also former Doors lead vocalist, Jim Morrison, to name but a few. Pick up a map

A statue on a tomb in the Cimetière du Père-Lachaise

Napoleon III's cousin; and the tomb of François Raspail, a much-imprisoned partisan of the 1830 Revolution, shaped to resemble a prison cell.

The oldest residents are the celebrated 12th--century lovers Abelard and Héloïse, while the most moving monuments include that of the romantic poet Georges Rodenbach, depicted rising out of his tomb, often with a freshly picked rose placed in his out-stretched hand, and, under a tiny willow tree, the grave of poet Alfred de Musset, bearing an inscription from one of his poems:

> "My dear friends, when I die
> Plant a willow at the cemetery
> I love its weeping leaves
> The pallor is sweet and precious
> And its shadow will lighten
> The earth where I shall sleep."

✠ 206 off C2
✉ 16 Rue du Repos, off Boulevard de Ménilmontant, 75020
☎ 01 55 25 82 10; www.pere-lachaise.com
🕐 Mid-March to mid-Nov Mon–Fri 8–6, Sat 8:30–6, Sun 9–6; mid-Nov to mid-March Mon–Fri 8–5:30, Sat 8:30–5:30, Sun 9–5:30
🚇 Père Lachaise, Philippe Auguste

at the entrance to see where they are buried.

In general, the more grandiose the tomb, the more obscure the occupant. Marcel Proust lies beneath a plain black marble slab in one of the cemetery's more modest quarters, and the notorious American dancer Isadora Duncan, who met an untimely death when her trailing scarf caught in the wheel of her Bugatti and broke her neck, is represented by a simple plaque among thousands of others lining the walls of the crematorium.

The exception to the rule is Oscar Wilde, whose grave is marked by a massive Epstein statue of a naked Egyptian-looking figure flying skyward: the playwright would probably have considered the whole thing perfectly ludicrous, and therefore quite fitting.

Look out also for these: the artist Géricault, reclining on his tomb, palette in hand, admiring his masterpiece *The Raft of Medusa*; the recumbent statue of 19th-century journalist Victor Noir, as he was found after being shot by

47 Musée Edith Piaf

Born Edith Gassion in the working-class Bastille neighbourhood in 1915, this beloved *chanteuse* so famous for her powerfully emotional voice, took her stage name from her nickname, "the little sparrow". By the age of 15, she was singing in cafés, on the streets and in the cabarets of Pigalle, taking her subject matter from the drugs, deaths and unhappy love affairs of her own life.

The atmospheric museum, opened in 1977 by Les Amis d'Edith Piaf, offers private tours around a two-room shrine to the

OFF THE BEATEN TRACK

Take a stroll along the **Canal St-Martin** (Metro: République/Goncourt/Château Landon/ Jaurès), one of Paris's hidden delights. This picturesque 5km (3-mile) stretch of water- way – a long-time favourite of artists, novelists and film directors – links the Seine with a network of canals on the outskirts. Walk along the tree-lined watersides fringing the canal, over locks and iron footbridges and past old warehouses, or sit in a café watching the traditional barges chugging by. It's like winding the clocks back to the 19th century. Or, if you'd rather be afloat, take a 3-hour cruise along the Canal from La Villette to the Seine. Canauxrama (tel: 01 42 39 15 00; www.canauxrama.com) and Paris-Canal (tel: 01 42 40 96 97; www.pariscanal.com) are both based at the Bassin de la Villette, 75019.

Right: A photograph of Edith Piaf taken in the 1940s

great diva, crammed with kitsch memorabilia, from a life-size card-board cut-out of the singer to her amazingly tiny suede shoes. The red walls are covered with original posters, photographs and portraits of *l'Ange Noir*, while immortal hits such as *La Vie en rose* (also the title of the 2007 film of Edith Piaf's life, as played by Oscar-winner Marion Cotillard) and *Je ne regrette rien* play on the gramophone.

✚ 206 off C3
✉ 5 Rue Crespin du Gast, 75011
☎ 01 43 55 52 72
🕐 Mon–Thu 1–6. Closed June, Sep.
Visits by prior appointment only
🚇 Ménilmontant 💵 Donation

Where to...
Eat and Drink

Prices

Expect to pay per person for a meal, excluding drinks:

€ under €25   €€ €25–€50   €€€ €51–€100   €€€€ over €100

404 €€

This fashionable establishment, with its chic Berber décor, serves excellent North African food. It is often busy and crowded, but the food is capably prepared and authentic. Several tagines and couscous dishes feature as main courses, with the pigeon or fish *pastilla* (a sweet and savoury pie) a must for anyone who has never tasted its delicious flavours.

➕ 206 A4

✉ 69 Rue des Gravilliers, 75003

☎ 01 42 74 57 81; www.404-resto.com

🕐 Daily Mon–Fri noon–2:30, 8–midnight, Sat–Sun noon–4, 8–midnight. Closed Aug

Ⓜ Arts et Métiers

L'Ambassade d'Auvergne €€

The rustic décor makes an appropriate setting for the authentic farmhouse cooking of the mountainous Auvergne region. Much of the produce used here comes from the region and is assembled to create warming and quite substantial dishes. Among the specialities are a wonderfully delicate cabbage soup ladled over a slice of Roquefort, *cassoulet* (stew) with puy lentils and *boudin aux chataignes*, a rich, delicious black pudding with chestnuts accompanied by a chestnut sauce. The tiny on-site shop sells specialities from the Auvergne.

➕ 205 F3 ✉ 22 Rue du Grenier St-Lazare, 75003 ☎ 01 42 72 31 22;
www.ambassade-auvergne.com

🕐 Daily noon–2, 7:30–10

Ⓜ Rambuteau

L'Ambroisie €€€€

Book at least a month in advance for a table in this elegant and exclusive restaurant that is the proud bearer of three Michelin stars. Presided over by chef Bernard Pacaud, it is set in an exclusive town house in the beautiful 17th-century Place des Vosges. The main dining room is lined with fabulous tapestries, which, together with stone floors and much dark wood, add to the period atmosphere.

➕ 210 C5 ✉ 9 Place des Vosges, 75004

☎ 01 42 78 51 45; www.ambroisie-placedesvosges.com 🕐 Tue–Sat noon–1:30, 8–9:30. Closed 2 weeks Feb, and Aug

Ⓜ Bastille/St-Paul/Chemin Vert

Au Pied de Cochon €€   Insider Tip

Parisians use this convivial brasserie as a convenient and satisfying pit-stop following lengthy shopping expeditions or a night out on the town. Tables can be booked until midnight or so, although the establishment claims to be open 24 hours a day. Established in 1947, Au Pied de Cochon originally served Les Halles market traders and it continues to offer classic fare, including the eponymous pigs' trotters, grilled or stuffed. The cheese-crusted French onion soup is wonderful, and for those who dislike offal, the seafood and grilled steaks are excellent. The house wine is from the owner's own vineyard.

➕ 205 D3 ✉ 6 Rue Coquillère, 75001

☎ 01 40 13 77 00; www.pieddecochon.com

🕐 Daily 24 hours Ⓜ Les Halles

Au Trou Gascon €€€

If Alain Dutournier's prestigious restaurant in the 1st *arrondissement* (Carré des Feuillants, ➤ 120) is fully booked or too expensive, try this more accessible but equally memorable establishment (with one Michelin star). The meat and fish-oriented dishes include regional specialities such as *cassoulet* and goose *confit*, but extend to flavoursome lamb or seared scallops. For the perfect conclusion, choose between Gascon cheese and one of the gorgeous, moist chocolate cakes.

✚ 210 off C4 ✉ 40 Rue Taine, 75012
☎ 01 43 44 34 26; www.autrougascon.fr
🕔 Mon–Fri noon–2, 7:30–10 🚇 Daumesnil

Aux Vins des Pyrénées €

This restaurant takes patrons back to the 1930s with gingham tablecloths and old family pictures on the walls. Fish and meat lovers are equally catered for with dishes such as salmon *millefeuille* and smoked duck breast on the menu. For dessert, try *crème brûlée* or half-baked chocolate cake. The comprehensive wine list includes a selection from the Pyrenees.

✚ 206 B1 ✉ 25 Rue Beautreillis, 75004
☎ 01 42 72 64 94
🕔 Sun–Fri noon–2:30, 8–11:30, Sat 8–11:30
🚇 St-Paul/Sully-Morland

Bofinger €€

A legendary brasserie, claiming to be Paris's oldest, close to Place de la Bastille, with an amazing turn-of-the-century belle époque interior. The classic dishes here are oysters and platters of shellfish served on crushed ice. Specialities include *Choucroute de la mer: lotte, saumon, haddock, langoustine* (seafood feast of monkfish, salmon, haddock and langoustine), also pig's trotters, duck *foie gras*, *steak tartare* and grills, with delicious home-made desserts and ices to finish. The three-course fixed-price menu is a popular choice and good value.

✚ 206 C1 ✉ 5–7 Rue de la Bastille, 75004
☎ 01 42 72 87 82; www.bofingerparis.com
🕔 Daily noon–3, 7–midnight 🚇 Bastille

Café Beaubourg €€

Waiters clad in slim black suits and 1980s-style split-level concrete, are hallmarks of this Costes brothers masterpiece. The place-to-be-seen terrace affords a splendid view of the Pompidou Centre. Don't be put off by the posiness of it all, because the food and drink are faultless, bountiful brunches, perfectly mixed cocktails, snacky delights such as *gazpacho*, or smoked salmon with blinis, and full-blown meals like the ever-popular seared *steak tartare*, not forgetting the fine array of delicious *pâtisseries*.

✚ 205 F2 ✉ 100 Rue St-Martin, 75004
☎ 01 48 87 63 96
🕔 Sun–Wed 8am–1am, Thu–Sat 8am–2am
🚇 Hôtel de Ville/Rambuteau

Chez Jenny €€

Named after the Alsatian Robert Jenny, who established this venue in 1930, Chez Jenny pays tribute to the Alsace region of France with frescoes of its landscapes. Alongside the traditional *sauerkraut*, the menu features specialities such as saveloy sausage salad and iced *Gugelhupf* (a version of *panettone*) with a vanilla-flavoured custard.

✚ 206 B4 ✉ 39 Boulevard du Temple, 75003
☎ 01 44 54 39 00; www.chez-jenny.com
🕔 Daily noon–midnight 🚇 République

Chez Marianne €

If you can't make up your mind which of the many tempting Jewish delis to plump for in this neighbourhood, choose Marianne's. The second dining room is calm and quaint, and in the summer there's a busy terrace. The service can be impatient but take your time to decide which of the delicious appetizers to have – you can concoct an assortment of four or more (be sure to have the hummus). The pastrami and smoked salmon are luscious.

Le Marais & Bastille

Too busy to sit down? There's also a take-away window where hungry visitors can refuel on the go.

➕ 210 B5 ✉ 2 Rue des Hospitalières St-Gervais, 75004 ☎ 01 42 72 18 86
🕐 Daily noon–midnight 🚇 St-Paul

Le Marché €€

Taking a seat at this eatery in the tree-shaded Place du Marché Saint Catherine is like being transported to a small town in the south of France. They often serve such suitably traditional fare as Magret de Canard and hare with rosemary. Foie gras and snails naturally also find a place on the menu. Very reasonable prices.

➕ 206 B2 ✉ 17 Rue de Saintonge, 75003
☎ 01 42 78 46 49 🕐 Mon–Fri noon–2:15, 8–10:30. Closed Aug, 1 week Christmas
🚇 Filles du Calvaire/St-Sébastien-Froissart

Le Gaigne €€/€€€

In a tiny dining room off the trendy Rue Rambuteau, master chef Mickaël Gaignon creates some of the *quartier*'s finest cuisine. White and green asparagus are paired with goat's cheese and presented on home-made blinis; squid are served up with aubergine caviar. Gaignon uses almost exclusively organic ingredients, sourced locally. The two-course lunchtime menu is a steal if you're on a budget.

➕ 206 A3 ✉ 2 Place du Marché Sainte Catherine, 75003 ☎ 01 42 78 46 49
🕐 Daily 11:30–11:30 🚇 Saint Paul

Le Marché des Enfants Rouges €

The "Market of the Red Children" is Paris's oldest covered market, dating from the 17th century. It takes its name from an orphanage formerly located near by. These days, the market's producers are ringed by a range of excellent *traiteurs* (delicatessens) – traditional French, as well as Japanese and Moroccan – and the modern wine bar L'Estiminet is particularly popular for Sunday brunch. Take your pick of cuisine, then head to one of the tables surrounding the market.

➕ 206 B3 ✉ 39 Rue de Bretagne, 75003
🕐 Tue–Thu 9–2, 4–8; Fri–Sat 9–8; Sun 9–2
🚇 Filles du Calvaire

Le Murano €€/€€€

This trendy restaurant at the Murano Urban Resort, one of Paris's avant-garde hotels on the northern edge of the Marais, has a chic clientele. The bold contemporary décor boasts deep red velvet seats, in striking contrast with the simple white table-cloths. Innovative dishes, based on classic French cooking, take inspiration from Eastern cuisine, associating seafood with meat (calves' sweetbreads with oysters, capers and lemon) as well as sweet and savoury flavours (*foie gras* with plum and pear chutney).

➕ 206 C3 ✉ 13 Boulevard du Temple, 75003
☎ 01 42 71 20 00; www.muranoresort.com
🕐 Daily noon–2:30, 7:30–midnight
🚇 Filles du Calvaire

L'Osteria €€

A lively, popular and often noisy Italian restaurant in the heart of the Marais. Venetian Toni Vianello's menus offer a choice of enjoyable dishes from his native region, including potato gnocchi with sage, Venetian-style calfs' liver cooked a melting pink, and a very moreish *osso bucco (cross-cut veal shanks in wine)*. The menu changes daily.

➕ 206 B2 ✉ 10 Rue de Sévigné, 75004
☎ 01 42 71 37 08 🕐 Tue–Fri noon–2:30, 8–10:30, Mon 8–10:30 🚇 St-Paul

Le Pharamond €€/€€€

This restaurant, established in 1832, is a Paris institution. The extravagant art nouveau interior is lined with ceramic murals, mosaics and enormous mirrors. The cuisine has strong links with the Normandy region, with dishes such as Caen-style tripe with cider and calvados, and mouth-watering chocolate cake.

➕ 205 E3 ✉ 24 Rue de la Grande-Truanderie, 75001 ☎ 01 40 28 45 18; www.pharamond.fr
🕐 Mon–Sat noon–2:30, 7:30–10:30
🚇 Les Halles/Châtelet

Where to ...
Shop

This part of the 2nd *arrondissement* was once the site of Les Halles, Paris's famous food market, which in 1969 was relocated to Rungis, in the suburbs south of Porte d'Italie. The rag trade is also based just north of here.

FOOD & DRINK

The **market** on Rue Montorgueil (Metro: Les Halles/Châtelet) is about all that remains of the original Les Halles, and is a good place for cheese, baguettes, fruits and vegetables.

Tiny *traiteur* **La Maison Stohrer** (51 Rue Montorgueil, tel: 01 42 33 38 20; www.stohrer.fr) is the original inventor of rum baba.

Across the Jardin des Halles, **Laura Todd** (2 Rue Pierre Lescot) makes mouth-watering organic brownies and muffins.

FASHION

Agnès B (2, 3, 6 and 19 Rue du Jour, 75001, for children's, men's, women's and baby clothes respectively, tel: 01 45 08 56 56; www. agnesb.fr; Metro: Les Halles) offers sharply cut clothes with original details.

There are other boutiques nearby selling designer threads, such as **Kabuki** (21 and 25 Rue Étienne-Marcel, tel: 01 42 33 55 65) for men and women, and **Notsobig** (38 Rue Tiquetonne, tel: 42 33 24 26) for children.

Just north of the Pompidou Centre, **Nagchampa** (158 Rue St-Martin, tel: 01 48 04 07 54) is packed with contemporary Indian-inspired clothing, leather bags and shoes.

For unique, vintage and one-off pieces, head to the Marais's back-streets. **Azzedine Alaia** (7 Rue de Moussy, 75004; tel: 01 42 72 19 19; Metro: Hôtel de Ville) specializes in flattering figure-hugging dresses, while Rue de la Verrerie stocks last season's designs at bargain prices.

For unique T-shirts, **Monsieur Poulet** (24 Rue de Sévigné, 75004; tel: 01 42 74 35 97; www.monsieur poulet.com; Metro: St-Paul) has the finest and funniest designs.

Dig through piles of vintage and used gear at **Free P Star** (61 Rue de la Verrerie), or try **La Piscine** (13 Rue des Francs-Bourgeois) for cut-price brand-name items, near Place des Vosges.

BOOKSHOPS

Red Wheelbarrow (22 Rue St-Paul, 75004; tel: 01 48 04 75 08; www. theredwheelbarrow.com; Metro: St-Paul) is an English-language bookshop.

Branches of **FNAC** (Level 3, Forum des Halles, 1–7 Rue Pierre Lescot, 75001; tel: 08 25 02 00 20; www.fnac.com/Paris-Forum-des-Halles; Mon–Sat 10–8; Metro: Les Halles, RER: Châtelet-Les Halles) sell MP3 players, DVDs, software, books (some in English) and electronics. The Forum des Halles branch has music books and a theatre and concert box office.

STATIONERY

Mélodies Graphiques (10 Rue du Pont-Louis-Philippe, 75004; tel: 01 42 74 57 68, closed Sun; Metro: Pont Marie/St-Paul) stocks fantastic stationery, including writing paper, sealing wax and stamps.

Papier+ (9 Rue du Pont-Louis-Philippe, 75004; tel: 01 42 77 70 49; www.papierplus.com; Mon–Sat; Metro: Pont Marie/St-Paul) is well worth seeking out for its unusual stationery supplies.

Where to ...
Go Out

Teeming with nightlife, Beaubourg and Châtelet-Les Halles offer contrasting kinds of entertainment, from classical and avant-garde music to cinemas, bars and wild nightclubs, and will have something to appeal to most visitors. Le Marais is the hub of Paris's gay scene; rainbow flags flutter over shop fronts, restaurants and bars, especially along the Rue Ste-Croix-de-la-Bretonnerie and the Rue Vieille-du-Temple, both lively main streets. Further east, partly egged on by the presence of the opera house, the Bastille area throbs with tiny theatres, jazz bars and salsa joints, each bursting at the seams most weekends.

CINEMAS

Le Nouveau Latina cinema (20 Rue du Temple, 75004; tel: 01 42 78 47 86; www.lenouveaulatina.com; Metro: Hôtel de Ville) has specialized in the films of Latin America, Spain, Portugal and Italy since 1913.

The renovated Forum des Images (2 Rue du Cinéma, Forum des Halles, 75001; tel: 01 44 76 63 00; www.forumdesimages.net; Metro: Les Halles) is an image bank of more than 5,000 films, from adverts to documentaries, all featuring Paris. The Forum also organizes film festivals alternate months, ranging from Le Festival de Films Gays Lesbiens Trans & ++++ de Paris, to Tout-Petits Cinéma, films targeted at children up to 4.

MUSIC

IRCAM (1 Place Igor Stravinsky, 75004; tel: 01 44 78 48 43/01 44 78 15 45; www.ircam.fr, closed July–Aug; Metro: Rambuteau/Hôtel de Ville) next to the Pompidou Centre, is for devotees of avant-garde music.

The home of the Opéra National de Paris Bastille (► 140) is in the controversial edifice at the southern end of Place de la Bastille: operas and symphony orchestras benefit from the exceptional acoustics.

At the grand neoclassical Théâtre du Châtelet (1 Place du Châtelet, 75001; tel: 01 40 28 28 40; www.chatelet-theatre.com, closed July–Aug; Metro: Châtelet), prices are often lower than elsewhere, and the repertoire includes ballet and the classics. With its extravagantly gilded interior, it's a perfect venue for baroque opera.

The Théâtre de la Ville (2 Place du Châtelet, 75004; tel: 01 42 74 22 77; www.theatredelaville-paris.com, closed July–Aug; Metro: Châtelet) is a showcase for contemporary dance and music.

NIGHTLIFE

Young European talent frequently heats up the stage at Le Sunset (60 Rue des Lombards, 75001; tel: 01 40 26 46 60; www.sunset-sunside.com, concerts Tue–Sun evenings; Metro: Châtelet) during memorable jam sessions for jazz and salsa lovers.

Kick-start the evening with a Macao Spring Punch at sexy Le China (50 Rue de Charenton, 75012; tel: 01 43 46 08 09; www.lechina.eu; Metro: Bastille).

More raucous revellers should head to Le Dépôt (10 Rue aux Ours, 75003; tel: 01 44 54 96 96; www.ledepot.com; daily 12am–8am; Metro: Étienne-Marcel), a huge dance factory and cult venue for the gay community in the heart of the gay district. Expect techno, house, disco and cabaret theme nights. Naked torsos, frenzied dancing and a sweaty atmosphere are guaranteed.

Montmartre

 **Little Treats**

For the Lovers
Couples from all over the world declare their love at the "Mur je t'aime" in a garden next to the **Place des Abbesses** (▶ 159).

Toulouse-Lautrec at the Moulin Rouge
The Moulin Rouge owns **posters by Toulouse-Lautrec** (▶ 158) – you can admire them in the foyer of the "Red Mill".

Montmartre Atmosphere
It's lovely to sit in one of the cafés or lounge in the shade of the trees in the peaceful **Place Emile-Goudeau** (▶ 190).

Getting Your Bearings

The hilltop settlement of Montmartre (often referred to by Parisians simply as La Butte or "The Hill") remains first and foremost a village, overlooking the busy metropolis sprawled at its feet but far removed in character. For this is the Paris of poets and writers, of Toulouse-Lautrec, of cabarets and cancan girls, of windmills and vineyards, of Renoir, Utrillo, van Gogh and all the other great artists who made it their home.

After the broad boulevards of downtown Paris, the streets here feel pleasantly intimate. Some bustle with visitors (especially around such tourist honeypots as Place du Tertre and the Sacré-Cœur), but others are so quiet that prowling cats are the only sign of life. And although many artists and writers have left the area, and its fabled nightlife no longer has the same charismatic charm, Montmartre still retains a nostalgic village atmosphere, thanks to its cobbled streets, its whitewashed cottages with tiny gardens tumbling down steep stairways lit by old-fashioned lamps, and its exquisite hidden squares that invite you to sit and watch the world go by or to admire street artists at work.

The mighty Sacré-Cœur Basilica stands atop the hill of Montmartre

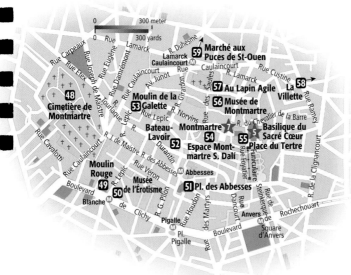

TOP 10

⭐ Basilique du Sacré-Cœur
➤ 154

⭐ Montmartre ➤ 156

At Your Leisure

People climbing the steps to the church

Perfect Days in...

The Perfect Day

If you're not quite sure where to begin your travels, this itinerary recommends a practical and enjoyable day out exploring Montmartre, taking in some of the best places to see. For more information see the main entries (➤ 154–163).

🕘 9:00am

Start off your day at the **48 Cimetière de Montmartre** (➤ 158), one of Paris's most romantic graveyards, which contains the neatly ordered tombs of countless musicians, artists, writers and poets who have been associated with La Butte over the centuries.

🕙 10:00am

From the cemetery, climb the steep hill to the heart of ★ **Montmartre** (➤ 156) or catch the **Montmartrobus** (➤ 159). Stop off halfway to refuel with a coffee and *pâtisserie* at one of the tempting outdoor cafés.

🕚 11:00am

To get a taste of Montmartre's rustic ambience, take time to explore its winding streets and back alleys, its long, steep stairways, its windmills, its famous vineyard (above, ➤ 156) and its tiny squares and terraces, so vividly portrayed in the canvases of van Gogh, Renoir, Utrillo and other artists.

🕐 12:30pm

Head to 55 **Place du Tertre**
(➤ 161) to watch the
street artists (below left)
at work in this once
prettiest of squares,
now overrun by tourists.
If the fancy takes you,
why not have your por-
trait sketched (it only
takes about 30 minutes)
or buy a painting to remind
you of your stay?

🕐 1:30pm

Insider Tip
Avoid Place du Tertre for lunch: the
restaurants are overpriced and overrated. Instead,
choose from one of the many restaurants in the surrounding
streets (➤ 164).

🕐 3:00pm

Visit the 56 **Musée de Montmartre** (➤ 161), which, through paintings,
documents, photographs and other artefacts, recounts the history of
the Montmartre district from its earliest days.

🕐 5:00pm

No visit to Montmartre would be complete without a visit to the
5 **Basilique du Sacré-Cœur** (➤ 154). Dominating the hill, its unmistakable
silhouette features a dazzling white dome and a massive bell tower,
which contains one of the world's heaviest bells. The terrace of the
basilica affords unforgettable views of the whole of Paris, especially
when the sun sets over the city.

🕐 7:00pm

During your day in
Montmartre, scan the
menus of likely eateries
you pass, targeting some-
where you like the look of
to return to in the evening.
Le Chamarré (➤ 164) or
Bistro Poulbot (➤ 164) are
good bets. Round off your
evening in an intimate live-
music bar, or if you fancy a
glitzy Las Vegas-style
night out with topless
dancers, 49 **Le Bal du Moulin
Rouge** (left, ➤ 158) is the
place to go.

 Basilique du Sacré-Cœur

Dominating the skyline of La Butte, the gleaming white Basilica of the Sacred Heart is one of the most conspicuous buildings in Paris – a confection of neo-Byzantine domes, turrets and towers which, viewed from afar at dusk or sunrise, looks more like a mosque than a Catholic cathedral.

During the Franco-Prussian War of 1870–71 – which led to the humiliating fall of the Second Empire under Napoleon III, and the final end of the monarchy in France – two laymen, Alexandre Legentil and Hubert Rohault de Fleury, vowed to build a church dedicated to the Sacred Heart of Christ should France be spared. Constructed as an act of penitence following the bloodshed of the war, the basilica took 40 years to build and was financed mainly by Parisian Catholics fearful of an anti-clerical backlash under the new republican regime. Astonishingly, every hour, day and night, since 1 August 1885 (even in 1944 as bombs shattered the windows), someone has been "on duty" here, to atone for the sins of the 1870 war.

Before entering the interior, note the three statues over the entrance depicting Christ flanked by Joan of Arc and St Louis, both on horseback. Inside, the mighty **gold mosaic** above the altar depicts Christ with the Virgin Mary, the Pope, the saints of France and even the project's initiators.

The highlight of Sacré-Cœur is the **climb to the top of the dome** (the second-highest point in Paris after the Eiffel Tower), for its dizzying views over the city (50km/31mi on a clear day) and down into the interior of the basilica.

The glorious neo-Byzantine exterior of Sacré-Cœur

TAKING A BREAK
Bistro Poulbot is a delightful place to take lunch (► 164).

🔲 200 C3 ✉ 35 Rue du Chevalier-de-la-Barre, 75018
☎ 01 53 41 89 00; www.sacre-coeur-montmartre.com
🕐 Basilica: daily 6am–10:30pm. Crypt and dome: daily April–Nov 9–6:45; Dec–March 9–5:45 🚇 Anvers, then walk to funicular 💶 Free; dome: €5

A HISTORIC PLACE OF WORSHIP
The Romans were the first to build a place of worship here – a temple dedicated to Mercury. The hill became known as Mons Mercurii, until early Christian times when it was renamed Mont des Martyrs, following the martyrdom of St Denis. Denis was the first bishop of Paris in the third century AD. He was beheaded by Romans at the top of the hill, whereupon he reputedly picked up his head, carried it to a nearby fountain to wash the blood from his face, then walked to the spot where he is now commemorated by the Basilique St-Denis.

INSIDER INFO

- Try to **attend Mass** (Mon–Fri 11:15am, 3pm (Fri only), 6:30pm, 10pm; Sat 11:15am, 10pm; Sun 11am, 6pm, 10pm; also other services). The adoration preceding the 10pm mass starts at 8:30; reserve your place by calling 01 53 41 89 03, 24 hours in advance. **You cannot walk about during the service**, but it brings an otherwise gloomy interior to life.
- Rather than climbing the steep steps up to the church, why not take the **sleek funicular** from square Willette instead? It runs all day (6am–12:30am) and costs one Metro ticket each way.
- The basilica **is most photogenic** when viewed from the gardens below.
- Also take a look at the **cathedral's famously splendid organ.** Extensively restored in 2011, the instrument was originally designed for Ilbarritz castle on the Atlantic Coast by Aristide Cavaillé-Coll, said to be the greatest organ-builder of the 19th century.

⭐ Montmartre

In the 19th century, Montmartre became a magnet for artists, writers, poets and musicians who gathered in this former hilltop village to enjoy the cabarets, dance halls and brothels that gave the *quartier* its thrillingly decadent reputation. Today's painters continue to thrive on the lively tourist trade, which has sprung up as hordes of eager visitors flood this picturesque district. However, in places it still manages to retain the relaxed, bohemian atmosphere of pre-war *gai Paris*.

Vineyards

Historically, La Butte was an important place of pilgrimage: Louis VI founded the Benedictine abbey of Montmartre here in 1133, of which only the church of St-Pierre now remains, forgotten in the shadow of Sacré-Cœur.

Consecrated in 1147, it is one of the city's oldest churches. Like most medieval abbeys in France, Montmartre became involved in wine production, and soon the hilltop was covered in productive vineyards.

In the 16th century, 30 windmills (of which only two remain, ► 160) were built to press the grapes and grind the grain produced by the surrounding villages. Place Blanche ("White Square") at the foot of La Butte takes its name from the clouds of chalky dust churned up by carts carrying crushed wheat and flour from the nearby windmills.

By the end of the 17th century, Montmartre was a thriving village, supplying the city with wheat, wine and so much gypsum ("plaster of Paris") that a popular saying emerged: "There's more of Montmartre in Paris than there is of Paris in Montmartre." The gypsum quarries closed during the 18th century, and at the same time Montmartre was annexed as part of Paris.

Browsing items for sale in Montmartre

Wine production also ceased, owing to increasing competition from vineyards in the south of France – though one **small vineyard** still remains. The Clos de Montmartre on Rue des Saules produces around 1,200 bottles of wine annually.

Look out for it on sale at the tourist office and, if you're fortunate enough to be in the area during the second weekend of October, you can join in with the themed **Fête des Vendanges de Montmartre**, during which

There are plenty of restaurants to choose from

you can sample French produce, listen to music and watch the harvest parade (www.fdvm.fr).

TAKING A BREAK

Watch the world go by at tiny **Le Consulat** (18 Rue Norvins, 75018; tel: 01 46 06 50 63; Metro: Abbesses). Once frequented by Picasso, Utrillo and fellow artists, it still serves simple, hearty fare on its sunny terrace.

➕ 200 C3
🚇 Abbesses/Anvers/Blanche/Lamarck-Caulaincourt

INSIDER INFO

- Visit the Syndicat d'Initiative (tourist office) for **up-to-date information about what's on** (21 Place du Tertre, 75018; tel: 01 42 62 21 21; www.montmartre-guide.com; daily 10–7, closed Sat–Sun 1–2pm).
- One of the quaintest corners of Montmartre is Villa Léandre, a tiny residential cul-de-sac of **creeper-smothered houses** and **tiny gardens** off Avenue Junot, in a style so English that number 10 bears a tiny "Downing Street, City of Westminster" sign.

  Insider Tip

- The sleazy Pigalle red-light district at the foot of La Butte – its garish neon lights, prostitutes, peep shows and erotica shops – are **best avoided by night**.
- You may be aware that *Amélie*, Jean-Pierre Jeunet's famous 2001 film starring Audrey Tautou, was set in Montmartre – but did you also know that her café (Café des Deux Moulins, 15 Rue Lepic, 75018; tel: 01 42 54 90 50) can be found here under the same name?

At Your Leisure

48 Cimetière de Montmartre

Montmartre's cemetery, established on the site of disused quarries, was first used as a mass grave during the Revolution. Here are the graves of composers Berlioz, Delibes and Offenbach, writers Heine, Zola (whose remains are now in the Panthéon), Stendhal and Alexandre Dumas the younger, artist Degas, film director François Truffaut, dancer Vaslav Nijinsky and other Montmartre celebrities. Pick up a plan of the graves at the main entrance, or download one from www.paris.fr before you visit.

➕ 200 A3 ✉ 20 Avenue Rachel, 75018
☎ 01 53 42 36 30
🕐 Mid-March to early Nov Mon–Fri 8–6, Sat 8:30–6, Sun 9–6; early Nov to mid-March Mon–Sat 8–5:30, Sun 9–5:30
(last entrance 15 min before closing)
🚇 Place de Clichy/Blanche

49 Moulin Rouge

The "Red Windmill" opened as a dance hall in 1889, when saucy, colourful dance shows were all the rage, as immortalized in the posters and paintings of the artist Toulouse-Lautrec. It soon gained a reputation for staging the hottest show in Paris and today it trades

The tomb of artist Gustave Guillaumet in the Cimetière de Montmartre

shamelessly on its worldwide reputation for scantily clad, cancan-dancing chorus girls.

➕ 200 B3 ✉ 82 Boulevard de Clichy, 75018
☎ 01 53 09 82 82; www.moulinrouge.fr
🕐 Spectacles nightly at 9 and 11.
Combined dinner and show at 7
🚇 Blanche 🍽 Expensive

50 Musée de l'Érotisme

The Erotic Museum, one of Paris's newest museums, and the only one that can be visited both day and night, is appropriately situated near Pigalle, a district long associated with the sex trade. Devoted to erotic art from different world cultures, it displays more than 2,000 items – paintings, models, statues and sex aids – from every continent, spanning the second century to the present day in an attempt to raise the smutty zeitgeist of the area to a loftier plane.

The Moulin Rouge

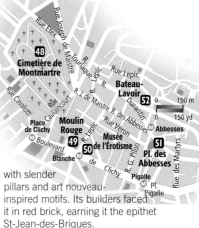

+ 200 B3 ✉ 72 Boulevard de Clichy, 75018
☎ www.musee-erotisme.com
🕑 Daily 10am–2am Ⓜ Blanche 💶 €8

51 Place des Abbesses

This tranquil triangular square boasts one of the city's few remaining art nouveau Metro entrances (another is at Porte Dauphine), a delicate swirling mass of glass and iron designed by Hector Guimard at the turn of the 20th century. At 40m (130 feet) it is also the deepest Metro station, with a spiral staircase decorated with frescoes (there's also a lift).

Insider Tip

Centuries ago, the square marked the entrance to the women's abbey of Montmartre. Legend has it that in 1590, handsome Henri de Navarre (later Henri IV, the "Vert Galant") kept Paris under siege from his garrison on the hill of Montmartre. At the same time he seduced the abbess, Claude de Beauvilliers. His lieutenants and the other nuns followed their example, and soon Parisians were talking about the "army's whore-house on the hill". Claude followed Henri to Senlis, where she foolishly introduced him to her pretty cousin, with whom he is alleged to have run off, granting Claude another abbey in recompense.

Dominating the square is St-Jean-de-Montmartre (1904), the first church built entirely of reinforced concrete – surprisingly graceful with slender pillars and art nouveau-inspired motifs. Its builders faced it in red brick, earning it the epithet St-Jean-de-Briques.

+ 200 C3 ✉ 75018 Ⓜ Abbesses

52 Bateau-Lavoir

An old timber piano factory here once housed a colony of up-and-coming painters including Pablo Picasso, Amedeo Modigliani, Kees van Dongen and Juan Gris. Local poet Max Jacob coined the name, meaning "Boat Washhouse", claiming the studios resembled a paint-spattered boat. It was here that Picasso and Georges Braque made their first bold attempts toward the concept of cubism.

The original Bateau-Lavoir burned down in 1970, to be replaced by a small, ugly concrete building (closed to the public) that still contains studios.

+ 200 B3 ✉ 13 Place Émile-Goudeau, 75018
Ⓜ Abbesses

GETTING AROUND

- Rather than puff your way up and down the hilly streets of Montmartre on foot, why not take the 🚂 Petit Train de Montmartre – a mini train that chugs past most of the sights on a 40-minute guided tour? Fun for all the family and a good option if you're pressed for time, it leaves Place Blanche, passing the key sights and stopping outside Place du Parvis du Sacré-Cœur (tel: 01 42 62 24 00; www.promotrain.fr), departs every 30 min 10–6, April–Sep until midnight, moderate. Single tickets, inexpensive, also available from Place Blanche to Sacré-Cœur.

- Alternatively, take the Montmartrobus, run by the RATP (www.ratp.info), the main Paris bus company, which takes a circuitous route all over La Butte every 15 minutes (7:50am–1am). A map is posted at each bus stop. The bus uses the same ticket system as the Metro (one ticket per trip) and you can board at any stop.

Montmartre

53 Moulin de la Galette

One of just two remaining wind-mills in Montmartre, the privately owned "Biscuit Windmill", built in 1622, was once the venue for an open-air cabaret frequented by van Gogh, Utrillo, Toulouse-Lautrec and Renoir, who portrayed it in his celebrated painting *Bal du Moulin de la Galette* (now in the Musée d'Orsay, ► 56).

It is said that Debray, a past owner of the mill, was strung up on its sails and spun to death after attempting to defend Montmartre against invading Cossacks in 1814, and his widow had to collect his scattered remains in a flour sack in order to take them to the cemetery. His son transformed the mill into the celebrated dance hall in the 1860s, naming it after the delicious *galette* biscuits made here using the flour ground in the mill.

Nearby, on the corner of Rue Lepic and Rue Girardon, the other windmill, the Moulin Radet, sits on top of a restaurant named after the Moulin de la Galette.

✚ 200 B3 ✉ rue Tholozé, 75018
🅰 Privately owned, not open to the public
🚇 Abbesses

A restaurant on Place du Tertre

Le Moulin de la Galette as seen from Rue Lepic

54 Espace Montmartre Salvador Dalí

More than 300 weird and wonder-ful works by the flamboyant Catalan surrealist artist Salvador Dalí are displayed here, including some of his less familiar paintings, lithographs and sculptures, in a small museum with black walls and a distinctly surrealistic feel. The artist took up residence in Paris in the late 1920s.

✚ 200 C3

✉ 11 Rue Poulbot, 75018
☎ 01 42 64 40 10; www.daliparis.com
🕐 Daily 10–6
🚇 Abbesses 💷 €6

55 Place du Tertre

Bustling crowds and the colourful canvases of street artists crammed into the tree-shaded centre of the square, combined with the aroma of fresh coffee, lure you to the animated Place du Tertre – a tiny café-bordered square where Montmartre's heart beats loudest.

During winter, this delightful 18th-century hilltop square (*tertre* means hillock) retains its rural atmosphere, but for the rest of the year it is one of the most hectic tourist spots in Paris: a place to eat mediocre, overpriced food surrounded by artists all clamouring to sketch you. (If their attentions are unwelcome be firm, and remember that if they produce an unsolicited portrait, you are not obliged to buy.)

On one corner of the square (at No 6), the unassuming bistro La Mère Catherine (tel: 01 46 06 32 69) dates from the Napoleonic era and was a favourite with the Russian troops who occupied the city in 1814. Their habit of banging the table and shouting "bistro!" ("quick!") here gave rise to the name for any unpretentious eating place. Today, this is one of several spots where you can occasionally sample Montmartre's own wine.
✚ 200 C3 ✉ 75018 🚇 Abbesses

56 Musée de Montmartre

This historic museum, set in picturesque grounds overlooking Montmartre's tiny vineyard (➤ 148), occupies the oldest house (1650) on La Butte. In its turn-of-the-20th-century heyday, it was home to an illustrious group of cabaret artistes, writers and painters, including Dufy, Utrillo and Renoir. Its models, lithographs, posters and paintings give a vivid insight into life during this bohemian period, and include a reconstruction of the Café de l'Abreuvoir and the composer Gustave Charpentier's study.
✚ 200 C3 ✉ 12 Rue Cortot, 75018
☎ 01 49 25 89 37; www.museedemontmartre.fr
🕐 Tue–Sun 11–6
🚇 Lamarck-Caulaincourt/Abbesses 💷 €9

57 Au Lapin Agile

This famous cabaret venue, situated bucolically beside the city's only vineyard, opened in 1860 as the Cabaret des Assassins, taking its name from a band of assassins who had allegedly broken in and murdered the owner's son. In 1880, artist André Gill painted a sign outside featuring a nimble rabbit (*lapin*) in a bow tie avoiding the cooking-pot – hence the play on his name, the *lapin à Gill* or, as the cabaret thereafter became known, the *lapin agile*.

Bought in 1903 by singer and cabaret entrepreneur Aristide Bruant, it thrived as a cabaret club. Verlaine, Renoir and Clemenceau would come here for a jolly sing-song, and Picasso paid for the occasional meal with paintings. Still atmospheric today, it is a popular venue for performers of traditional French *chansons*.
✚ 200 C4 ✉ 22 Rue des Saules, 75018
☎ 01 46 06 85 87; www.au-lapin-agile.com
🕐 Tue–Sun 9pm–2am
🚇 Lamarck-Caulaincourt 💷 €24

58 🚼 La Villette

La Villette was for many years an abattoir and livestock market for the whole of Paris. New refrigeration techniques, developed in the 1960s, rendered the area obsolete, and in 1984 its 55ha (136 acres) were turned into a vast and spectacular urban park and science city.

Highlights in this astonishingly ambitious, eclectic complex include La Cité des Sciences (a huge, dynamic science museum), Le Zénith (a pop-concert hall; www.zenith-paris.com), La Géode (a spherical cinema) and La Cité de la Musique (which houses the Conservatoire National Supérieur de Musique et de Danse, a concert hall and also a museum of musical instruments).

The main crowd-puller is undoubtedly the Cité des Sciences et de l'Industrie – a cathedral-sized science and technology museum built on the site of the old Villette slaughterhouses. In the main part of the museum (on the first and second floors), called Explora, visitors can engage in a variety of scientific activities: experiencing and understanding optical illusions, chatting to a robot, flying a flight simulator and, in a new exhibition, learning how satellites have revolutionized our perception of the earth and space exploration, to name only a few. On the ground floor, La Cité des Enfants introduces children to basic scientific principles through fun games and dazzling hands-on displays (sections for ages 2–7 and 5–12).

The park itself is also full of surprises, with maze-like playgrounds, a canal and a dozen red cube-shaped buildings providing childcare, cafés, information and other services. There's even a 1950s submarine to explore.

The unmissable **La Géode** (► ill.) looks like a giant, shiny steel marble, but inside you cannot help but be thrilled by the cinematographic special effects of the world's largest hemispherical movie screen.

The mirror-like sphere of La Géode contains a cinema

Antiques and bric-a-brac at the Marché aux Puces de Saint-Ouen

🕂 201 off F2 ✉ Parc de la Villette, 75019
☎ 01 40 03 75 75; www.villette.com.
Musique: 01 44 84 44 84; www.cite-musique.fr.
Sciences: 01 40 05 80 00; www.cite-sciences.fr.
Géode: 01 40 05 79 99; www.lageode.fr
🎧 Musique: Tue–Sat noon–6, Sun 10–6.
Sciences: Tue–Sun 10–6 (Sun until 7).
🍴 Several cafés for various budgets
🚇 Porte de la Villette
🎟 La Villette: free;
La Cité de la Musique: €9;
La Cité des Sciences: €8

59 Marché aux Puces de Saint-Ouen

The city's most famous flea market lies at St-Ouen, set up outside the city walls by rag merchants in the late 19th century in order to avoid paying tolls levied in the city. St-Ouen had the added advantage of attracting the inhabitants of La Butte, passing by on their way to and from the dance halls, and it was an instant success.

Today's flea market covers 7ha (17 acres). The 2,000-plus stalls are grouped into 13 individual *marchés*, each with its own specialities. You name it, you'll find it here, from bric-a-brac, second-hand clothes and fake Chanel handbags to pricey antiques and glamorous lingerie.

Keep a close watch on your bags and personal possessions and pay in cash. Haggling is strongly recommended.

🕂 200 B5 ✉ Streets around Rue des Rosiers, 93400 St-Ouen
☎ 01 40 12 32 58; www.parispuces.com
🎧 Sat 9–6, Sun 10–6, Mon 11–5
🚇 Porte de Clignancourt (not Porte de St-Ouen)

OPEN-AIR GALLERY

Montmartre in the tourist season is a big open-air picture gallery, with **every square and railing hung with paintings**, and artists working at their easels while you watch.
🎒 If your kids would like to have a go, head for the **Musée d'Art Naïf** (Naive Art Museum, www.hallesaintpierre.org) in the Halle Saint-Pierre, near the base of the Sacré-Cœur funicular, which has regular hands-on workshops, mainly for children.

Where to...
Eat and Drink

Prices

Expect to pay per person for a meal, excluding drinks:

€ under €25   €€ €25–€50   €€€ €51–€100   €€€€ over €100

Au Pied du Sacré-Cœur €/€€

This restaurant, serving traditional French cuisine, is true to its name, being at the foot of the Montmartre landmark, Sacré-Cœur. Choose from dishes such as terrine of rabbit with raisins and cognac or the house speciality, escalope of *foie gras* with balsamic vinegar. The décor is stylish and inviting, and in summer you can dine alfresco on the terrace.

🔳 200 B4 ✉ 85 Rue Lamarck, 75018 ☎ 01 46 06 15 26; www.aupieddusacrecoeur. free.fr 🕐 Tue–Sun noon–3, Mon–Sun 7– midnight 🚇 Lamarck-Caulaincourt

Au Virage Lepic €

This cosy bistro along one of lower Montmartre's most atmospheric streets has a few outdoor tables, perfect for summer evenings, and the food is reliable and utterly delicious. The wine list includes an excellent house champagne and is strong on clarets, the perfect accompaniment for the meaty main courses, such as leg of lamb with thyme. Puddings include a gratin of pears and other variations on familiar themes. It's best to reserve ahead.

🔳 200 B3 ✉ 61 Rue Lepic, 75018 ☎ 01 42 52 46 79 🕐 Wed–Mon 7pm–11pm 🚇 Blanche/Abbesses

Bistro Poulbot €€/€€€

Scenes of old Montmartre are depicted on the walls of this charming little restaurant. Véronique Melloul, who took over this traditional bistro in early 2008, presents sophisticated menus with a mouth-watering appeal, matched by beautiful presentation. The stunning *carte* changes frequently, and may include citrus-glazed *filet mignon (fillet steak)*, served with a perfect onion tart topped with tomato-olive sorbet. Save space for Melloul's unique desserts, such as pineapple and raspberry ravioli.

🔳 200 C4 ✉ 39 Rue Lamarck, 75018 ☎ 01 46 06 86 00; www.bistropoulbot.com 🕐 Tue–Sat 12:30–2, 7:30–10. Closed Aug, Christmas hols 🚇 Lamarck-Caulaincourt

Brasserie Wepler €€

Standing right on the busy Place Clichy, Wepler combines the tradition and ambience of the late 19th century with a solidly classic and familiar menu that includes a splendid seafood platter. Shellfish (the oysters are particularly good) is not the only speciality, however. Try the substantial French onion soup, *bouillabaisse*, duck *foie gras*, *choucroute*, steak *tartare* and grilled sirloin. Nougat glacé, *crème brûlée* and chocolate profiteroles stand out among the desserts.

🔳 200 A3 ✉ 14 Place de Clichy, 75018 ☎ 01 45 22 53 24; www.wepler.com 🕐 Daily noon–12:30am 🚇 Place de Clichy

Le Chamarré €€/€€€   *Insider Tip*

Boasting a flowering terrace and contrasting contemporary cuisine to set it off, Le Chamarré is one of the neighbourhood's newest arrivals. But chef Antoine Heerah has already won plenty of kudos. Traditional mains are given an exotic flourish: roast lamb is served with *Créole gambas* (prawns) and mangetout, guinea-fowl with peanuts and pink rice from Kerala.

🞣 200 C4 ✉ 52 Rue Lamarck, 75018
☎ 01 42 55 05 42; www.chamarre-montmartre.com ⏰ noon–11:30 🚇 Lamarck-Caulaincourt

Chez Toinette €/€€

Delicious evening meals are served here by candlelight. Beef *carpaccio* seasoned with ground nutmeg is the speciality starter, while most of the main courses have a definite southern flavour, be they fish, meat or game. House wines are very reliable and good value, but probably the highlight is the choice of desserts, with an emphasis on fruit tarts. Make sure you book.

🞣 200 B3 ✉ 20 Rue Germain-Pilon, 75018
☎ 01 42 54 44 36 ⏰ Mon–Sat 8pm–11pm.
Closed Aug 🚇 Abbesses

La Famille €€

If you enjoy inventive cuisine, you will relish the fusion dishes of young Basque chef Inaki Aizpitarte, whose short, constantly changing menu (four choices for each course) combines French (and especially Basque) ingredients with more exotic flavours, resulting in dishes such as peach *gazpacho*, oyster *ceviche*, pan-fried *foie gras* with *miso* sauce and chocolate pot with Espelette chilli pepper. Away from Montmartre's tourist throng, the tiny, simple interior and hip music add to the atmosphere, and the restaurant is especially popular for its low-cost "mini" tapas dinner, which is offered on the first Sunday of every month.

Insider Tip

🞣 200 C3 ✉ 41 Rue des Trois-Frères, 75018
☎ 01 42 52 11 12 ⏰ Tue–Sat, 1st Sun of month 8pm–11.30pm 🚇 Abbesses

Le Restaurant €/€€

Over the 20 years since he opened Le Restaurant, Yves Peladeau has established a loyal clientele for his imaginative, contemporary cuisine. Herbs and spices play an important part in his creations, adapted from French, North African and Mediterranean recipes. Dishes are a well-balanced fusion of unusual flavours, such as *gambas* (prawns) and green pea soup, juniper-infused rabbit with cabbage purée or salmon *tartare* with matchstick potatoes. Diners on a budget can pop in at lunchtime for Le Restaurant's bargain set menu.

🞣 200 B3 ✉ 32 Rue Véron, 75018
☎ 01 42 23 06 22; www.lerestaurant.fr
⏰ Daily noon–2:30, 7–11:30.
Closed 24 Dec–3 Jan 🚇 Blanche/Abbesses

Rose Bakery €/€€

Although technically a British café, the tiny Rose Bakery has captured the hearts – and tastebuds – of Montmartre's local community. Run by Anglo-French couple Rose and Jean-Charles, the restaurant's lunch counter overflows with seasonal ingredients. Put together your own organic salad, or stop in for a pot of tea and one of their fabulous miniature carrot cakes.

🞣 200 C2 ✉ 46 Rue des Martyrs, 75009
☎ 01 42 82 12 80 ⏰ Tue–Sun 11–4
🚇 Pigalle/Anvers

La Table d'Anvers €€

Located at the foot of Montmartre and overlooking the peaceful square d'Anvers, this restaurant offers traditional French cooking at affordable prices. Some of the tasty, carefully prepared dishes, such as the rabbit pâté and the delicious *pot-au-feu* (meat and vegetable soup), served in wintertime, are classics. Others denote a distinctive Mediterranean influence: pan-fried chicory with Parmesan and truffle essence, or roast sardines stuffed with feta cheese and served with mashed potatoes seasoned with olive oil. The restaurant also offers an interesting range of wines – most are available by the glass.

🞣 201 D2 ✉ 2 Place d'Anvers, 75009
☎ 01 48 78 35 21; www.latabledanvers.com
⏰ Mon–Fri 10am–midnight, Sat 7pm–midnight.
Open Sat lunch and Sun on public hols
🚇 Anvers

Where to ...
Shop

La Butte has a character all of its own, with some especially good French foodie shops. Avoid shopping around Place du Tertre.

Coquelicot des Abbesses bakery (24 Rue des Abbesses, 75018; Mon–Sat 10–7:15, Sun 11–7; Metro: Abbesses), the wine shop **Cave des Abbesses** at No 43 and the traditional **Charcuterie** at No 30 should provide all you need for a delicious picnic.

For angel-themed gifts such as well-crafted ornamental dolls, try **La Boutique des Anges** (2 Rue Yvonne Le Tac, tel: 01 42 57 74 38; Mon–Sat 10:30–7:15, Sun 11–7; Metro: Abbesses). At the northern boundary is the **Marché aux Puces de Saint-Ouen** (► 163).

Where to ...
Go Out

Montmartre is no longer the hub of city nightlife, but visitors still want a taste of its bohemian past.

CABARETS

For those with a good knowledge of French, singing cabarets make a great night out with their mix of popular music and sharp-edged repartee. The famous **Au Lapin Agile** (► 161; 22 Rue des Saules, 75018; tel: 01 46 06 85 87; www.au-lapin-agile.com; Tue–Sun 9pm–2am; Metro: Lamarck-Caulaincourt) opened in 1860 and is still one of the best.

Montmartre is best known for the **Moulin Rouge** (► 158; 82 Boulevard de Clichy, 75018; tel: 01 53 09 82 82; www.moulinrouge. fr; shows nightly at 9 and 11; Metro: Blanche). The venue has enjoyed a revival since the eponymous Hollywood movie. Today, productions are very much geared towards the tourist market – but are lavish and visually spectacular, though very expensive.

Cabaret Michou (80 Rue des Martyrs, 75018; tel: 01 46 06 16 04; www.michou.com; nightly dinner/show 8:30, show 10:30; Metro: Pigalle) is a popular, if expensive, dinner/cabaret hosted by the irrepressible Michou. Book in advance, especially for dinner.

Nearby, the music-hall shows at intimate **La Nouvelle Eve** (25 Rue Pierre Fontaine, 75009; tel: 01 48 74 69 25; www.lanouvelleeveparis. com, closed Nov–March; Metro: Blanche) celebrate avant-garde and more traditional performances.

NIGHTCLUBS

Folies Pigalle (11 Place Pigalle, 75009; tel: 01 48 78 55 25; daily 11pm–4am; Metro: Pigalle) is a nightclub emblematic of Paris's red-light district. The mid-20s crowd dances to the sound of house in a highly charged ambience.

For a great atmosphere and reasonably priced drinks, try **Le Divan du Monde** (75 Rue des Martyrs, 75018; tel: 01 40 05 06 99; www.divandumonde.com; daily 7pm–6am; Metro: Pigalle/ Abbesses), formerly a nightspot frequented by both Picasso and Toulouse-Lautrec. This small and inviting concert venue runs theme nights, with an emphasis on world music. **Pigalle Rock Party** on Saturdays (11pm–6am) blends heavy electro and rock remixes.

Excursions

Excursions

On those rare occasions when the delights of Paris are overcome by the hustle, bustle and heat of urban life, the surrounding tranquil countryside of the Île-de-France provides a perfect escape, offering several excellent and varied excursions all within easy reach, thanks to the city's comprehensive public transport system.

Swap sophisticated French culture for a day at the American fantasy world of Disneyland® Resort Paris at Marne-la-Vallée – a must for the kids. Or, if time is limited, spend half a day at Versailles, on the south-western outskirts of Paris. It is hard to believe that when it was built, this massive palace was not large enough for the Sun King's nobles and servants. If time permits, visit the romantic château at Chantilly, or the historic

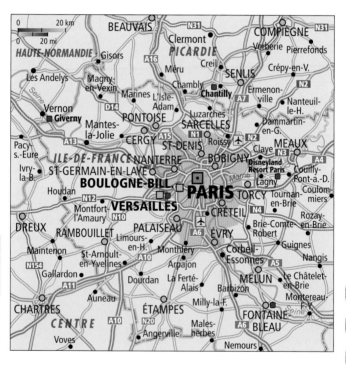

château of Fontainebleau, nestling in a former royal hunting forest. Giverny, home of painter Claude Monet, along the Seine west of Paris, is a place of pilgrimage for garden- and art-lovers, to see the gardens that so in-spired the artist. The pretty village gives a rich taste of Normandy country life.

Giverny

This delightful little riverside village, 80km (50mi) northwest of Paris, is the one of the most visited attractions in Normandy. Crowds of art- and garden-lovers flock to see the home of Claude Monet and the world's most famous lily pond, immortalized in some of the best-known paintings of Impressionist art.

One of the wooden Japanese bridges in Claude Monet's water gardens

Monet moved from the nearby Paris suburb of Argenteuil to this little pastel-pink house with green shutters in 1884, after spotting the village out of a train window and deciding it was where he wanted to live. Initially he rented the house, but once he became more widely known and his canvases had begun to sell well, he was able to buy it for the sum of 22,000 francs. He then laid out his gardens, considered by many of his contemporaries to be his greatest masterpiece.

Glorious Garden

Monet also purchased a further plot of land at the bottom of the main garden on the banks of the River Epte, where he created his **water garden**, with its water lilies and its Japanese bridge entwined with wisteria. Despite visitor numbers, the gardens manage to retain a magical quality. You can almost feel the presence of the grand old master of Impressionism working on his huge, flower-filled canvases: as he used to say, "I am good for nothing except painting and gardening."

The main garden, the **Clos Normand** still follows Monet's original design, with its dazzling palette of colours, changing from season to season. Each month is dominated by a particular colour, as is each room in his immaculately preserved house, with its bright yellow dining room and its cool blue kitchen, decorated from wall to wall with his

collection of Japanese prints. Just a stone's throw from the house is Monet's huge **atelier** where he painted his famous water-lily series, *Décoration des Nymphéas*. The studio has been restored and is hung with gigantic reproductions of the artist's finest works. There is also a shop. The great "garden painter" remained in his beloved pink house in Giverny until his death in 1926.

Monet lived in this house from 1883 until he died in 1926

✉ 84 Rue Claude Monet, 27620 Giverny
☎ 02 32 51 28 21; www.fondation-monet.com
🕐 House and gardens: April–Oct Tue–Sun 9:30–5:30;
also open Easter Mon, Whitsun Mon
💶 €9.50

INSIDER INFO

- Arrive at least **half an hour before the gardens open** to beat the jostling crowds of snap-happy tourists, all attempting to capture their own impression of Monet's water lilies.
- Picnics are sadly banned inside the gardens. Take your sandwiches along the River Epte or try one of the cute eateries in the village instead.
- Credit cards are accepted at the ticket desk, but there are no ATMs in the village itself.
- Visit the **Musée des Impressionnismes** (99 Rue Claude Monet, tel: 02 32 51 94 65; www.museedesimpressionnismesgiverny.com; April–Oct Tue–Sun 10–6; Adults €7, Children 0-7 free of charge, 7–12 years €3, ages 12 and up €4.50, free 1st Sun of month). It hosts temporary exhibitions that concentrate on the artists who passed through Giverny to pay pilgrimage to Monet, including Whistler and Sargent, as well as more recent impressionists.

Getting there Trains leave **Gare St-Lazare** for the 50-minute ride to Vernon (train information tel: 36 35; www.voyages-sncf.com). From here, regular buses and taxis run to Giverny. When the weather's fine, you can also rent a bicycle from one of the restaurants at the station and enjoy the fresh air while pedalling along the 6km (4mi) cycle route to Monet's garden.

Versailles

The monumental palace of Versailles, situated 23km (14mi) to the southwest of Paris, is on most visitors' list of absolute must-see attractions. And it's all thanks to the vision of one individual – Louis XIV, the Sun King – whose extravagant taste, passion for self-glorification and determination to project both at home and abroad the absolute power of the French monarchy (then at the height of its glory) created one of France's great treasures.

Versailles is surrounded by huge gardens; the Latona Fountain in the foreground

A New Court

Two decades into his 72-year reign (1643–1715), Louis decided to adapt his father's modest hunting lodge and weekend retreat into a palace large enough to house some 20,000 courtiers and ministers. He commissioned the greatest artists and craftsmen of the day: architects Louis Le Vau and Jules Hardouin-Mansart planned the build-ings; Charles Le Brun designed the interior and the great landscaper André Le Nôtre set to work outside, flattening hills, draining marshes and relocating forests to lay out the fine gardens. Some 30,000 workers toiled on the 580m (1,900ft) long structure for more than 50 years. No expense was spared, but it wrought havoc on the kingdom's finances.

The palace became the centre of political power in France and the seat of the royal court from 1682 until 1789 when Revolutionary mobs massacred the palace guard and seized the despised King Louis XVI and Marie-Antoinette, dragging them to Paris and eventually to the guillotine.

The vast palace complex is divided into **four main parts**: the palace itself with its wings, great halls and chambers

(only certain parts are open to the public); the extensive gardens; and two smaller châteaux in the grounds, used as royal guesthouses – the Grand Trianon and the Petit Trianon.

The château and gardens are usually busy with visitors

The sumptuous interior of the palace has undergone surprisingly few alterations since it was constructed, although the majority of the furnishings disappeared during the Revolution. Most visited are the **Grands Appartements** (State Apartments) on the first floor, which contain the royal bedchambers and the **Galerie des Glaces** (Hall of Mirrors). This grandiose gallery with 17 giant mirrors facing tall arched windows was used for state occasions, and, in 1919, was the scene of the ratification of the Treaty of Versailles, which ended World War I. In the north wing is Mansart's beautiful two-storey **Chapelle Royale** and the **Opéra**, a late addition completed in 1770, in time for the marriage of Louis XVI and Marie-Antoinette. For financial reasons, it was built entirely of wood, then painted to resemble marble.

✉ 78008 Versailles
☎ 01 30 83 78 00; www.chateauversailles.fr
🕐 Grands Appartements: Tue–Sun 9–5:30 (April–Oct until 6:30).
Grand Trianon and Petit Trianon: April–Oct daily noon–6:30; Nov–March noon–5:30. Gardens: April–Oct daily 7am–8:30pm; Nov–March 8–6.
Last entrance 30 min before closing. Closed some public hols
💶 Palace: €15. Grand Trianon and Petit Trianon (combined ticket): €10. (Entrance to Versailles is free Nov–March on the first Sun of every month and to under-18s of any nationality and EU citizens under 26 years of age at any time.) Gardens: free; except April–Oct Sat–Sun.
Audio guide included in cost of ticket

FORMIDABLE FOUNTAINS

The vast grounds, covering 100ha (247 acres), are as overwhelmingly ornate and rigidly planned as the palace interior, with marble-paved courtyards, colonnades, urns, sculptures, an orangery, a canal, and lakes and ponds in a variety of shapes and sizes dissecting the velvety lawns and orderly flowerbeds. The gardens are most famous for their many fountains, which spring to life in early April until October (Sat–Sun 11–12, 3:30–5:30, and on Sat mid-June to early Sep 9–11:20pm for special water displays with music, fireworks and lasers). Be sure to see the Bassin de Neptune (Fountain of Neptune), with its sea god, dragons and cherubs, and the Bassin d'Apollo (Fountain of Apollo), depicting the sun god emerging from the water in his chariot surrounded by sea monsters.

INSIDER INFO

■ Avoid the crowds by arriving early in the morning or around 3:30–4. If you have a **Paris Museum Pass** (▶ 38) or have purchased an advance ticket via the Versailles website, you can go straight to Entrée A (Entrance A). The palace is busiest at weekends and on Tuesdays.

■ **Pick up a plan** of the palace grounds at the main entrance.

■ It's impossible to see everything in one visit. If this is your first time, **concentrate on the Grands Appartements**, either at your own pace with an audio guide or with one of the frequent guided tours (in various languages).

■ If you can't face the huge queues, **you can still have a great day** in the **grounds**, enjoying the fountains and architecture. Why not bring a picnic?

■ If rushed, visit the main palace and **forget the smaller châteaux**, the Grand Trianon and the Petit Trianon, in the northwest corner of the gardens.

Hidden Gem The **Hameau de la Reine** (Queen's Hamlet), Marie-Antoinette's place of rustic refuge from courtly life, makes a delightful contrast after the grandeur of the palace. This beautiful collection of stylised country buildings – including a farmhouse, a dovecote and a dairy - was where the fabulously wealthy Queen liked to dress up and pretend to live the life of a simple shepherdess. To reach it, catch a tram from the north side of the main complex.

Getting there To get there, it's best to catch the **RER (Line C)** to Versailles-Rive Gauche (around 35 minutes, requiring a Zone 1–5 ticket) or a **main-line train** (about every 15 minutes) from Gare Montparnasse to Versailles-Chantiers (around 20 minutes). Alternatively, trains from Gare St-Lazare head to Versailles-Rive Droite (about 35 minutes) via La Défense. All three stations are within walking distance.

To the Glory of the Sun King

Nowhere else has a ruler's worldview been brought to life so rigorously and impressively while retaining an absolute sense of taste and harmony as at the Sun King's fairytale castle.

❶ Chambre du Roi The Sun King's bedroom, decorated with opulent sculptures and located at the centre of the palace, was the stage for the "lever (and coucher) du roi". Close confidantes brought the King the latest news while he got up, was examined by the court physician, and was shaved and powdered. Then came the "Grand Lever" in front of dozens of "spectators", during which the King drank his chocolate and finished dressing. A balustrade divided the "private" and "public" sections of the room.

❷ Water Parterre River gods, nymphs and putti inhabit the pools in front of the main facade.

❸ Bosquets Romantic beech-hedge bosquets ("small woods") in various designs form intimate spaces for festivities and amusements on both sides of the garden's main axis.

❹ Orangerie The Orangerie sits under the south parterre, framed by the "staircase of 100 steps". Thanks to its double glazing, the temperature never drops below 5° C (41° F). Over 1,000 exotic trees in containers lead to the almost 700 metre-long "Swiss pond".

❺ Opéra Royale Restored between 2007 and 2009, this splendid opera hall with its gold-bronze and mirrored walls was added to the North Wing in 1770 by Ange-Jacques Gabriel in honour of the future King Louis XVI's marriage to Marie-Antoinette. Made entirely out of wood, its acoustics are outstanding. Ingenious technology means that the auditorium – which holds more than 700 guests – can also turn into a ballroom. Apart from during performances, you can only visit the hall on thematic guided tours in August. These are held by prior arrangement on Tue–Sun at around 9.45am, tel. 01 30 83 78 00; www.chateauversaillesspectacles.fr.

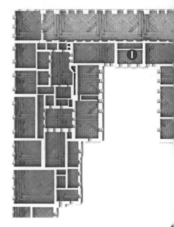

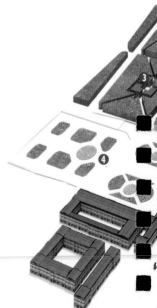

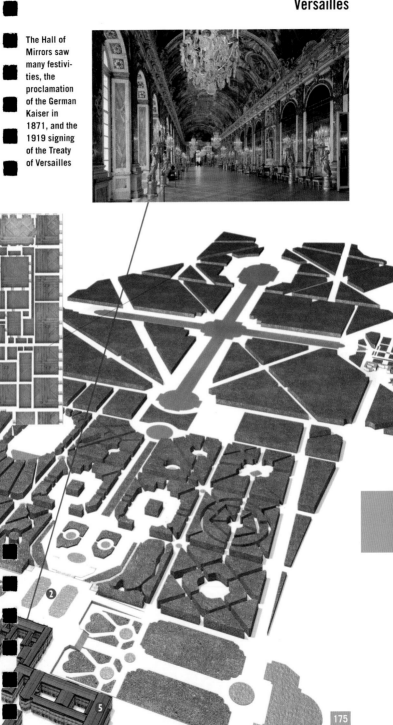

The Hall of Mirrors saw many festivities, the proclamation of the German Kaiser in 1871, and the 1919 signing of the Treaty of Versailles

2

5

Chantilly

Chantilly, 48km (30mi) north of Paris, has always enjoyed a reputation for fine cuisine (even though its most famous chef, François Vatel, committed suicide in the château because the fish he had ordered for Louis XIV arrived late), and the name of the town is indelibly associated with fresh whipped and sweetened cream, created by Vatel, and ordered in the best restaurants worldwide as *crème Chantilly.*

Visitors to Chantilly today come not for the cream but for its fairy-tale Renaissance château. Walking around the ornately **medieval interior** it's hard to believe the structure is only just over a century and a quarter old.

The original mansion was razed during the French Revolution and rebuilt from scratch between 1875 and 1885 by the Duc d'Aumale. The heirless duke bequeathed the property to the state in 1884 along with its **magnificent art collection** – one of the finest in France – which contains notable works by Botticelli and Piero di Cosimo. The surrounding grounds feature English, French and water gardens, plus an ornamental village, said to have inspired Marie-Antoinette's hamlet at Versailles.

On the chateau's doorstep is Chantilly Racecourse, an opulent set-up that contains the **Musée Vivant du Cheval (Living Horse Museum)**. The museum is closed for restoration until 2014, but there are animation and horse shows in the **Grandes Écuries** (Grand Stables) (early April–early Nov Wed–Mon 10–5; early Jan–early April 2–5; Dec 2–6).

✉ BP 70243, 60631 Chantilly
☎ Château and Musée Vivant du Cheval: 03 44 27 31 80;
www.chateaudechantilly.com, www.museevivantducheval.fr
🕐 Apr–Oct Wed–Mon 10–6; Nov–March 10:30–5
🚆 Numerous trains from Gare du Nord to Chantilly-Gouvieux.
The journey takes around 30 min and the château is about 25 minutes' walk from the station, or you can take a taxi or (infrequent) bus
🎫 €14

The château, reflected in the encircling water

Disneyland® Resort Paris

First opened in 1992, 👫 Disneyland® Resort Paris is now Europe's most visited theme park. It has 52 top attractions, among which is probably the world's most impressive Disney castle, *Le Château de la Belle au Bois Dormant* (Sleeping Beauty's Castle).

Bright pink and fit for a princess: The Sleeping Beauty Castle at Disneyland® Resort Paris

A dream destination for kids from all over Europe, the resort now has 15 million visitors per year, placing it among the top three most visited sights on the continent. Disneyland® Park offers such thrilling rides as **Big Thunder Mountain**, Indiana Jones and the Temple of Peril (including 360-degree loops backwards) and, scariest of all, **Space Mountain Mission 2**. Peter Pan's Flight, It's a Small World and the Mad Hatter's Tea Cups are geared to toddlers, while top attractions **Pirates of the Caribbean** and **Buzz Lightyear Laser Blast** will appeal to young children. A whole host of American-style eateries, shops and parades ensure non-stop entertainment.

There is also the thrilling **Walt Disney Studios® Park**, which opened in 2002 with tram tours that go behind the scenes of hit movies and live Disney stage shows. It's not an inexpensive option, but for most children it has to be the ultimate treat. Booking in advance and checking for offers on the official website can bring the price down hugely, as can staying in one of the on-site hotels, which routinely give out free resort tickets as part of the package.

It's best to avoid weekends and mornings when the inevitable crowds are at their worst. Those with limited time can purchase a **Fastpass** and bypass the queue. A daily Eurostar train links London St Pancras directly with the park.

✉ 77777 Marne-la-Vallée ☎ 01 60 30 60 30; www.disneylandparis.com
🕐 Open 365 days a year. Times vary according to season;
phone for the latest information
🚇 The RER (line A) takes around 35 min to reach Marne-la-Vallée/Chessy;
the entrance to Disneyland® is 100m (110 yards) from the station exit
💵 €64 (the 2- or 3-day "Park Hopper" is good value)

Fontainebleau

If you can't face the crowds at Versailles, come to this château instead. As a **UNESCO World Heritage Site**, it is equally grand but surprisingly overlooked. This splendid palace, 65km (40mi) south-east of Paris, started out as a hunting lodge and became a royal residence in the reign of Louis VII.

The present edifice was commissioned by François I. So entranced was he by Italy's Renaissance that he hosted the era's best artists at the château and so ended with a galaxy of fine art, including da Vinci's *Mona Lisa*, on the walls.

The Gallery of François I is home to an impressive collection of fine art

Successive kings left their mark, often an entire wing, as a legacy. Henri II and Catherine de Médicis littered the ornate interior with engravings of the letters H & C. The **stunningly landscaped grounds**, which rival Versailles, were put in place by Henri IV. They include parkland studded with grottos of rare trees, lakes, swans and peacocks, and one of France's finest swathes of primeval forest, bisected by a canal.

Napoleon renovated Fontainebleau to its current standing after the French Revolution. He was proclaimed Emperor here by Pope Pius VII in 1804, snatching the papal crown from Pius's hands and plonking it on his own head. He kept the pope a prisoner here from 1812 to 1814. Fontainebleau remains one of France's largest former royal residences (1,900 rooms), celebrated for its **furnishings** as much as its grounds.

✉ 77300 Fontainebleau
☎ 01 60 71 50 70; www.musee-chateau-fontainebleau.fr
🕐 Château: April–Sep Wed–Mon 9:30–6; Oct–March 9:30–5; last entrance 45 min before closing. Gardens: May–Sep daily 9–7; March–April, Oct 9–6; Nov–Feb 9–5
🚉 Trains leave Paris's Gare de Lyon approx every hour for Fontainebleau-Avon. Regular buses run from the train station to the château. Total journey time: about 1 hour 💶 €11

Walks & Tours

1 RIVER TRIP
Tour

TIME 1 hour
START POINT Square du Vert-Galant
END POINT Pont Neuf ✛ 209 E5

Paris is an ideal city to visit by river cruise. Hour-long cruises run both day and night along the main sightseeing reaches of the Seine, presenting a new and magical perspective on many of the city's most famous monuments and bridges. This trip follows the route of the Vedettes du Pont Neuf.

begun as World War II broke out, boasts special telescopic lights; designer Raymond Subes continued his work in secret, completing the lamps in 1941.

2–3
After the Pont Royal (a gift from Louis XIV to the people of Paris),

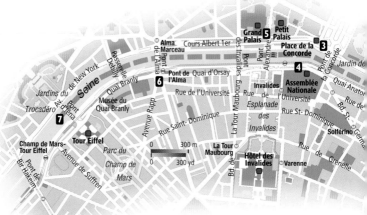

1–2
Set sail from the square du Vert-Galant below the Pont Neuf on the **Île de la Cité** (▶ 182). Initially, the boat heads westwards under the Pont des Arts (the city's first cast-iron bridge, constructed in 1804 and rebuilt in 1984), which occasionally provides an unusual setting for sculpture exhibitions. As you pass the **Louvre** (▶ 102) on your right, Paris's largest museum and for centuries the home of kings and queens, the boat glides under the Pont du Carrousel. This bridge,

on the left you will see the **Musée d'Orsay** (▶ 56), where the city's most important collection of Impressionist art is housed in a converted railway station.

3–4
Two bridges later is the Pont de la Concorde, built in 1791, during the French Revolution. To the right is the immense **Place de la Concorde** (where the guillotine was erected, ▶ 114), one of the finest examples of sophisticated 18th-century Parisian town-planning.

The river tour passes the Conciergerie, part of the Palais de la Cité

The 3,300-year-old obelisk at its centre is the city's most ancient monument. To the left is the 18th-century neoclassical **Palais Bourbon**, home of the Assemblée Nationale (the lower house of the French Parliament).

4–5

The most decorative bridge comes next: Pont Alexandre III, built to commemorate the Franco-Russian alliance in 1893 and named after Tsar Alexander III. The ornate candelabra are copies of the lamps on Trinity Bridge in St Petersburg. It is flanked by the **Grand Palais** and **Petit Palais** (➤ 115), both equally lavish in their architectural style, in stark contrast with the more sober

classicizing baroque architecture of the **Invalides** complex (➤ 63) on the Left Bank opposite.

5–6

Two bridges after Pont Alexandre III, look for the statue of a soldier on the central pier of the Pont de l'Alma, used to measure the level of the Seine when it is in flood.

6–7

Have your camera ready before you round the next curve of the Seine, because the **Eiffel Tower** (➤ 53) now looms large, offering breathtaking photographic opportunities. Remarkably, this extraordinary edifice manages to remain in harmony with the perfect symmetry and the beautiful vista of the **Champ de Mars** (➤ 54)

Walks & Tours

One of the tour boats passing under the Pont des Arts

beyond, and of the fountain-filled Jardins du Trocadéro which roll down towards it on the Right Bank – another stroke of French town-planning genius.

7 – 8

The boat will turn here and head eastwards, returning to the Île de la Cité. Notice the many boats and barges moored alongside the wharfs, some converted into bars and restaurants, others now used as houseboats. When you reach the island, the boat will bear right, passing under several bridges including the Petit Pont, the smallest in the city, spanning just 33m (108ft), and passing **Notre-Dame** (▶ 76), one of the high spots of the cruise, on your left.

8 – 9

Continuing onwards, the boat now encircles the tranquil **Île St-Louis** (▶ 88), where graceful willows bow to meet the waters of the river: it is hard to believe that this island, where elegant residences now line the waterfronts, was once a swampy wasteland. As the dramatist Pierre Corneille wrote: "An entire city, built here with pomp, seems miraculously to have sprung out of an old ditch" (*Le Menteur*, 1643).

9 – 10

The boat returns past the northern side of Île de la Cité, lined with the imposing facades of the Hôtel Dieu, Paris's oldest hospital and the site of a major battle between the Paris police and German forces in 1944. It also passes the splendid **Palais de Justice** (▶ 82), the city's first public clock (still working six centuries on), and the medieval, turreted **Conciergerie** (▶ 82) – former royal palace-cum-prison, where Marie-Antoinette spent two months before losing her head in 1793.

10 – 11

The final bridge on the cruise is the **Pont Neuf** (▶ 19). Despite its name (meaning "new bridge"), it is the oldest bridge in Paris, dating from the 17th century, and was the first to be built with no houses on it. The many grimacing heads that decorate it are supposed to represent the friends and ministers of Henri IV who built it – a somewhat dour-looking bunch. The cruise ends just beyond the bridge, at its start point beside the beautiful **square du Vert-Galant**.

TAKING A BREAK

There is a snack bar on board and a toilet at the embarkation quay but not on board.

WHEN TO GO

Small **Vedettes du Pont Neuf** boats run mid-March to Oct daily at 10:30, 11:15, 12 and every half-hour from 1:30 to 7, and at 8, 9, 9:30, 10, 10:30; Nov to mid-March Fri–Sun at 10:30, 11:15, 12, then every 45 min from 2 to 6:30 and at 8, 9 and 10. On 24 Dec and 31 Dec the last departure is at 5:45. For further information tel: 01 46 33 98 38; www.vedettesdupont neuf.com. The large *bateaux-mouches* follow a similar route and depart from the Pont de l'Alma.

2 LE MARAIS
Walk

DISTANCE 3.5km (2mi)   **TIME** 3 hours
START POINT Place de l'Hôtel de Ville ➕ 205 F1
END POINT Place St-Gervais ➕ 205 F1

From after the Revolution until the 1950s, this district, which had once been favoured by kings and courtiers, was one of the city's poorest areas. Now rediscovered and with its gracious aristocratic mansions restored, the chic and sophisticated Marais *quartier* has uniquely preserved most of its pre-Revolutionary architecture. A stroll through its streets is rather like walking around a giant open-air museum.

The walk starts near the Hôtel de Ville in the square of the same name

❶–❷

Start in Place de l'Hôtel de Ville. From the northeastern corner, head one block eastwards (past the BHV department store) along Rue de Rivoli then turn left into Rue des Archives. At No 24 (on your right) you will find the tiny sand-coloured **Cloître des Billettes**, the only surviving medieval cloister in Paris, now a school. It was built in the flamboyant Gothic style and dates from 1427. Frequent temporary exhibitions mean the vaulted courtyard is often open to the public. Further on at No 40 is **Maison Cœur**, one of the oldest houses in Paris, built by the granddaughter of Jacques Cœur, Charles VII's celebrated minister of finance in the 15th century.

❷–❸

Continue along Rue des Archives to reach the restored, early 18th-century **Hôtel de Soubise**, home to the Archives Nationales, on the corner of Rue des Francs-Bourgeois. The **Musée de l'Histoire de France**, housed in its rococo salons, makes an unbeatable introduction (in French) to the history of France (tel: 01 40 27 60 96; Mon, Wed–Fri 10–12:30, 2–5:30, Sat–Sun 2–5:30).

❸–❹

Turn right along Rue des Francs-Bourgeois, a street lined with private homes that derives its name from the almshouses for the tax-exempt poor that stood here in the 14th century. On your right is the church of **Notre-Dame-des-Blancs-Manteaux**, named after the white habits worn by the Augustinian friars who founded a convent here in 1258. Further on, at the intersection with Rue Vieille-du-Temple, stands the **Hôtel Hérouet**, an unusually ornate Gothic-style building, adorned with turrets and stone carvings, built originally by Jean

Walks & Tours

Hérouet, treasurer to Louis XII in 1510, and cleverly reconstructed in the 19th century.

4–5

Turn right here down Rue Vieille-du-Temple, then left into Rue des Rosiers. This area, known as the Pletzl, is one of the city's liveliest Jewish neighbourhoods, and the street is lined with tempting kosher delicatessens, restaurants and falafel vendors.

5–6

Just before the end of Rue des Rosiers, turn left into Rue Pavée, so-named because it was the first "paved street" in the capital. On the corner of Rue Pavée and Rue des Francs-Bourgeois stands the **Hôtel de Lamoignon**, built in 1585 for Diane de France (illegitimate daughter of Henri II), and now home to the **Bibliothèque Historique de la Ville de Paris.** Step inside the courtyard so that you can fully appreciate the mansion's grandeur.

6–7

Turn left along Rue des Francs-Bourgeois past countless alluring fashion boutiques and designer shops – but don't be too distracted by the window displays, or you will miss the architecture of the splendid mansions that house them. The first turning to the right takes you up Rue Elzévir, past the **Musée Cognacq-Jay** (tel: 01 40 27 07 21; Tue–Sun 10–6), a little-known treasure trove of 18th-century French *objets d'art*, lovingly assembled by Ernest Cognacq and his wife Marie-Louise Jay, founders of La Samaritaine, once Paris's largest department store.

Insider Tip

7–8

Turn right into Rue du Parc Royal, lined with grand pastel-coloured mansions, past a small park (square l'Achille), and right again down Rue de Sévigné, past the main entrance to the **Musée Carnavalet**, an impressive homage to Parisian history (▶ 138). The church looming large at the end of the street is **St-Paul-St-Louis** (▶ 184).

8–9

Turn left into Rue des Francs-Bourgeois to reach **Place des Vosges**, a stunning arcaded square of red-brick town houses, with manicured lawns and elegant fountains (▶ 130). Leave Place des Vosges by the southwestern corner, passing through the ivy-hung courtyard of the **Hôtel de Sully,** a stylish mansion built in 1624. It is now not only the

Musée Carnavalet can be visited on the walk route

linking Rue de Rivoli with Place de
la Bastille. Cross over and continue
westwards past the imposing
facade of **St-Paul-St-Louis,** a
17th-century Jesuit foundation
whose numerous art treasures
include Delacroix's *Christ in the
Garden of Olives*.

🔟–⓫
Fork left into Rue François-Miron,
one of the first roads to cross the
marshy area of the *marais*, passing
its popular shops and ancient
half-timbered houses to reach
Place St-Gervais and the church of
St-Gervais-St-Protais – a beautiful
Gothic church with the earliest
classical facade in Paris,

headquarters of the **Centre des
Monuments Nationaux (Monum)**
(the organization responsible for
preserving many of France's
historic monuments), but
also holds dedicated

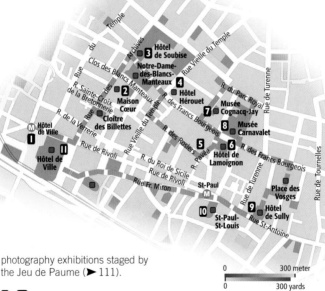

photography exhibitions staged by
the Jeu de Paume (➤ 111).

9️⃣–🔟
Turn right on to one of the city's
oldest streets, Rue St-Antoine, in
medieval times a favourite place
for jousting and for ceremonial
entries into the city. Henri II was
fatally wounded here in 1559 when
he took part in a tournament to
celebrate his daughter's wedding.
Today it is a main thoroughfare

a three-storey exercise in the hier-
archy of the classical orders. Inside
is the organ on which François
Couperin composed his two great
masses. The walk ends here in
Place St-Gervais, at the back of the
Hôtel de Ville, the town hall.

3 ST-GERMAIN
Walk

DISTANCE 3km (2mi) **TIME** 3 hours	
START/END POINT Église St-Germain-des-Prés ✚ 209 D5	

This relaxing walk leads you through the artists' quarter of the Left Bank, down into the Odéon district and the Jardin du Luxembourg, capturing the frequently changing character of St-Germain-des-Prés en route.

1–2

Start at the ancient church of **St-Germain-des-Prés** (▶ 60). Walk eastwards along Boulevard St-Germain and turn left up Rue de Buci, venue of a lively food market, then left again along Rue de Bourbon-le-Château.

2–3

Cross Rue de l'Echaudé and Rue Cardinale, with their charming small boutiques, and continue up Rue de l'Abbaye, taking the first right into Rue de Furstemberg, named after Cardinal von Furstemberg, a 17th-century abbot of the monastery of St-Germain. This leads to Place Furstemberg, a charming, tiny stage-set of a square, complete with a tree, iron lamp post and park bench.

Tucked into the left-hand corner is the former home and studio of romantic artist Delacroix, today a small **museum** (►64).

3–4

Continue to the end of Rue de Furstemberg. Turn left into Rue Jacob, then right into Rue Bonaparte past the famous **École Nationale Supérieure des Beaux-Arts**, which numbers Degas, Matisse, Monet and Renoir among its former students.

4–5

Continue up Rue Bonaparte to the river. Turn right along the embankment past *les bouquinistes*. These quaint green bookstalls lining the Seine date back three centuries to the time when second-hand booksellers piled up their wares on the riverbank.

On your right, note two imposing buildings: the **Institut de France**, home to the illustrious Académie Française, which since 1635 has been the watchful guardian of the French language, and the **Musée de la Monnaie**, formerly the Paris mint and now a coin museum and temporary exhibition space (tel: 01 40 46 55 35; Tue–Fri 11–5:30, Sat–Sun noon–5:30, moderate).

5–6

At the Pont Neuf, turn right and head south down Rue Dauphine to the Carrefour de Buci. Turn left into Rue St-André-des-Arts, and immediately right into Cour du Commerce-St-André, a narrow cobbled passageway that was once a hive of Revolutionary activity. Megalomaniac residents Marat and Danton (Nos 8 and 20 respectively) used to meet at **Le Procope**, with anatomy professor Dr Guillotin (who proposed the use of his later notorious "philanthropic beheading machine" to prevent unnecessary pain). He lived at No 9.

6–7

The exit from the passage is on Boulevard St-Germain. Go straight over the road, across the Carrefour de l'Odéon and into Rue de l'Odéon, passing the neoclassical **national theatre** to your left at the top of the hill.

7–8

Cross Rue de Médicis and enter the idyllic **Jardin du Luxembourg** (►65) – an old favourite with Parisians, especially students, and an ideal place to relax for a while or even have a picnic.

8–9

Leave via the park's Rue de Vaugirard exit. Turn right then immediately left down Rue Férou to Place St-Sulpice with its splashy, flamboyant fountain.

The austere neoclassical **church of St-Sulpice**, dominating the square, boasts France's largest organ, and some spectacular frescoes by Delacroix.

9–10

From the church's main portal, cross the square (past the fountain) and turn right up Rue Bonaparte. This popular shopping street leads back to the **church of St-Germain-des-Prés** and the end of the walk.

TAKING A BREAK

One of Paris's most famous cafés, **Les Deux Magots** (► 29, 64) is conveniently situated at the start/end of the walk.

WHEN TO GO

Weekday mornings are best, before the Jardin du Luxembourg teems with schoolchildren and lunching office workers.

4 MONTMARTRE
Walk

DISTANCE 3km (2mi)   TIME 3 hours
START POINT Place Blanche ✚ 200 B3
END POINT Place des Abbesses ✚ 200 B3

Explore the back streets of Paris's historic hilltop "village", with its leafy cobbled streets and steep stairways lined with iron lamps, its quaint white-washed cottages and country gardens, its picturesque café-lined squares and its sweeping panoramas, and you will soon understand why so many generations of artists, writers and poets have fallen in love with this atmospheric neighbourhood.

❶–❷

From Place Blanche climb up Rue Lepic past tempting delicatessens and cafés. Turn left at the top and branch right, still on Rue Lepic. Van Gogh lived in an apartment at No 54 from 1886 until 1888, taking his inspiration from the windmills and gardens of Montmartre.

❷–❸

Continue to climb Rue Lepic, following the road round to the right. Note the steep flights of steps on your left leading up to countrified private villas, and high above you (opposite the intersection with Rue Tholozé), the **Moulin de la Galette** (➤ 160), once the venue for a notorious open-air cabaret. A few steps beyond (on the corner with Rue Girardon), Montmartre's only other remaining windmill – **Moulin Radet** – is now part of a restaurant.

❸–❹

Turn left here, and cross Avenue Junot, where artists Utrillo and Poulbot once lived at Nos 11 and 13. Soon after, turn left into **square Suzanne-Buisson**, a lovely secluded park where St Denis allegedly washed his decapitated head in a fountain before he died (➤ 154). Today a statue of the saint marks the spot, overlooking a boules pitch.

People walking up the shaded steps leading to Sacré-Cœur cathedral

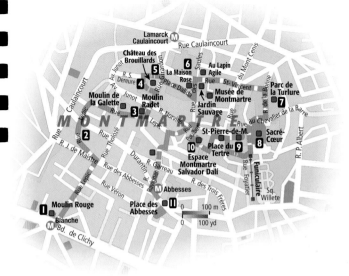

4–5

Turn right at the statue, descend past the rose garden on your left into Place Casadesus, in Rue Simon-Dereure, and turn right up several steps into allée des Brouillards. Here, the 18th-century **Château des Brouillards** on your right was once used as a shelter for homeless artists. Pierre-Auguste Renoir lived and worked in one of the houses on the left from 1890 to 1897.

5–6

At the end of allée des Brouillards, carry straight on up the cobbled Rue de l'Abreuvoir, once a country lane used by horses and cattle en route to the watering trough *(abreuvoir)* which stood on the site of No 15. Number 14 was formerly the Café de l'Abreuvoir, frequented by many great artists in Montmartre's heyday. Continuing up the hill, Impressionist painter Camille Pissarro rented No 12 between 1888 and 1892. Note

the charming sundial on the wall of No 4, with a picture of a rooster promising *Quand tu sonneras, je chanteray* ("When you [the sun] strike, I'll crow"). The restaurant at No 2, **La Maison Rose** (The Pink House), was made famous in an early Utrillo canvas.

6–7

Turn left immediately after La Maison Rose and head down steep Rue des Saules, past the city's last remaining **vineyard** (► 156) to the legendary **Au Lapin Agile** (► 161). Turn right along Rue St-Vincent, skirting the vineyard and a tiny **Jardin Sauvage** ("wild garden"; open April–Sep Sat–Sun 1:30–6:30; Oct Sat–Sun 1:30–5:50), designed to preserve the natural flora and fauna of Montmartre. Cross Rue du Mont Cenis, where composer Hector Berlioz once lived at No 22, and continue uphill to Rue de la Bonne and the entrance to neat and shady Parc Marcel Bleustein-Blanchet with its magnificent city vistas.

The original art nouveau "Métropolitain" sign at Abbesses Metro station, designed by French architect, furniture designer and writer Hector Guimard

just before a descending flight of steps will lead you across the cobbled Place du Calvaire to Rue Poulbot and the **Espace Montmartre Salvador Dalí** (► 160), which houses a permanent display of more than 300 works by the eccentric, mustachioed Spanish artist, as well as some temporary exhibitions of surrealist art.

🔟–⓫

Follow Rue Poulbot round to Rue Norvins. Turn left, then almost immediately left again, and head straight downhill, keeping the grassy square of Place Jean-Baptiste Clément on your right. Turn right at the intersection into Rue Ravignan, and follow the road round to the left into **Place Émile-Goudeau**, past the **Bateau-Lavoir** (► 159) on your right.

Leave the square down a small flight of steps. Cross over Rue Garreau and continue downhill on Rue Ravignan. A left turn at the next intersection will take you straight to the art nouveau Metro stop at **Place des Abbesses** (► 159) and the end of the walk.

🔼–🔽

Stroll through the park, which merges into **Parc de la Turlure**, leaving it by Rue du Chevalier de la Barre round the back of the **Sacré-Cœur** (► 154), and carrying on into Rue du Cardinal Guibert, which runs alongside the basilica to its entrance on Place du Parvis du Sacré-Cœur. (Note that the entrance to the crypt and the dome is in Rue du Cardinal Guibert.)

🔼–🔽

On leaving the Sacré-Cœur, head right along Rue Azaïs, admiring the distant views of Paris as you go. A right turn up Rue St-Eleuthère will lead you to the church of **St-Pierre-de-Montmartre**, consecrated by Pope Eugene III in 1147 and one of the oldest churches in the city.

🔼–🔟

As you leave the church, continue straight ahead into **Place du Tertre** (► 161), once a delightful 18th-century village square and now a veritable tourist honeypot filled with of artists and street caricaturists. Leave the square via Rue du Calvaire. A right turn

TAKING A BREAK

Avoid the tourist cafés in Place du Tertre. Try **Bistro des Dames** (18 Rue des Dames, 75017; tel: 01 45 22 13 42; daily lunch and dinner) for good bistro food and a great ambience, with the bonus of a small garden. Or have a picnic in the Parc de la Turlure.

WHEN TO GO

Avoid Sunday, when the district is crowded.

Practicalities

Practicalities

WHAT YOU NEED

		UK	USA	Canada	Australia	Germany	Ireland	Netherlands	Spain
● Required ○ Suggested ▲ Not required	Some countries require a passport to remain valid for a minimum period beyond the date of entry – contact their consulate or embassy for details								
Passport/National Identity Card		●	●	●	●	●	●	●	●
Visa (regulations can change – check before you travel)		▲	▲	▲	▲	▲	▲	▲	▲
Onward or Return Ticket		▲	▲	▲	▲	▲	▲	▲	▲
Health Inoculations		▲	▲	▲	▲	▲	▲	▲	▲
Health Documentation (▶ 196, Health)		○	○	○	○	○	○	○	○
Travel Insurance		○	○	○	○	○	○	○	○
Driving Licence (national)		●	●	●	●	●	●	●	●
Car Insurance Certificate		○	n/a	n/a	n/a	○	○	○	○
Car Registration Document		○	n/a	n/a	n/a	○	○	○	○

WHEN TO GO

High season Low season

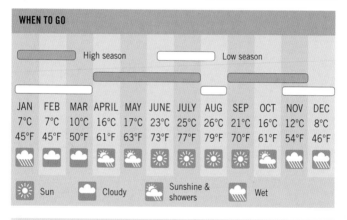

JAN	FEB	MAR	APRIL	MAY	JUNE	JULY	AUG	SEP	OCT	NOV	DEC
7°C	7°C	10°C	16°C	17°C	23°C	25°C	26°C	21°C	16°C	12°C	8°C
45°F	45°F	50°F	61°F	63°F	73°F	77°F	79°F	70°F	61°F	54°F	46°F

☀ Sun ☁ Cloudy ⛅ Sunshine & showers 🌧 Wet

Temperatures are the **average daily maximum** for each month. The best time to visit Paris is June, a glorious month when the days are longest, with the most sunshine and average daytime temperatures a comfortable 23°C (73°F). The city reaches peak tourist capacity in hot, sunny July. August sees the Parisian exodus to the countryside, leaving the city emptier than usual. It is the hottest, most humid month and the city is prone to sudden storms. September and October have a high percentage of crisp days and clear skies, but rooms can be difficult to find as this is the peak trade-fair period. Winter temperatures rarely drop below freezing, but it rains frequently, sometimes with hail, from November to January.

GETTING ADVANCE INFORMATION

Websites
■ Paris Tourist Office:
www.parisinfo.com
(visitors with disabilities should also consult
www.infomobi.com)

■ Paris Tourism:
www.paris-tourism.com
■ French Tourist Office:
www.franceguide.com
■ Paris Angloinfo
www.paris.angloinfo.com

In the UK
French Tourist Office
Lincoln House, 300 High
Holborn, London WC1V 7JH
☎ 09068 244123;
www.uk.franceguide.com

GETTING THERE

By Air Paris has two main airports – Roissy Charles de Gaulle and Orly (both www.adp.fr). Numerous carriers operate direct flights from the US and Canada, including American Airlines, Delta and Air Canada. From the UK, British Airways and easyJet operate a regular service; from Australia, Qantas and Cathay Pacific are the major carriers. France's national airline, Air France (tel: 0820 320 820 in France, 0871 663 3777 in the UK, www.airfrance.com) has scheduled flights from Britain, mainland Europe and beyond, to both main airports. Approximate flying times to Paris: London (1 hour), Dublin (1.5 hours), New York (8 hours), West Coast USA (12 hours), Vancouver (10 hours), Montreal (7.5 hours), Sydney (23 hours), Auckland (21 hours). Ticket prices tend to be highest in spring and summer (Easter to September). City-break packages may offer even more savings if a Saturday night is included. Check with the airlines, travel agents and the internet for current best deals and offers.

By Rail There are six major railway stations, each handling traffic to different parts of France and Europe. French Railways (www.raileurope.co.uk/sncf) operates high-speed trains (TGVs) to Paris from main stations throughout France. The Eurostar passenger train service (tel: 08705 186186 in Britain, www.eurostar.com) from London's St Pancras International via the Channel Tunnel to Paris Gare du Nord takes 2 hours 15 minutes.

By Sea Ferry companies operate regular services from England and Ireland to France, with rail links to Paris. Crossing time: 35 minutes to 6 hours (England); 14–18 hours (Ireland).

TIME

France is on Central European Time, one hour ahead of Greenwich Mean Time (GMT +1). From late March, when clocks are put forward one hour, until late October, French summer time (GMT +2) operates.

CURRENCY AND FOREIGN EXCHANGE

Currency The French unit of currency is the Euro (€). Coins are issued in denominations of 1, 2, 5, 10, 20 and 50 cents and €1 and €2. There are 100 cents in €1. Notes (bills) are issued in denominations of €5, €10, €20, €50, €100, €200 and €500.

Exchange You can exchange travellers' cheques at some banks and at bureaux de change at airports, main railway stations or in some department stores, and exchange booths. All transactions are subject to a hefty commission charge, so you may prefer to rely on cash, debit and credit cards. Travellers' cheques issued by American Express and VISA can also be changed at many post offices.

Credit cards You can use your debit and credit cards to withdraw money from French cash machines *(Bancomat)* twenty-four hours a day. Banks accept all major credit cards, as do most hotels, restaurants, car rental companies and many shops. Banks are open Monday to Friday from 10am until 5pm, and some banks also open their doors until midday on Saturdays. French banks generally close at around noon on the eve of public holidays.

French Tourist Offices: int.rendezvousenfrance.com

In the US	In Australia	In Canada
825 Third Avenue, 29th floor (entrance on 50th Street), New York NY10022 ☎ 514/288 1904	Level 13 25 Bligh Street Sydney, NSW 2000 ☎ (02) 9231 5244	1800 avenue McGill College Suite 1010 Montreal, Québec H3A 3J6 ☎ 514-288 2026

Practicalities

NATIONAL HOLIDAYS

1 Jan	New Year's Day
Mar/Apr	Easter Sunday and Monday
1 May	May Day
8 May	VE (Victory in Europe) Day
6th Thu after Easter	Ascension Day
May/Jun	Whit Sunday and Monday
14 Jul	Bastille Day
15 Aug	Assumption Day
1 Nov	All Saints' Day
11 Nov	Remembrance Day
25 Dec	Christmas Day

ELECTRICITY

 The power supply in Paris is 220 volts. Sockets accept two-round-pin (or increasingly three-round-pin) plugs, so an adaptor is needed for most non-Continental appliances. A transformer is needed for appliances operating on 110–120 volts.

OPENING HOURS

○ Shops
● Offices
● Banks
● Post Offices
● Museums/Monuments
● Pharmacies

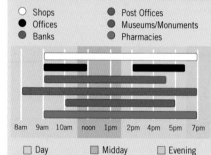

8am 9am 10am noon 1pm 2pm 4pm 5pm 7pm

☐ Day   ☐ Midday   ☐ Evening

Shops Some shops close 12–2pm, and all day Sun and Mon. Food shops open 7am–1:30pm and 4:30–8pm, and may open Sun until noon.
Banks Some open extended hours.
Museums City museums usually close Mon. Most national museums close Tue, except Versailles and Musée d'Orsay.

TIPS/GRATUITIES

Restaurant, café and hotel bills must by law include a service charge so a tip is not expected, although many people do leave a few coins in restaurants.

Taxis	€0.50–€1.50
Tour guides	€3–€5
Porters	€0.50–€1.50
Cloakroom attendants	small change
Hairdressers	€3–€5
Lavatory attendants	small change

NO SMOKING

France has banned smoking in all public buildings, as well as bars and restaurants. Although the smoky indoor Parisian café is no more, many places have set up outdoor terraces, where it is acceptable to smoke.

TIME DIFFERENCES

Paris (CET)
12 noon

←
London (GMT)
11am

→
New York (EST)
6am

→
Los Angeles (PST)
3am

→
Sydney (AEST)
9pm

STAYING IN TOUCH

Post Post offices (www. laposte.fr) are identified by a yellow or brown "La Poste" sign. The main office at 52 rue du Louvre is open Mon–Sat 7:30am–6am, Sun 10am–6am. The branch at 71 avenue des Champs-Élysées is open Mon–Fri 8am–7pm, Sat 8am–noon.

Public telephones To use most **public phones**, you will need to buy a phonecard *(télécarte)*. These are sold in units of 50 and 120 and can be bought from France Telecom shops, post offices, tobacconists and railway stations. Cheap rates generally apply Mon–Fri 7pm–8am, Sat–Sun all day.

All telephone numbers in France are comprised of ten digits. Paris and Île de France numbers all begin with 01. There are no area codes; simply dial the number.

International Dialling Codes: Dial 00 followed by

UK:	44	**USA/Canada:**	1
Ireland:	353	**Australia:**	6

Mobile providers and services Although mobile coverage is excellent, it may be worth investing in a French SIM card. Prices start around €5 from both Orange (www.orange.fr) and SFR (www.sfr.fr). American visitors who do not own a GSM-enabled cell phone are advised to purchase a new handset (from around €25, including French telephone number and initial credit).

WiFi and Internet Most of Paris is covered by free wireless internet; public zones include parks, open areas and squares. In turn, almost all hotels, restaurants and cafés also offer free internet service. Access is fast and reliable. A list of internet cafés can be found on www.parisinfo.com.

PERSONAL SAFETY

Petty crime, particularly theft of wallets and handbags, is fairly common in Paris. Be aware of scruffy, innocent-looking children as well as groups of streethawkers: they may be working the streets in gangs, fleecing unwary tourists. Report any loss or theft to your nearest police station, or call 01 53 71 53 71. To be safe:

■ Watch your pockets and your bag on the Métro, in busy tourist areas like Beaubourg and the Champs-Élysées and in museum queues.

■ Cars should be well secured.

■ Keep a minimum of cash and valuables on you at any time; store them instead in your hotel safe.

■ Avoid walking alone along dark streets at night, particularly in areas that can be dodgy at night, like Les Halles and Pigalle.

Police assistance:
☎ **17 from any phone**

POLICE 17
FIRE 18
AMBULANCE 15
DOCTOR (24-hour call-out for a fee) 01 47 07 77 77

Practicalities

HEALTH

 Insurance Citizens of EU countries receive free or reduced-cost emergency medical treatment with relevant documentation (European Health Insurance Card), but private medical insurance is still advised and essential for all other visitors.

 Dental Services As for general medical treatment (► above), nationals of EU countries can obtain dental treatment at reduced cost. Around 70 per cent of standard dentists' fees are refunded, but private medical insurance is still advised for all.

 Weather During hot weather, make sure to wear protective clothing and sunglasses, use sun cream and drink lots of fluids.

 Drugs Pharmacies – recognized by their green cross sign – provide first aid and prescribe a wide range of drugs, although some are available by prescription (ordonnance) only.

 Safe Water Tap water is safe to drink, but never drink from a tap marked eau non potable (not drinking water). Mineral water is widely available.

CONCESSIONS

Students/Youths Holders of an International Student Identity Card (ISIC) are entitled to discounted admission to museums and sights, air and ferry tickets and meals in some student cafeterias. Most sights and museums are free for visitors under 18 (or under 26 from the EU).

Senior Citizens If you are over 60 you can get discounts (up to 50 per cent) in museums, on public transport and in places of entertainment. Purchasing a Carte Senior (www.senior-sncf.com) can give discounts of up to 50 per cent on train travel. You may get a discount simply by showing your passport.

TRAVELLING WITH A DISABILITY

Many older public facilities and attractions lack amenities for people with disabilities, although most hotels with two or more stars have lifts. Few Métro stations have lifts.

Infomobi (tel: 08 10 64 64 64, www.infomobi.com) provides free information and specific public transport maps (which can be downloaded from their website).

CHILDREN

France is seen as being child-friendly, and lots of places offer discounts for younger visitors. Special attractions for kids are marked out with the logo shown above.

TOILETS

Some older establishments have a squat toilet, but there are modern pay toilets throughout Paris. Café toilets are for customers only.

TAXES AND CUSTOMS

France's VAT (TVA) is 19.6 per cent on most goods. Visitors from outside the EU may be entitled to tax rebates.

EMBASSIES AND HIGH COMMISSIONS

UK	**USA**	**New Zealand**	**Australia**	**Canada**
☎ 01 44 51 31 00	☎ 01 43 12 22 22	☎ 01 45 01 43 43	☎ 01 40 59 33 00	☎ 01 44 43 29 00

Useful Words and Phrases

SURVIVAL PHRASES

Yes/no **Oui/non**
Good morning/evening **Bonjour/bonsoir**
Hello **Salut**
Goodbye **Au revoir**
How are you? **Comment allez-vous?**
Please **S'il vous plaît**
Thank you **Merci**
Excuse me **Excusez-moi**
I'm sorry **Pardon**
You're welcome **De rien/avec plaisir**
Do you have...? **Avez-vous...?**
How much is this? **C'est combien?**
I'd like... **Je voudrais...**
Directions
Is there a phone box around here? **Y a-t-il une cabine téléphonique dans le coin?**
Where is...? **Où se trouve...?**
   ...the nearest Métro **le Métro le plus proche**
   ...the telephone **le téléphone**
   ...the bank **la banque**
   ...the lavatory **les toilettes**
Turn left/right **Tournez à gauche/droite**
Go straight on **Allez tout droit**
The first/second (on the right) **Le premier/le deuxième (à droite)**
At the crossroads **Au carrefour**

IF YOU NEED HELP

Could you help me, please? **Pouvez-vous m'aider, s'il vous plaît?**
Do you speak English? **Parlez-vous anglais?**
I don't understand **Je ne comprends pas**
Could you call a doctor quickly, please? **Pouvez-vous appeler un médecin d'urgence, s'il vous plaît?**

RESTAURANT

I'd like to book a table **Puis-je réserver une table?**
A table for two please **Une table pour deux personnes, s'il vous plaît**
Do you have a fixed-price menu? **Vous avez un menu?**
Could we see the menu? **Nous pouvons voir la carte?**
Could I have the bill please? **L'addition, s'il vous plaît**
A bottle/glass of... **Une bouteille/un verre de...**

MENU VOCABULARY

apéritifs appetizers
boissons alcoolisées alcoholic beverages
boissons chaudes hot beverages
boissons froides cold beverages
carte des vins wine list
coquillages shellfish
entrées first courses
fromage cheese
gibier game
hors d'œuvres starters
légumes vegetables
plats chauds hot dishes
plats froids cold dishes
plat du jour dish of the day
pâtisserie pastry/cake
plat principal main course
potages soups
service compris service included
service non compris service not included
spécialités régionales regional specialities
viandes meat courses
volaille poultry

NUMBERS

0	zéro	11	onze	22	vingt-deux	110	cent dix
1	un	12	douze	30	trente	120	cent vingt
2	deux	13	treize	31	trente et un	200	deux cents
3	trois	14	quatorze	40	quarante	300	trois cents
4	quatre	15	quinze	50	cinquante	400	quatre cents
5	cinq	16	seize	60	soixante	500	cinq cents
6	six	17	dix-sept	70	soixante-dix	600	six cents
7	sept	18	dix-huit	80	quatre-vingts	700	sept cents
8	huit	19	dix-neuf	90	quatre-vingt-dix	800	huit cents
9	neuf	20	vingt	100	cent	900	neuf cents
10	dix	21	vingt et un	101	cent un	1,000	mille

Useful Words and Phrases

agneau lamb
ail garlic
ananas pineapple
anguille eel
banane banana
beurre butter
bifteck steak
bière (bière pression)
  beer (draught beer)
bœuf beef
boudin noir/blanc
  black/white
  pudding
bouillabaisse
  seafood soup
brochet pike
cabillaud cod
calmar squid
canard duck
cassoulet meat and
  bean stew
champignons
  mushrooms
chou cabbage
choucroute -sauer-
  kraut
chou-fleur
  cauliflower
choux de Bruxelles
  Brussels sprouts
citron lemon
civet de lièvre
  jugged hare
concombre
  cucumber
confiture jam
coquilles Saint-
  Jacques scallops
cornichon gherkin
côte/côtelette chop
côtelettes dans
  l'échine spare ribs
couvert cutlery
crevettes grises
  shrimps
crevettes roses
  prawns
croque monsieur
  toasted ham and
  cheese sandwich
cru raw
crustacés seafood
cuisses de grenouilles
  frogs' legs

cuit (à l'eau) boiled
eau minérale
  gazeuse/
  non gazeuse
  sparkling/still
  mineral water
écrevisse crayfish
entrecôte sirloin
  steak
épices spices
épinards spinach
épis de maïs corn
  (on the cob)
escargots snails
farine flour
fenouil fennel
fèves broad beans
figues figs
filet de bœuf fillet
filet mignon fillet
  steak
filet de porc
  tenderloin
fines herbes herbs
foie gras goose/
  duck liver
fraises strawberries
framboises
  raspberries
frit fried
friture deep-fried
fruit de la passion
  passion fruit
fruits de saison
  seasonal fruits
gaufres waffles
gigot d'agneau leg
  of lamb
glace ice cream
glaçons ice cubes
grillé grilled
groseilles
  redcurrants
hareng herring
haricots blancs
  haricot beans
haricots verts
  French beans
homard lobster
huîtres oysters
jambon blanc/cru/
  fumé ham (cooked/
  Parma style/
  smoked)

jus de citron lemon
  juice
jus de fruits
  fruit juice
jus d'orange orange
  juice
lait demi-écrémé/
  entier
  semi-skimmed/
  full-cream milk
langouste crayfish
langoustine scampi
langue tongue
lapin rabbit
lentilles lentils
lotte monkfish
loup de mer
  sea bass
macaron macaroon
maïs sweetcorn
marron chestnut
menu du jour/à la
  carte menu of
  the day/à la carte
morilles morels
moules mussels
mousse au chocolat
  chocolate mousse
moutarde mustard
myrtilles bilberries
noisette hazelnut
noix walnut
noix de veau fillet
  of veal
œuf à la coque/dur/
  au plat
  soft/hard-boiled/
  fried egg
oignon onion
origan oregano
pain au chocolat
  croissant with
  chocolate centre
part portion
pêche peach
petite friture fried
  fish (whitebait or
  similar)
petits (biscuits)
  salés savoury
  biscuits
petit pain roll
petits pois green
  peas

pintade guinea fowl
poire pear
pois chiches chick
  peas
poisson fish
poivre pepper
poivron green/red
  pepper
pomme apple
pommes de terre
  potatoes
pommes frites
  chips
poulet (blanc)
  chicken (breast)
prune plum
pruneaux prunes
queue de bœuf
  oxtail
ragoût stew
ris de veau
  sweetbread
riz rice
rôti de bœuf (rosbif)
  roast beef
rouget red mullet
saignant rare
salade verte lettuce
salé/sucré salted/
  sweet
saumon salmon
saucisses sausages
sel salt
soupe à l'oignon
  onion soup
steak tartare
  minced raw beef
sucre sugar
thon tuna
thym thyme
tripes tripe
truffes truffles
truite trout
truite saumonée
  salmon trout
vapeur (à la)
  steamed
venaison venison
viande hâchée
  minced meat/mince
vin blanc/rouge/rosé
  white/red/rosé wine
vinaigre vinegar
xérès sherry

Street Atlas

For chapters: see inside front cover

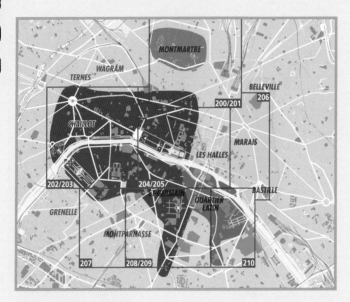

Key to Street Atlas

ℹ	Information	📖	Library
Ⓜ	Museum	Ⓜ	Metro with station
🎭	Theatre / Opera house	(RER)	Rapid transit train station
⚑	Monument		Pedestrian precinct
⊕	Hospital		Public building / Building of interest
✡	Police station	★	TOP 10
✉	Post office	26	Don't Miss
✝ ✡	Church / Synagogue	22	At Your Leisure

1 : 13.500

0	500	1000 m
0	500	1000 yd

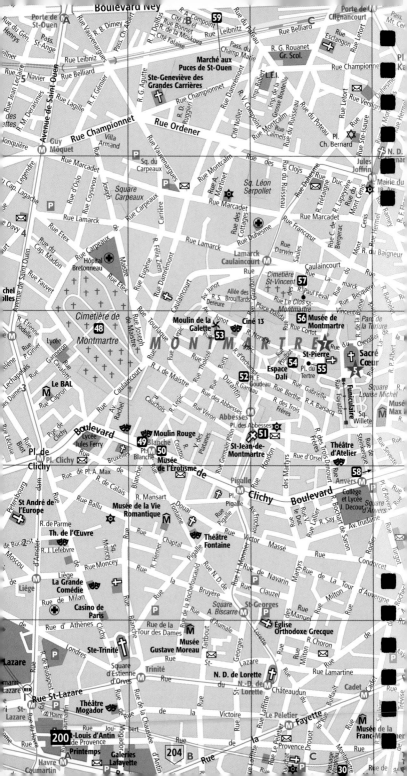

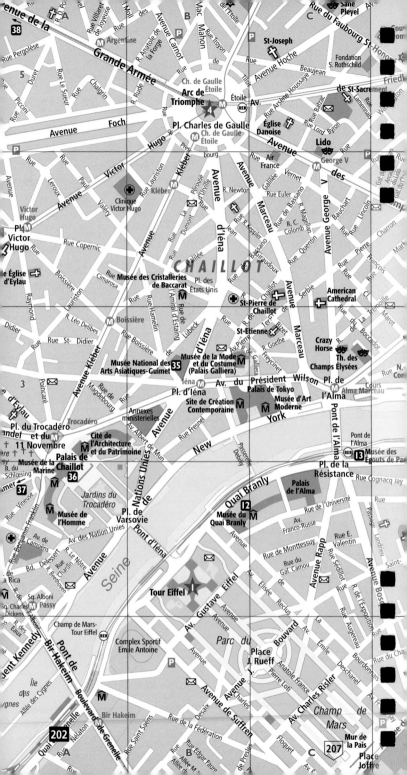

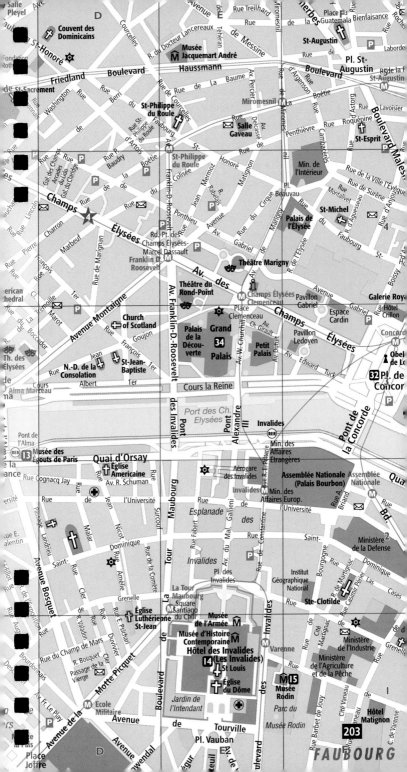

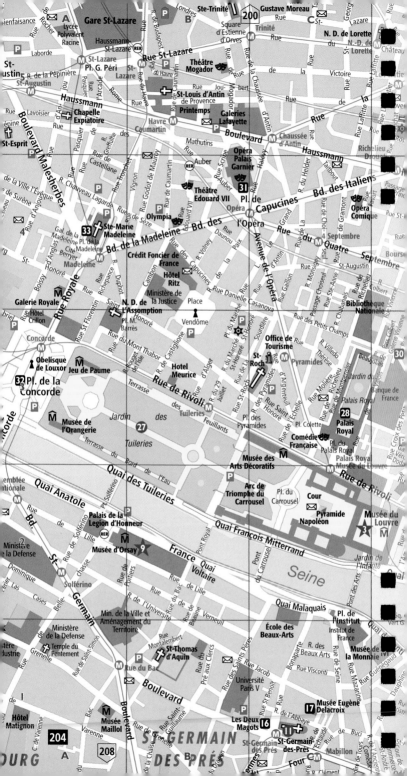

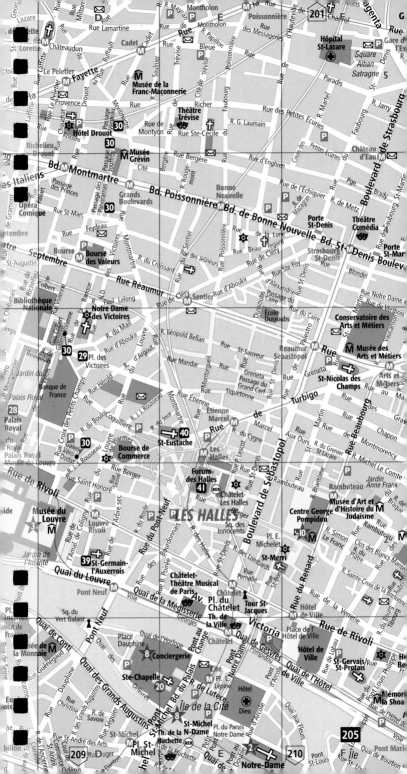

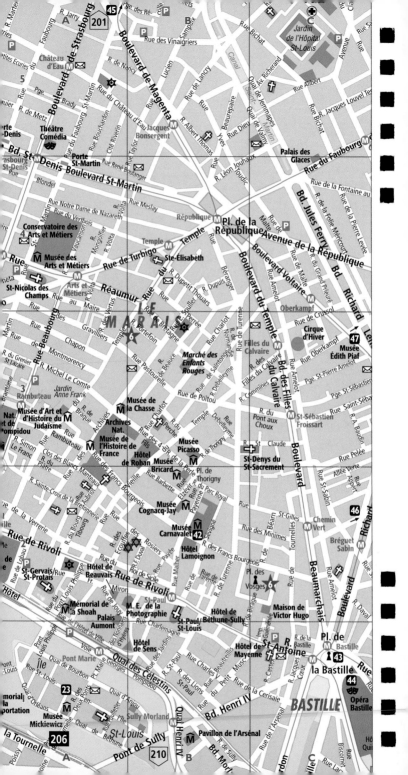

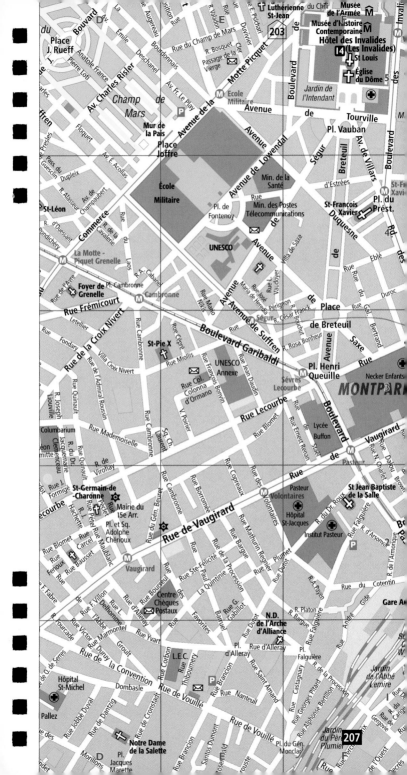

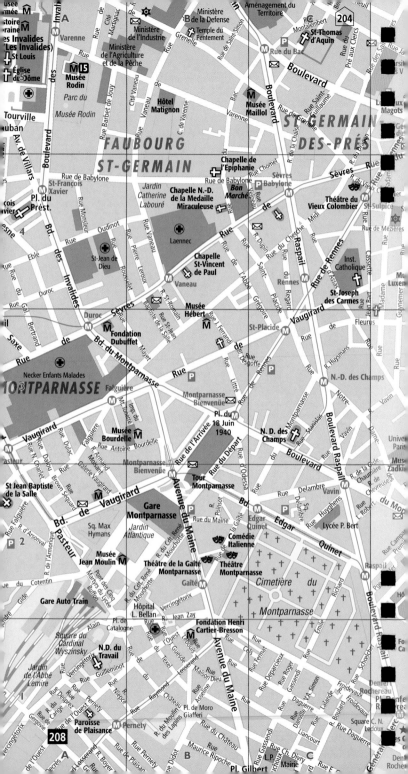

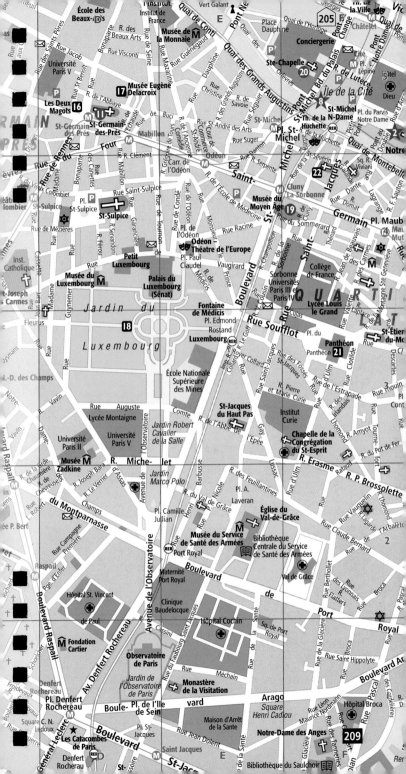

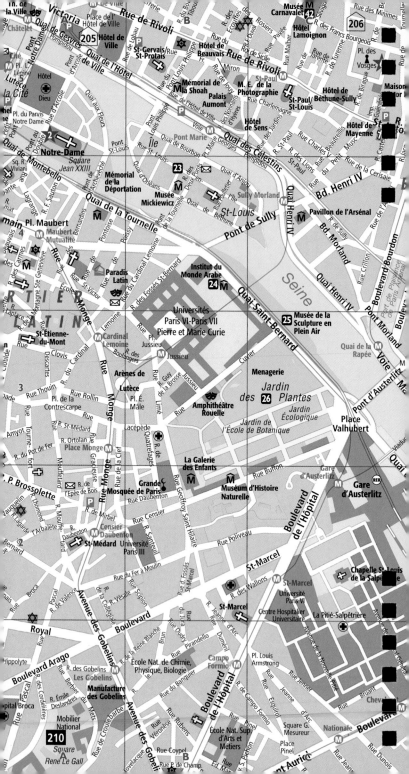

Street Index

Street Index

Street Index

Street Index

Index

Index

Picture Credits

Credits

1st Edition 2015

Worldwide Distribution: Marco Polo Travel Publishing Ltd
Pinewood, Chineham Business Park
Crockford Lane, Chineham
Basingstoke, Hampshire RG24 8AL, United Kingdom.
© MAIRDUMONT GmbH & Co. KG, Ostfildern

Authors: Teresa Fisher, Mario Wyn-Jones, Adele Evans,
Waltraud Pfister-Bläske
Editor: Annegret Gellweiler, Guido Huss, Anja Schlatterer,
Anette Vogt (red.sign, Stuttgart)
Revised editing and translation: Jon Andrews, jonandrews.co.uk
Program supervisor: Birgit Borowski
Chief editor: Rainer Eisenschmid

Cartography: © MAIRDUMONT GmbH & Co. KG, Ostfildern
3D-illustrations: jangled nerves, Stuttgart

Printed in China

Despite all of our authors' thorough research, errors can creep in.
The publishers do not accept any liability for this. Whether you
want to praise, alert us to errors or give us a personal tip –
please don't hesitate to email or post:

MARCO POLO Travel Publishing Ltd
Pinewood, Chineham Business Park
Crockford Lane, Chineham
Basingstoke, Hampshire RG24 8AL
United Kingdom
Email: sales@marcopolouk.com

FSC
www.fsc.org
MIX
Paper from
responsible sources
FSC® C020056

10 REASONS
TO COME BACK AGAIN

1. Sit in a café, let a croissant melt in your mouth, and enjoy Paris's **cosmopolitan flair**.

2. Admire the crazy – but surprisingly accident-free – **traffic** weaving around the triumphal arch.

3. Enjoy the sunshine accompanied by Maillol's sculptures of nudes in the **Tuileries Gardens**.

4. The **cheerful waiters** dressed in long aprons who joke around with their guests in the **bistros**.

5. Pastel coloured mint and rose **macaroons**, once a favourite of Marie-Antoinette.

6. **Elegant Parisian women** managing to stay cool while fixing their makeup on a busy Metro.

7. The view from the steps of the **Sacré-Cœur Basilica with the whole of Paris at your feet**.

8. **Eat oysters** in a brasserie overflowing with mirrors and Art Noveau décor.

9. Gaze out from the Louvre in the evenings at the **glowing pyramids** outside.

10. Rummage around for unique souvenirs at the **flea market in the Village Saint Paul**.